Marriage and the Counsel of God

Marriage and the Counsel of God

Michael A. Eschelbach

PUBLISHERS
Eugene, Oregon

MARRIAGE AND THE COUNSEL OF GOD

Copyright © 2007 Michael A. Eschelbach. All rights reserved. Except for brief quotations in critical articles or reviews, no part of this book may be reproduced in any manner without prior written permission from the publisher. Write: Permissions, Wipf and Stock Publishers, 199 W. 8th Ave., Suite 3, Eugene, OR 97401.

ISBN 13: 978-1-55635-346-8

Manufactured in the U.S.A.

Contents

1. Introduction / 1
2. Preliminary Outlines and Supplementary Materials / 3
3. Genesis
   Model of Paradise Created and Destroyed / 31
4. The Ten Commandments in Marriage
   The Model Revisited / 75
5. The Creed
   The Nature of God Related to Marriage / 129
6. The Lord's Prayer
   Petitions For an Eternal Union / 161
7. Baptism
   Confidence in the Potential of Your Spouse / 197
8. The Lord's Supper
   Weekly Restoration of Confidence / 207
9. Confession and Absolution
   The Two Vital Signs of a Relationship / 213
10. Concluding Remarks
    How to Keep This Mindset in the Mix / 221

Movies Index / 223

Examples Index / 224

Biblical Text Index / 226

Topics Index / 231

1
Introduction

THERE ARE as many reasons to pursue marriage counseling as there are people to seek it. But there are four directions from which forces compel us to counsel before pursuing a marriage or before seeking to terminate one: forces from above, beside, below, and within. First, the force from above is God. God created us to live in communion with Himself and each other. He defined that communion even more specifically by creating new life through the union of husband and wife. The wisdom of our creator is the first and most compelling force to seek the fulfillment that comes within a relationship that is lived according to His design.

Second, a good marriage is important to the community of people around us, near and far. The world itself, whole nations and small communities, is only able to recognize and devote significant effort toward noble causes when marriages and families are sound and vibrant. Christian congregations provide an environment of mutual support when marriages within it are healthy and encouraging. Extended families also benefit from the common effort to know the blessings of relationships according to God's design.

Third, a good marriage is essential to those below—the children. Children learn about their relationship to God by observing their fathers and mothers. The fallen human nature of children needs a united perspective and response from parents. The souls of children need the united yet multifaceted witness of parents.

Finally, each person involved in a relationship has a soul that yearns to know the union that God intended. The distorted thinking of human nature and the aggressive nature of perversion (especially through the media) make a life within God's Word and grace essential if goodness is to be discovered and protected. Our souls need truth to know what makes life and grace to inspire us to that life. Such absolute truth and grace can only be found in the Word of God.

God's Word as the only reliable response to human need in relationships is the origin of this book and the reason for its title, *Marriage and the Counsel of God*. What follows is the product of more than twenty-five years of study coupled with more than twenty years of marriage counseling (pre and post). The clarity of God's design for relationships as communicated in the Bible and fidelity to that provide the most reliable means of developing, sustaining, and restoring good marriages. The text generally follows Martin Luther's chief parts of the Christian faith from his Small Catechism: The Ten Commandments, The Creed, The Lord's Prayer, Baptism, Lord's Supper, and the Office of the Keys. However, longer sections of scripture are considered where appropriate and other matters of counseling are treated in supplementary sections. For example, the counseling proper begins with a careful treatment of Genesis 1–3 since that is the foundation and source of everything else the Bible has to say about marriage and relationships. Ephesians 5 is treated in greater detail under the second article of the Apostles' Creed because Christ provides the other great witness to God's intent for relationships.

The companion workbook to this volume should be given to each of the individuals seeking counseling. They are to complete the battery of questions (2.b.) before counseling begins and then continue to read ahead and make notes on the subsequent materials. As the counselor leads the individual or couple through these materials the counselee(s) can refer to their notes for questions, disagreements, or interest in further discussion.

2
Preliminary Outlines and Supplementary Materials

2.a.i. Preliminary Concerns—Outline

I. Preliminaries
    A. Consent of those responsible to God for your well-being
        1. Parents of the woman
        2. Parents of the man
        3. Pastor
            a. Eligibility in regard to the state
                i. Marriage license
                ii. STD counseling
            b. Eligibility in regard to family
            c. Eligibility in regard to the Church
                i. Of one faith
                ii. In the image of Christ and His Church
                iii. With obvious and consistent morality/virtue
    B. Proposal and acceptance
        1. With full capability to fulfill what is required
        2. With a full understanding of what is being proposed
        3. Freely and without deceit or duress

II. Preparations
    A. Counseling to insure all of the above
    B. Final consent of pastor
    C. Rehearsal . . . date/time_____
    D. Wedding arrangements in human modesty to the glory of God
            date/time_____

      1. Texts
      2. Music
      3. Apparel, marriage party (people), conduct before, during, and after
      4. Photography: before, during, after
      5. Reception
   E. Use of the church
      1. Pastor
      2. Organist
      3. Musicians
      4. Cleaning

III. Post wedding pattern of living
   A. Faithful involvement in the life of God's Church
   B. Personal devotions (pulse)
   C. Private confession and absolution (blood pressure)
   D. Faithfulness to vows—in every respect

2.a.ii. Preliminary Concerns—Outline and Explanation

I. Preliminaries

There is preliminary work to do before counseling and even before working through this page.

First, everyone benefits from a clear consistent reminder that weddings are not a pay/per service, nor are pastors "free-agents" available for hire. You will want to put this in writing with the support of the congregation and elders. You will help everyone by treating this subject in detail in adult Bible class, college and high school Bible studies, and in catechism classes. The pastor represents God, the congregation, and other responsible parties (parents and the state, for example). If the pastor is to be of real benefit to a couple he must have time to genuinely assess the situation. Everyone benefits from knowing that they may not come to the pastor with a wedding date and expect to squeeze counseling into that. Nor can the counseling reach its maximum effectiveness unless the couple is willing to consider that the other "intended" may not be the right person to marry after all. Letting this be known ahead of time provides several benefits.

Couples with no interest in spiritual matters will seek another facility for their wedding. Couples who are uncertain will find a setting where they can really consider their future together with godly counsel. Still other couples who are already faithful will find opportunity to continue to grow together. Note: I never refuse a wedding nor to counsel. Never, ever refusing avoids anger and misunderstanding (especially spread by gossip). Rather than refusing, I simply express my responsibility to be genuinely helpful and the conditions within which I might fulfill that on behalf of the couple. We are always the advocates, never the adversaries of any individual. If the couple is not interested in godly counsel, then it will be their decision to refuse to move forward.

Second, now that the couple knows they may not impose a "deadline" we may explain that this course of counseling also does not have a set number of sessions. This time together with the counsel of God takes as long as the situation requires. If negative answers are discovered in the matters that follow, some time may be required to resolve the problem. Consent of parents or moral living simply cannot be forced with time constraints. If the marriage is to be sound and supported, then that support must come by conviction and the Spirit of God. On the other hand, I have found this counseling to take between twelve and eighteen hour-long sessions. I have even completed this counseling all in one day (a long day) with a couple that I knew well and was very mature in the Scriptures and their faith.

Third, the couple will work through the following in order to know their posture for proceeding. If obstacles are discovered they will need to be removed. The following also provides an overview of the whole process, including wedding plans and post-wedding follow up. When I take a couple through this course of counseling I make a life-long commitment to that marriage, in as much as I am able to do so.

A. Consent of Those Responsible to God for Your Well-Being

The fourth commandment includes a concern for parents' consent to a marriage. Parents' responsibility is extended in the civil realm through the requirement of a marriage license and spiritually through the involvement of a pastor. Couples do well to welcome the more objective perspective of those who care the most about their future. Young people are often fearful of this involvement, as if parents are eager to chain their children to an ogre for a spouse. The truth is, as in shopping for a car, loved ones are not concerned with the "model" you choose but with the reliability. Choose any model you want, but choose a model that will not leave you stranded!

If an individual objects to this involvement, that is a matter to resolve all in itself. This kind of issue is already affecting the proposed relationship and will affect it in the future. For this reason, such matters need to be discovered and resolved before proceeding.

1. Parents of the Woman

According to Genesis 2, as we will see in detail, the "man leaves his father and mother, and is joined to his wife." For this reason, the service traditionally includes the consent of the father of the bride. What's happening in a marriage is a transfer of responsibility from father to husband. Why would a loving father relinquish his responsibility to another unless or until he knows that man will be a good caretaker for his daughter?

2. Parents of the Man

Traditionally, the question in the service is just asked of the parents of the bride. However, the fourth commandment and general Christian concern for the well-being of all makes it appropriate for the parents of the man to give their consent as well.

3. Pastor

There is nothing in civil or biblical law that requires the involvement of a pastor in marriages or weddings. What is required for a marriage in the eyes of God is the same as for the state: public declaration of relationship between a man and a woman. The husband will be responsible for the woman and the woman will be responsible to the man. Both state and church will hold them accountable for this public commitment. A civil wedding is no less acceptable to God than a church wedding and a pastor need not be involved. If a couple is interested only in the physical setting for a wedding then the pastor would refer them to the church council about "using" the church for a wedding—and the pastor is not involved.

Nevertheless, marriage is a deeply spiritual estate. God's Word and Spirit are essential for conduct that produces good relationships and marriages that endure. If a couple wants the pastor to be involved then they need to respect his perspective and conscience. This course of counseling may convince the pastor that he cannot, in good conscience, give his consent to a marriage nor be a part of it. This does not mean the couple cannot pursue a marriage, and a marriage may work out in the end. But the pastor's role depends on conditions he has no control over. His approval or disapproval must be respected as given in the deepest interest of love for the man and the woman.

a. Eligibility in Regard to the State

i. Marriage License

States and counties vary in their requirements for marriage. A couple does well to find out what requirements they must meet well in advance. The state's involvement is for civil order, providing public declaration of the relationship, and binding the couple under civil law accordingly.

ii. STD Counseling

In some states, you can't get a marriage license unless you have some kind of counseling in regard to sexual conduct and health. In my experience the counseling that is provided by local health departments is incredibly useless and offensive. They may show you all sorts of things that are in fact pornographic. By their treatment of the matter they often promote the very attitude toward sexual conduct that is producing the diseases they are counseling you to prevent. At the same time they often mock traditional values and especially chastity as ridiculous and even unhealthy. One county had sex education materials that listed "having to abstain from sexual activity for short periods of time" as a negative "side effect" of abstinence.

Therefore, you will want to know that these same civil authorities will allow you to pursue this counseling with your own physician. This allows you to find a physician who shares your values and have a conversation that is more productive.

b. Eligibility in Regard to Family

Here "in regard to family" has two parts. First, this means the pastor may not proceed with counseling if the parents do not give their consent. The exception to this would be if the family's refusal was itself unreasonable and unchristian.

Second, this means that neither individual is already married. In one instance in my experience both man and woman were divorced, but the reasons for their divorces were not biblical; they confessed that they simply "didn't get along" with their former spouse. In another instance, a man was still legally married to a woman in another state. In any case, these issues must also be resolved if the counseling is to proceed.

c. Eligibility in Regard to the Church

i. Of One Faith

Here is a place to take sort of a hard and relaxed line at the same time. The most important thing is not that both are members of the same denomination or even the same congregation. Formal membership tells us very little about a person or their faith. On the other hand, many people actually have the same faith or eagerly grow into the same faith, even though they are still considered members of different churches. Only time and serious conversation will allow us to discover where the man and woman are in relationship to the truth/faith and therefore in relation to each other.

Discovering whether the couple is of the same faith and/or helping them grow into the same faith is not something you can make happen or expect to conform to a deadline. The same obstacle to discovery and real progress will be present if the couple is sexually active. Any pre-commitment in the relationship will compromise the objectivity of assessing faith and the spiritual unity of the couple. This is another reason not to accept the constraint of a wedding date.

I am willing to take as long as it takes to discover whether the couple shares one faith or not, knowing that a five or ten week membership class isn't going to do much for a couple, especially when they just see that as a hurdle they need to get across so they can get where they want to be. That's the other reason I tell couples, "Don't bring me a wedding date." We can't know what we need to about the faith of the individuals, the viability of the proposal, nor my disposition toward the wedding if we have time constraints.

Example: The best marriage I have ever seen was with a young lady who was a member of my congregation, but I didn't educate; she was there when I got there, and already through the system, so to speak. She was dating a young man who was Roman Catholic nominally, but that's all. And we talked about these things for weeks and weeks and weeks as we counseled before they were married. What told me about their condition was their disposition toward the counseling and their involvement in the life of the Word/church. He was never absent from worship, stayed for adult Bible study, and was steady and active in a men's weekday breakfast Bible study. He was responsive in counseling, asking questions and discussing his understanding. So they were married, even though he had not yet been formally received as a member of the congregation. Thus it was no surprise that his disposition and activity remained consistent after the wedding, as before. It was not until two years later, after services one morning, when he came to me and said, "What do I need to do to become a member here?" I said, "Well, the fact is, you've been a member here for I don't know how long. I've just been waiting for you to make a formal declaration of the fact."

ii. In the Image of Christ and His Church

Neither man nor woman may be expected to know automatically what is required of them according to biblical design in Genesis 2 or Ephesians 5. That realization will come in the course of the counseling. But at this point, it is necessary that they both consent to the idea that there is a design, according to creation and redemption, which a marriage must follow in order to realize its potential. This is an early moment were the counselor may discover that strong convictions regarding feminism or evolution must be resolved before any other progress can be made.

Example: In one case, I was not the couple's pastor but they had asked me to perform their wedding. I had not worked through these preliminary questions but discovered in the course of counseling that the woman's feminist convictions made her absolutely unwilling to accept the word "obey" in the wedding vows. Though I spent great time and effort in explaining that "obey" is something everyone does, according to their nature and role, still she could not get past the idea or the word. In the end, I explained that I could not perform a ceremony that omitted the word since then I would be leaving the biblical text and uncertain of what I was doing/performing. If the wife to be is not asked if she will obey according to Ephesians 5, perhaps they are just as married, but I could not be sure—especially as my presence is precisely for the purpose of certainty in regard to the biblical marriage. In consideration of each other's convictions, I gave the homily at the ceremony, but the ceremony was provided by their own pastor, who did not have such reservations.

iii. With Obvious and Consistent Morality/Virtue

Integrity is essential for the man and woman intending to marry and for the whole community within which they live. If Christian weddings are provided for couples whose sexual activity or living arrangements obviously contradict the Christian faith, then the wedding and the church are marginalized. This is the place where I ask the couple if they are living together and if they are sleeping together. The two separate questions are important. We may not assume that a couple living together is sexually active, even though that is the assumption of the world and a problem in itself (Ephesians 5:3). We may also not assume that because a couple is not living together they are remaining chaste. Productive counseling cannot take place if the couple is already physically committed or sexually active. The necessity of preserving the sexual indulgence becomes the motivating force for the man, and the need to know that intimacy was not a mistake becomes the motivating force for the woman. The disposition of counselees in such circumstances has made it clear that securing the wedding was all that mattered. Consequently, serious issues that were discovered in counseling were glossed over or dismissed by the couple.

Example: There was once a young lady who was a member. The young man she intended to marry was not. In our first meeting we came to this question and discovered that they were sexually active. I explained to them why this was not good for them and how it would be an obstacle for our progress in counseling. I left them with some options on how we might proceed and waited to hear from them. I didn't hear from her until about three months later. She wrote me a long note about how angry he became during their drive back to where they were going to school. When they returned to her apartment he became violent and even punched holes in her walls and kicked in her door. All of that because he realized that his personal sexual gratification was in jeopardy of being suspended until after the wedding. The young lady was, of course, both upset and relieved. She was upset at the thought that she could give herself so intimately to a man who was so selfish and violent. She was relieved because she found out in time to terminate the engagement and relationship.

What are the Christian counselor's options when a couple admits to cohabitation or sexual activity? Here again it is essential to be positive, offering options that will resolve the impediment rather than being negative and refusing any further involvement. Any couple can understand and accept how their condition or disposition will affect the involvement of one who represents God according to His Word. The thing that couples and their families cannot accept is how condemnation and rejection as a first response is in any way consistent with the gospel. So, what are the options?

Physical intimacy (sexual and living arrangements) is the obstacle to be removed. This obstacle can be removed in either of two directions. The couple can formalize their relationship by obtaining civil recognition or by separating and maintaining chastity. Formalizing the relationship provides integrity for the situation, but removes the pre-emptive aspect of the counseling. Separating protects the pre-marriage benefit of the counseling but is often resisted or seen as unreasonable.

If the couple simply will not separate, then obtaining a marriage license and formalizing the relationship is simple. This does not mean there will be no counseling or a wedding ceremony. Quite the opposite. Now counseling, though "post" rather than "pre," can be pursued without time or emotional constraints and a wedding (recognition/affirmation of a civil marriage) can be arranged which everyone can support. In one case, I formalized the civil marriage in a private ceremony, immediately after the couple obtained the license, and then a year later performed the ceremony in a wedding service.

If the couple wants a traditional wedding, then separation is the key. If they claim that they live together for economic reasons, then the pastor and congregation need to be prepared to muster whatever help is necessary to provide for those economic requirements (find them temporary living space, pay off a lease, etc.). If the couple is sexually active, then a commitment must be offered to refrain. In any case, the pastor does well to be always in a helpful mode, offering solutions that provide a path for integrity in the relationship.

B. Proposal and Acceptance

1. With Full Capability to Fulfill What Is Required

This is where you ask the questions about an individual's freedom to be married.

1. Are you trying to get away from something?
2. Do you think this is a business partnership?
3. Are there other competing interests that we should know about?

Some people seek marriage to escape a bad situation at home, or in search of security, or to avoid loneliness, or even to obtain some physical advantage. Any such force in a person's life will blind them to real issues of marriage. Exposing such issues in no way means the end of the relationship, but realizing them IS essential if we are to know what kind of relationship we are dealing with.

2. With a Full Understanding of What Is Being Proposed

Does the man understand that proposing means he is committed to giving his life, sacrificially, permanently, and selflessly for the well-being of the wife? Does he understand that doing so means following the Word and example of Christ by inspiration of the Spirit of Christ? Does he accept the biblical model of manhood? Is the man ready to do so without reservation? This reality of what is being proposed must be considered before the proposal can be taken seriously.

Similarly, does the woman understand that by accepting his proposal, she will be submitting herself to his care? Does she accept the biblical model of womanhood according to Ephesians 5 and 1 Peter 3? Accepting his proposal does not mean that she relinquishes the protection that Scripture affords a wife. It simply means that short of abuse, adultery, or abandonment, she accepts the leadership and care this man will provide.

3. Freely and Without Deceit or Duress

"Freely" here refers to civil law. This means he or she is not a fugitive of the law, an illegal alien, already married, or in some other way hiding something from the other. A marriage that is being sought because of a pregnancy falls in this category. In many instances, the marriage of biological parents is absolutely not in the best interest of man, woman, or child. This question also means that neither he nor she is being "bullied" into this commitment. Some individuals are very persuasive or dominant emotionally, consciously or unconsciously forcing the other along a course they are not sure of.

Example: I have had cases where the man or woman felt very uncertain about the proposed marriage and very afraid of making that known. In each case I made it clear that such fears or reservations will not be resolved unless they are expressed, and that they could do so with my advocacy. Once expressed, the other person has to realize that to obtain a marriage by duress is not to have a marriage at all. In fact, I asked the other, "Why would you want a relationship with a person who does not feel the same way about you?"

And freely without deceit or duress. I've had an incident not in my past but in my friend's past where a guy had a marriage somewhere out west, and just left, found another girl, and was going to get married again. So you've got to ask these things. And then it's just some nuts and bolts to think about when you're making arrangements.

II. Preparations

    A. Counseling to Insure All of the Above

    B. Final Consent of Pastor

    *C. Rehearsal . . . date/time*_____

    D. Wedding Arrangements in Human Modesty to the Glory of God
    *date/time*_____

    1. Texts

    2. Music

The Bible speaks about marriage but not about weddings. Therefore the wedding service cannot be prescribed, per se. Nevertheless, if the wedding is to take place in the church, it must be a service of worship to God, within which the union of a man and woman in marriage will be solemnized. The invocation, sacred music, readings, and liturgy that are biblical provide the content. Personal expressions of feelings, family traditions, popular music, and expressions need not be forbidden, but properly take place at the reception.

Example: I once officiated at a wedding for two particularly spiritual people. All the guests and family came to the late service on Sunday morning. After service and the greeting of the congregation, then the guests, wedding party, and guests who came only for the wedding entered the sanctuary. The service was short, covering only the essentials because we had just been together for worship, then we proceeded to the reception.

3. Apparel, Marriage Party (People), Conduct before, during, and after

I have found it necessary over the years to speak about conduct at the rehearsal, where everyone can hear what is said. Though the groom and bride may be deeply spiritual, this does not necessarily prevent a guest in the wedding party from embarrassing them by his or her conduct. The most serious problem is drinking before the ceremony. This not only looks bad for guests and neighbors, but it throws the whole solemnity of the occasion into question. Sunglasses, printing on lapels or the soles of shoes, cell phone calls, etc. need to be prohibited in the clearest language. My practice regarding inappropriate conduct is to let the family know that my participation in the service will end when the antics begin. I will simply leave, and leave the wedding party to work out how to proceed.

4. Photography: before, during, after

I highly recommend doing photography before the wedding for two reasons. One, everyone looks better since they are freshly dressed. Two, this allows the wedding party to proceed to the reception sooner, which is better for the guests.

5. Reception (Not much to be done here)

E. Use of the Church

Couples need to be prepared for specific fees and expectations of a congregation in regard to the use of the premises. The couple will also want to inquire ahead of time about honorariums and fees for services expected.

1. **Pastor**
2. **Organist**
3. **Musicians**
4. **Cleaning**

III. Post Wedding Pattern of Living

An annual visit with the couple is ideal. When the visit is approaching, the husband and wife will both be assessing their conduct and experience within the marriage. They will be considering whether they want to bring up issues or whether they should let them go. They may gain a new appreciation for what they have in their marriage but had begun to take for granted.

In the materials to follow, explanation will be provided regarding the essential nature of involvement in a Christian congregation, personal devotions, and private confession and absolution. For now, consider the following summary. Since the Word of God provides the life of the Christian, the presence of that Word in a marriage is the pulse of that marriage. Confession and absolution restore what is damaged by our failure to live according to God's design and relieve the pressure that builds under guilt and resentment. Therefore, confession and absolution keep the pressures from building to a point of bursting, when a spouse bursts out in anger or frustration over matters that need not have built up. We know that because of the condition of our human nature we will fail to live as God intends us to. Even more troublesome than that is our nature's desire to justify itself. Therefore it is helpful to revisit each spouse's unreserved determination to live according to God's design as husband or wife, a determination inspired by and made approachable by His Word and Spirit.

> A. *Faithful Involvement in the Life of God's Church*
> B. *Personal Devotions (pulse)*
> C. *Private Confession and Absolution (blood pressure)*
> D. *Faithfulness to Vows—In Every Respects*

2.b. Questions for Couples to Answer before Counseling

After working through preliminary concerns, each counselee works through these questions individually. If possible, have them answer the questions in electronic form and send them to you as attachments. Then you can import both sets into a table, making it easy to compare answers. Review this before going through the corresponding section with the couple in counseling, noting significant issues, questions, or positive conditions already in place.

The first fifteen questions are introductory and general in nature—getting to know the couple. You may have covered much of this material in your preliminary session. Having them fill this out now allows you to assess the effect of that preliminary session and the need for more work in these areas.

After this the questions are numbered in reference to the counseling materials.

The first number refers to the chief part: 1. Ten Commandments, 2. Creed, 3. Lord's Prayer, 4. Baptism, 5. Lord's Supper, 6. Confession and Absolution. The second number refers to the next subsection of that chief part. For example, 1.1 refers to the first commandment, 2.2 refers to the second article of the Creed, 3.4 refers to the fourth petition of the Lord's Prayer, and so forth. Subsequent numbering does not refer to parts of the Small Catechism, but is only a continuation of the outline form and to allow for identification during counseling.

Material below is included in the corresponding workbook.

The purpose of these questions is to help you take time to consider the thoughts, attitudes, and characteristics you will bring to marriage. The better we know each other, the less chance there is for misunderstanding and the more appropriately we can implement God's counsel to us concerning marriage.

Please take your time to thoughtfully answer these questions. Each of you should answer these questions separately and in electronic form if possible. This will allow you to reconsider, edit, and revise your answers. This will also allow your counselor to import your answers into a table for comparison. We will refer to both as opportunity arises in the course of our counseling.

1. How much study / preparation do you think is necessary before planning to get married?
2. How much concentrated study / effort do you think is necessary after the wedding?
3. Why do you want to be married in a church?
4. What are the most important factors to you in planning your wedding (in order of priority)?

(Depending on your answers, you may wish to stop here)

5. How long have you known each other?
6. How well would you say you communicate with each other?

Preliminary Outlines and Supplementary Materials

7. Why do you want to get married?
8. When did you become engaged?
9. Have you been engaged before?
    a. How long ago?
    b. What happened?
    c. Is this fully resolved?
10. Have you been married before?
    a. How long ago?
    b. For how long?
    c. What happened?
    d. Is this fully resolved?
11. Do you have any physical handicaps or disabilities that might affect your marriage and have you faced these to your mutual satisfaction?
12. Are you acquainted with the emotional characteristics of your intended spouse?
13. What concerns do you have / what changes would you like to see?
14. How do you feel about the social circles in which your intended spouse has lived?
15. How will your courtship contribute to your marriage?

1.1.1 What is your religious affiliation?
1.1.2 What is your intended spouse's religious affiliation?
1.1.3 What is the history and nature of your involvement in your church?
1.1.4 What are your thoughts regarding being of one faith with your spouse-to-be?
1.2.1 Can people have the same faith and belong to different churches? Explain.
1.2.2 What is / has been God's part in your relationship?
1.3.1 How are you observing the "Sabbath" in your relationship?
1.3.2 Worship life?
1.3.3 Bible studies?
1.3.4 Daily devotions / Bible reading?
1.4.1 How do your parents feel about this marriage?
1.4.2 Have you met with your parents to discuss the marriage?
1.4.3 Have your parents met with each other?
1.4.4 How do you think you will get along with your intended spouse's family?

1.5.1 Have you ever had a fight?
1.5.2 How often?
1.5.3 What are they about?
1.5.4 How do you resolve them?
1.6.1 Are you living together at this time?
1.6.2 Have you lived together in the past?
1.6.3 Are you / have you been sleeping together?
1.6.4 What is love?
1.6.5 How did you come to your views on love, romance, and marriage?
1.6.6 Do you plan to have children?
1.6.7 What have you determined about the place of children in your marriage?
1.6.8 What are your views on birth control?
1.7.1 What are your plans for career?
1.7.2 What priority will those plans have in your life?
1.8.1 Are your thoughts toward your intended spouse always positive?
1.8.2 When are they negative?
1.8.3 How do you deal with these thoughts?
1.9.1 Are you content with your life?
1.9.2 What changes would you like to make?
1.9.3 What part do you see your intended spouse playing in the life you would like to lead?

2.1.1 What part does God play in your physical life?
2.1.2 What part do you think God has played in your relationship?
2.1.3 What do you believe about the nature of "marriage"?
2.1.3.1 What is the essence of the relationship?
2.1.3.2 What is the purpose of the relationship?
2.1.3.3 What are the roles of each spouse?
2.1.3.4 How long does this relationship last?
2.1.4 How familiar are you with what the Bible says about marriage?
2.1.5 How do you plan to provide for your physical needs once you are married?
2.1.6 How do you plan to provide for your spiritual needs once you are married?
2.1.7 How will you handle the various responsibilities of maintaining a home?

Preliminary Outlines and Supplementary Materials

2.1.8 Where do you plan to live after you are married?
2.1.9 What is your view on debt?
2.1.10 How does that compare to the view of your intended spouse?
2.2.1 How are you saved?
2.2.2 How does your understanding of salvation affect your relationship with your intended spouse?
2.2.3 How does/will your relationship bear witness to your faith?
2.3.1 Where does faith come from?
2.3.2 What part does faith play in your life?

3.0.1 How often do you pray?
3.0.2 What do you pray for?
3.0.3 What does it mean to pray to "OUR" Father?
3.1.1 What is God's name?
3.1.2 How will God's name be "set apart" in your marriage?
3.2.1 What is the "Kingdom of God"?
3.2.2 How will it come to your marriage?
3.2.3 How might His kingdom come to others through your marriage?
3.3.1 What is God's will for you as an individual?
3.3.2 What is God's will for you in relation to your intended spouse?
3.4.1 What is "daily bread"?
3.4.2 What are the most essential things for your life?
3.4.3 What do you think are the most essential things for the life of a marriage?
3.5.1 Do you distinguish between the kinds of things that people do wrong? How?
3.5.2 What is forgiveness?
3.5.3 What role do you play in forgiving others?
3.6.1 What temptations do you struggle with?
3.6.2 What temptations do you see in your intended spouse's life?
3.6.3 How do you / will you deal with temptations?
3.7.1 What kind of protection does God provide for your relationship?
3.7.2 How would you react if your intended spouse was seriously injured or killed before your marriage?

4.1.1 What is baptism?
4.1.2 How does baptism work, what does it do?
4.1.3 Who should be baptized?
4.1.4 What part, if any, does baptism play in your relationship?

5.1.1 What is "Holy Communion"?
5.1.2 Who should come to Communion?
5.1.3 Should anyone ever NOT come to Communion?
5.1.4 How is real Communion established and sustained?
5.1.5 What part will Communion play in your marriage?

6.1.1 What will you do if your marriage begins to go badly?
6.1.2 What is your thinking about divorce?
6.1.3 What do you think about separation?

7.1 What are the "vital signs" of marriage?

Preliminary Outlines and Supplementary Materials

2.c.i. Flowchart of Preliminary Marriage Matters—Outline

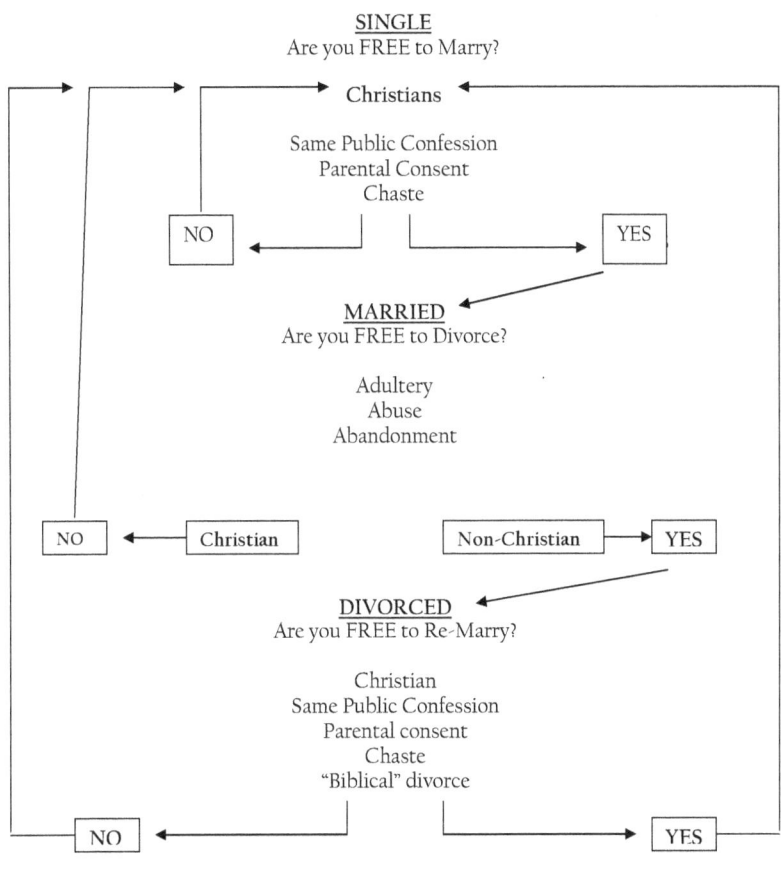

2.c.ii. Flowchart of Preliminary Marriage Matters—with Explanation

SINGLE
Are you FREE to marry?

This question was considered above under preliminary concerns. The question has three areas of interest:

1. Regarding civil law—Are either of the individuals already married? Is there any kind of legal encumbrance or litigation against either person that we should all know about? Are they of legal age?
2. Regarding physical circumstances—Marriage is not necessarily the best solution to a pregnancy or to economic expediency. ("It's cheaper to live together," or "This way I can be on his or her insurance.")
3. Regarding emotional and other circumstances—Is someone fleeing a bad situation at home? Is one or both of the individuals trying to get something they lack? Is one or the other creating a burden of commitment, even though the other has fears or serious reservations?

Christians

You may not be able to know the answer to this question until the end of all the counseling. However, it is helpful to know how each person assesses their own relationship to Christianity and to God. Note that this question is entirely before and separate from the question of public confession/membership.

Same Public Confession

Once the individual's own faith has been identified and articulated, we can consider what that means in comparison to any church body they hold membership in or identify with. This is a good time to talk about integrity; that is, consistency between one's inner beliefs and one's outward confession and conduct. The marriage union (as well as all other relationships) depends on honesty (not trust) between the individuals. If words and conduct are not consistent with inner convictions, then we really never know the person we are trying to bond with. Discrepancies between the private and public person are like dirt on a surface meant to be bonded to another. No glue can hold.

Once we have determined the convictions of each individual, we can consider how they compare to each other, to the Word of God/orthodox Christianity, and to the options available in which they might confess that publicly and in communion with others.

Parental Consent

This was also included above in preliminary concerns. Here we simply need to know whether both sets of parents have given their consent. If they have not, we need to pursue the cause. If their cause has merit, we need to work that out with the couple. If their cause does not have merit, they must either recognize that and give consent, or realize that their refusal cannot be accepted as an obstacle to the marriage.

Example: I have had both cases. In one case, a mother refused consent. Upon investigation her objections were absolutely legitimate. The couple refused to honor her concerns and flew to Vegas for a quick wedding. They are still legally married, but that marriage has never been good or joyful for either of them. In another case, I had parents raise objections that a long conversation was able to relieve. This system of counseling offers great relief to most parents, as they see the depth, comprehensiveness, and biblical character of the material.

Chaste

The individuals must be chaste. If they have not been, the situation needs to be resolved and confession and absolution provided. They may choose to resolve this by marrying immediately, in which case this becomes "post" marriage counseling. If they separate they need to make arrangements to insure that they can remain chaste.

MARRIED
Are you FREE to divorce?

Marriage is an extension of and witness to God's relationship with His people. Consequently, Christian marriage is dependant on the individual's relationship with God. A person's relationship with God has eternal consequences; a marriage to another person does not. For these reasons, Paul makes clear in 1 Corinthians 7 that a believer's union with God always takes priority over their relationship with another person. Yet union with God includes love, which motivates love and reconciliation between people, if possible. Therefore,

1. A Christian is free to divorce if their spouse puts their relationship with God in peril.
2. A Christian is also free to divorce is their spouse terminates the marriage in fact by:

a. Committing adultery (this includes not only the physical act of intercourse with another, but conduct which demonstrates that a spouse is devoted to another person).
b. Abuse of any kind that puts a spouse's health in jeopardy.
c. Abandonment, which is really a combination of adultery and abuse as defined above.
3. Nevertheless, a marriage need not necessarily be terminated for any of these reasons, if the offending spouse is penitent and willing to amend and if the offended spouse is capable of seeking reconciliation.
4. If the offending spouse is claiming a Christian faith, then we have cause to investigate:
    a. Is this confession of the offending spouse of a character that would urge reconciliation?
    b. Is this confession just a sham, in which case the offending spouse is no Christian at all, and the offended spouse is free to divorce anyway?

(This explains why the flow chart appears as it does. According to 1 Corinthians 7:10–12, if both parties claim a Christian faith, then we have every reason to believe that reconciliation may be achieved.)

Adultery

Abuse

Abandonment

DIVORCED
Are you FREE to re-marry?

If individuals who come for marriage counseling have been married already, we must know the circumstances of the termination of their first marriages. Here, some special care is appropriate:

1. That we not impose any kind of physical or spiritual penalties that the Bible does not impose.
2. That we not disturb or disrupt absolution and healing that has already been established.

3. That we also not gloss carelessly over situations where, from God's perspective, a previous marriage is still in place. Doing so would make us a party to adultery and encourage the very destruction of marriages we are trying to prevent.

Thus, only in cases where none of the biblical causes for divorce exist would we pursue this issue. Even so, if the former spouse(s) have already remarried or if they are unwilling, we cannot force reconciliation. The rest of the categories below have been addressed above.

Christian
Same Public Confession
Parental Consent
Chaste
"Biblical" Divorce

At any point along this process, if we find a "no" answer, then we return to previous, more fundamental questions. If we are not dealing with two Christians, we need to go back and resolve that, for we have no reason to be a part of uniting believers to unbelievers (2 Corinthians 6:14). If there is resistance to chaste conduct, the question of Christian faith is raised again. If there is a divorce, at many points we may again be forced to consider the question of an individual's Christian faith. When seeking re-marriage, we may need to go back and evaluate reasons for a previous divorce, or the individual's disposition may again put their religious convictions in question.

When all aspects of concern are resolved, then the "yes" answer is appropriate and the couple or individual may pursue their course.

2.d. Critical Diagnostic before Proceeding
(Workbook p. 8)

The four passages that follow were not originally part of the text or process of pre/post marriage counseling. They came into the process as a necessary response to unresponsive participants. In both pre and post marriage counseling, little good can be accomplished unless both parties are interested. Even if he or she is interested, the general "know-it-all" aspect of fallen human nature hinders consideration of biblical texts and principles.

Many see my summary of the passage's significance as "overstating" the case. My experience has been that such "overstating" is necessary in order to be taken seriously and to make the point clear. Marriage, according to the counsel and image of God, is completely radical to human opinion and contemporary culture. Thus, it is better to treat the topic of our disposition toward God's counsel as a whole, before trying to obtain the good of it for a marriage in particular.

Note: In all the material to follow, the bold print is a part of the scriptural reference that indicates the significance of that text. The non-bold print that follows is a brief explanation of that significance. The more familiar you are with the entire passage, the more meaningful the reference will be.

I. John 6

"The Spirit is the life-maker; the flesh profits nothing. The words I have spoken to you are Spirit, and they are life."

God's Word helps, my thoughts/attitude harm.

A counselee once asked at this point, "Are all of my thoughts and attitudes always contrary to God's thoughts and attitudes?" The answer to that question has several parts. First, such "overstatements" are often necessary in order to make the case at all. Unless people hear a challenge, they will usually pay little attention to the point. Lack of attention is exactly what troubles most marriages. Second, if we leave any room for personal opinion or ego to feel justified, the counsel of God is bound to be ignored, or at least compromised. If a fallen human nature is allowed to think, "Well, surely the thoughts I have that I think are right, are right," then all of the self-justification that troubles marriages is also left in place. Third, more often than not when you're dealing with relationship problems, even if the person is doing the right thing, it is often done for the wrong reason. Particularly in marriages, a lot of manipulating goes on, especially on the male side of the equation. Men tend to seek out and seek to retain a relationship with a woman for three reasons. They seek a cook, maid, and mistress. In every case I have counseled, the wife has expressed this exact sense of things—in every case! These three services are what men want; otherwise they'd be perfectly happy with no woman in their lives. In order to maintain those services they will do things that are right, but not for the right reasons. Often, when a wife comes to me in search of counseling, the first thing I discover is a woman who is angry on top of everything else. Why is she angry? Because when she told her husband she had had enough and was seeking help, he sent her flowers or bought her chocolates. But that is like trying to put a band-aid on a car accident. He is hoping to buff out a few scratches; she is convinced the car is totaled. To ignore the reality of these thoughts and dispositions is to blur, at best, the rest of the material to follow.

On the other hand, there is a way in which the assertion about our thoughts/attitudes would not be true. In one sense, our thoughts and attitudes don't always harm because at some point our minds and hearts are tracking after God's design. Although such points occur, I would argue, within a larger selfish orientation that is contrary to God. So, in general, man's orientation since the fall is to move away from God, contradicting His will. But in as much as His Word and Spirit are at work in a believer, there will be times when that believer's thinking is consistent with His.

At the outset then, we want to establish a new "default system" in our thinking. If my disposition is, "my thinking is probably wrong here," then I have the freedom to consider other information more objectively. I can listen to my spouse, to my counselor, and to the biblical texts in front of me. Christians have the same liberty in regard to criticism and condemnation. If we know our human nature and the grace of God that provided a remedy for that, why wouldn't we be the first to consider that "I'm probably wrong here"? We may well be wrong and if so, there is confession, absolution, and grace to make amends. If we are not wrong, what have we lost by showing true consideration to others who find themselves in conflict with us? Consideration from one person invites consideration in return. Consideration allows for discovery and discovery allows for solutions.

A. Proverbs 3:5–7: " . . . Do not be wise in your own eyes . . ."

My understanding/lack of genuine understanding has affected my marriage negatively.

Our own understanding of things, opinions, and instincts make trouble for us precisely because they come without any effort. Pride, selfishness, impatience, resentment and every other element contrary to a good relationship is always perched in the front of our minds. Two steps are necessary to keep this from forever ruining our relationship with the one we claim to love. First, as above, we need to come to terms with the fact that our natural understanding of things is skewed since the fall. Sometimes I remind couples that all of their best thinking has brought them to what they now claim is the most miserable experience in their life. Except for divorce, they have no idea what to do about it. Second, we need to be ready to keep those perched opinions from pouncing. So James wrote, "Let every man be slow to speak, slow to anger, quick to listen" (James 1:19). Taking time to compare biblical wisdom against our own, or seek biblical wisdom before responding makes for good marriages. If we fail at this point, knowing this truth about ourselves can at least make us more willing and ready to take back words we say in haste, beg pardon, and take the appropriate time to consider.

B. Proverbs 16:25: "There is a way that seems right to man . . ."

What I feel justified in thinking/saying/doing on my own behalf only makes things worse.

Solomon recognized this as such a significant problem that he repeated this observation twice (the other place is Proverbs 14:12). Even if we take a moment to consider our own opinions about things, they are bound to seem right to us because they are OUR opinions. When our thinking seems right to us we become more hasty to defend our own and more hasty to attack others. Instead of inquiry we get accusation, instead of investigation we get prosecution, instead of discovery we get defense. If we are determined to follow the paths that seem right to us, the result is death, death of our relationships and of our own self.

Example: The husband who finds it natural and easy to manipulate his wife thinks he is right to do so. He thinks that because he provides for his wife and because she "knew what she was getting into" when she agreed to the marriage that he is entitled to the gratification he seeks. He wants dinner, she is unhappy. He lectures about all he does to provide, she complies in a sense of fear and helplessness. But the dinner lacks an atmosphere of joy and companionship, so the meal does little more than fill the stomach. Eventually the wife finds the courage to leave—her husband has killed the relationship. Even if she doesn't leave, such a practice will make his senses dead.

A more subtle example is the generally loving husband in a generally happy relationship. However, he wants sexual activity more than she does.

So he hints, then holds, then flirts. She hints in return (or makes plain) that she is not in the mood. Then he pouts, or takes her out to dinner or buys her a trinket—and then she feels guilty if she does not indulge his sexual appetite. But she will not enjoy the intimacy because the essence of it was to be selfless, not self indulgent. Afterwards he finds it less gratifying than he thought, because it was taken, not given. She feels taken advantage of. Over time, though his appetite still urges him on, neither of them find any love or joy in their physical intimacy. There is a way that seems right to a man, but its end is the way of death.

C. Isaiah 55:1–13: " . . . for my ways are not your ways . . ."

> **My ways are contrary to life and powerless to make things better; God's ways are always life giving and provide the energy to affect what they describe/command.**

The final, absolutely radical proposition is that our ways and thoughts are completely foreign to God's design, and His ways and thoughts completely foreign to us. God's remedy for our own fall is the primary example. In every human situation, our idea of a solution is to terminate the problem. God's response to our problem was to sacrifice Himself (Paul takes this up in 1 Corinthians 1:18–31). Note the significance of the first part of the Isaiah text: "Why do you spend money for what does not satisfy?" Human thinking since the fall is going to contradict God's design for humanity. Popular thinking is always going to be the most contradictory. Not surprisingly then, the more people try to find fulfillment in self-gratification, the more it eludes them. Americans spend more money than any other people and are arguably the least satisfied. God's ways are not just different than our ways, they are the inverse, the opposite; they are universes away from our thoughts. How then can we know them except by living in His revealed Word? We depend on His wisdom to keep the sun shining, though science cannot explain how it can continue to do so without an external source of fuel. We depend on God's wisdom to keep our heart beating and lungs breathing. (Science calls these "involuntary muscles," but what does that mean?) If we so obviously depend on God to sustain our physical existence, wouldn't we depend on Him even more for the more intricate and complicated aspects of it? How do I know how to relate to His creation or to other human beings within it unless I listen to His instruction? Where can I find the energy to overcome my nature to contradict His instruction except from His Spirit, which is inseparable from His Word?

Human nature has the natural inclination to right itself, to have the top of our head up. We have a parallel instinct to justify ourselves and always to return to our own pattern of thinking. The Christian faith requires us to keep that inclination neutralized, off balance if you will. Only the Word of God can keep that contradictory nature off balance and inspire the soul with a better posture. In relationships, especially marriages, it is a posture that gives and nurtures by the power of God, who does the same for us.

3

Genesis
Model of Paradise Created and Destroyed *(Workbook p. 10)*

> *"Or do you not know that your body is the temple of the Holy Spirit who is in you . . . and you are not your own?"*
>
> 1 Corinthians 6:19

THE REALITY that we are a work of God's creation makes all the difference. We have been created according to a particular design ("in the image of God") and with a particular purpose. If we live according to this design and purpose then we will experience life. To the extent that we contradict that design, life will be absent and we will know dying and death instead. Now that evolutionary theory has been accepted as fact for so many decades, the whole idea of design has been replaced with accident. Everything is accidental, without design or purpose. The only purpose knowable in an evolutionary society is immediate self-gratification. An evolutionary society is also without any absolutes—no right and no wrong. Therefore, anything we want for ourselves must be right and we are entitled to it. Without design, human beings are left to grope about in the dark for meaning and purpose (Genesis 19:11). Without design, there is no meaning to gender or real purpose in a marriage except for personal satisfaction. Note then how the ideal of traditional marriage is seen as completely arbitrary and archaic, heterosexuality makes no sense, and children are not the purpose of the marriage but another possession of the individual.

On the other hand, in harmony with biblical testimony, all creation exhibits design and bears witness to the Creator (Psalm 19; Romans 1). We were created as the climax of God's work. We were made in His image and animated with His own Spirit. In as much as His Spirit and design (described in Holy Scripture) are available to us, we can begin to recapture what has been lost. The Holy Spirit regenerates us (Titus 3) and brings us into union with the Word of God. That Word of God is unlimited in its potential to fulfill God's purposes in and through us, especially in marriage and family relationships. Looking carefully at God's design for us according to the creation account makes the details of our roles recognizable and understandable. The kingdom of God comes through His Son, the Word of His Son, and His Spirit. Having that kingdom come, even now in our time, in our lives and in our marriages rightly inspires both optimism and determination.

Example: No one who is responsible for authenticating items can possibly be familiar with all forms of fraud or counterfeit. Those who are trained to detect counterfeit money do not spend their time looking at all the fakes, but at learning to know every detail of the genuine article. Similarly, the better and more fully we know God's design and will for men and women, the more easily we will recognize those forces that are contrary to it. Knowing they are contrary to God's design sets the will to reject alongside the ability to detect.

A. Genesis 1:26–31

" . . . in the image of God, . . . male and female, He created them . . ."

The image of God is the relationship intended between man and woman; man is responsible for, woman responsible to. (See 1 Corinthians 11:3.)

"In the image of God, He created *him*; male and female, He created them." There is a shift in number in those verses. First the text says, "God created *man* ["Adam" in Hebrew] in His own image, in the image of God He created him [singular]," meaning human beings in distinction from every other animal. The Greek translation of the Old Testament confirms this by using "anthropos." Then the text shifts right away to "male and female, He created them," which means that human beings are all made in the image of God, more specifically as male and female.

What then is the "image" of God? Most people answer, "to be holy" or "righteous." But those terms have no meaning without a standard. What is the content of "holy"? What is "righteousness"? The meaning of "image" is filled out as the text continues. For now, consider the emphasis that the text makes about relationship. There is a relationship established between male and female human beings, which is an extension of the very nature of God. Paul confirms and articulates this image in the 1 Corinthians passage. God the Father has a relationship with the Son (expressed in detail by Jesus in the Gospel of John), the Son of God in the person of Jesus Christ has a parallel relationship with man, and man has a parallel relationship with woman. (This pattern also exists between parents and children, governments and people, and masters and servants.) That being in a relationship with another is essential to the image of God will be confirmed again in Genesis 2. This is the fact that exposes the whole argument over equality as blind and self-defeating. In the first place, when we are talking about human beings, we are comparing beings that are all generated from the same source in the same way; we are not comparing a person to a dog or cat. Paul makes this case in Acts 17:26: "He has made from one blood every nation under heaven . . ." However, evolutionary thinking makes gender accidental. So here is the irony: the same worldview that produces feminism also defeats it. Feminists believe that they are equal to men, but they cannot prove it by any absolute standard. As females, they are the product of accident and unless they can demonstrate their equality in constant competition with men, their claim is unsupported. Notice that any time and as soon as you leave the truth of divine revelation you will find yourself under the burden of the law. You must prove, on your own, what is impossible for a contingent being to prove. What have I proven about my value or ego in the whole course of my life, if in the end I am dead and return to dust? Therefore, the way forward for women is not a belief in their gender (feminism), but a belief in design—that being female has meaning because of the creator's intent.

" . . . let them have dominion . . ."

One purpose of man and woman in their relationship is to have dominion—to take care of the created world (**not** to alter, accumulate greedily, find discontentment with, etc.).

Since the fall, the term "dominion" has generally had a bad connotation. When people think about dominion they usually think of foreign powers exercising rule over another people and not for their well-being. We think of the British Empire or the colonization of America or the Caribbean Islands or lots of places where powerful and aggressive people came and took over. These people claim that all things under their control belong to them and that people under their control have few, if any, rights. Often cruel abuses against the conquered are experienced to satisfy the petty self-indulgence and ego of the dominant. But this is not what God means by the term. Dominion, as you can see in the word, has to do with the Lord—"Dominae" in Latin. So, dominion or lordship has God's care and providence as its origin. The Lord or dominant one provides rather than being provided for. The Lord supports everyone else, rather than being supported by everyone else. It is amazing to consider that while Jesus was taking particular time and interest to support the lives of people He ministered to, and especially while He was dealing with the assaults of His enemies, He was at the same time sustaining their lives and the whole universe they lived in. This is the image of God that man was created to parallel. Dominion means to bear the burden of support for, to care and provide for the well-being of another. This understanding is essential when we come to the proposition that the husband has dominion over the wife.

Example: Many couples feel lost or utterly defeated when they decide to have children and find out they cannot. Certainly there is reason to sympathize, but there is also a problem exposed. If our lives are genuinely about dominion, what difference does it make if the children are "mine"? If we understand dominion, then what we know is that real fulfillment comes not from me controlling the context in which I relate to others, but in finding a way to relate to others as they come to me. If a couple understands this at the beginning, then they need not endure the anxiety or disillusionment of not having children of their own. They may instead turn their attention to other contexts by which God would provide them with an opportunity to provide for the life of children. The world is full of people and children who long for and desperately need someone to have dominion over them. If a marriage is a union of providers and caretakers, there can never be disappointment. For this very reason I find teaching to be such a fulfilling mission. There is so much good to be done and so much to provide, especially for the kind of teachers who make sacrifices for the good of the students. Indeed, time has shown that some teachers have many more children than most couples.

> "... God blessed them ... 'Be fruitful and multiply...'"

Man and woman are to help God in His creative activity through the bearing and raising of children.

There are two words in both Hebrew and Greek that are translated "blessed." The word used here means "to become what God intends." For example, according to God's will and promises, He blessed Abraham. That blessing produced descendants from a couple who could have none. Jesus blessed a few loaves of bread and a few fish and fed a multitude. What we are witnessing here is how the biology of human reproduction was set into motion and the cause of its functioning today. Men and women's bodies produce the components of human life and conceptions take place because of God's Word/will. Note how in Scripture, people recognize that ability or inability to conceive is always and obviously controlled by God (Genesis 30:2).

(Related question: Why then does God allow conception in bad circumstances? This is no different than the larger question of why God allows any physical action that is not good. A partial answer provided here is this: The solution for humanity since the fall is not for God to prevent every physical consequence of contradicting His design, but to provide an eternal solution in the midst of His physical providence and our troubles.)

The other aspect of this passage is the obvious characteristic of a living God—He cannot be fruitless. If man is made in His image, then the life of man must have real significance. This real significance comes in man and woman's role as agents of God's continuing creative activity, in their care in raising a child, and in the eternal nature of the child's life. There is an old joke and challenge to Christianity that says, If God is almighty, can He make a rock so big that even He cannot lift it? The nature of this challenge is to dismiss the proposition of God as illogical, therefore impossible. But the challenge is easily overcome with this aspect of God's character. "No, God cannot make a rock so big even He cannot lift it."

Not because He is not almighty, but because He is not futile; for what would be the purpose of making a larger rock and lifting it? (Interestingly, one philosopher suggests that because God is almighty, He *can* make a rock so big even He can't lift it, and then lift it! [Harry Frankfort in *The Philosophy of Religion: An Anthology*. Edited by Louis P. Pojman. Toronto: Wadsworth, 2003; p. 255])

Being fruitful and multiplying then not only parallels God's nature in creative activity, but also provides the circumstance in which we realize what it means to have dominion and to love. Our children, other people and their children, a whole world filled with people who have various ways of contradicting God's design, the whole mess of a fallen world (the product of 6,000 years of multiplication) are the means by which we realize what it is to be fruitful—to provide for the temporal and eternal welfare of these lives.

Example: Many people assume that overpopulation is one of the greatest threats to the future of humanity. But it is not the number of people that threatens, but the kind of people. What is the difference between the murderer, who does so because he thinks his life depends on it, and the advocate of population control (birth control, abortion, euthanasia) who does so for the same reason? In reality, the world can sustain many more people than inhabit it. What we realize in our experience is our unwillingness to devote our lives to fruitfulness as the proper response to multiplication. Note, for instance, that the U.S. pays farmers not to grow crops in their fields and often throws away tons of milk and dairy products in order to support better prices for the farmer. But why not give these products to the hungry? Simply because fallen human beings cannot or will not let it happen!

> " . . . 'See I have given you every herb . . . and fruit for food . . .'"

In paradise there is no need for others to be sacrificed for me. Everyone and everything can fulfill its purpose for others and live.

Before the fall everything necessary was given. Plants produced the food we need as a part of the way they lived. Nothing had to be taken, nothing stored, nothing died. The witness to God's providence is constant through the Bible, as God always provided food for people who were in the worst of circumstances: the children of Israel in the desert, Elijah the fugitive, the people who followed Jesus for three days in the deserted places but brought nothing to eat. Isaiah 55 and John 6:27 both address the fact that God freely gives what we need to live.

Genesis 2:15–18
". . . God took the man and put him in the garden to tend and keep it . . ."

Man alone, before there was woman, was given the responsibility to care for and tend the garden. This purpose and responsibility has not changed.

God made Adam in His image, meaning that God made Adam with a purpose. After creating Adam, God created a specific place where Adam would realize that image of God by tending and keeping it—just as God would continue to tend and keep His entire creation, but human beings in particular. Note how the image of God and the relationship between God and man is underscored by this circumstance. On the one hand, man is like God, having responsibility for the care of a living environment. On the other hand, man is not God, so he bears no burden of inventing any new creation; he is only to appreciate God's work and honor God by caring for it. Jesus drove this point home with Peter before and after His resurrection. Matthew 17:1–5 records the transfiguration of Jesus before Peter, James, and John. Peter responds to the revelation by offering to create—to build shelters for Jesus, Moses, and Elijah. The voice of God the Father interrupts Peter with a combination of rebuke and instruction: "This is My beloved Son; listen to Him!" Listening to God, rather than pretending that we can create for Him is half of the lesson. The other half comes in John 21:15–17, where Jesus commands Peter three times to feed/tend His sheep. Caring for the sheep (not manipulating, counting, measuring, or sacrificing them) is the image of God that man was created to live for.

Note also that rivers flowed and precious things were found in the Garden of Eden. Rivers rather than lakes are not without significance, because rivers are an example of living water. Rivers provide fresh water,

water safe to drink, cool and "refreshing" water. Rivers are also a powerful source, giving man a sense of what Jesus means when He says He provides living water in His Word—live giving, refreshing, powerful. Precious things are found in the Word of God, more precious and enduring than gold (1 Peter 1:7; Matthew 13:44–46).

Yet the image of God is not yet fulfilled in man's environment because he is not yet responsible for anything of eternal, divine significance. Some person, some human life and soul that is dependent on man for its well-being will be required if man is really going to be like God. So the narrative continues.

> ". . . but of the tree of knowledge . . . you shall not eat . . ."

Man was given a place to demonstrate his trust in God by diligence in his purpose and refusal to seek more knowledge than God had given. God's choices for us are always good; ours are always bad for us and others.

This proposition was already encountered in the preliminary section. Here it is revisited as an issue that was raised in the garden of Eden. God provides a tree of life with the command to eat freely of it. By way of contrast, He also includes the tree of the knowledge of good and evil and a command NOT to eat of it—for that will mean death. Now, the tree of life is of knowledge also, but of knowledge that contributes to life. The tree of the knowledge of good and evil presents man with information and opportunity he has no absolute capacity to discern or resist. Since the fall of Adam, our minds are continually muddled with knowledge we lack the capacity to judge accurately. Our emotions, passions, pride, selfishness, and contradictory nature make it impossible for us to recognize what is really evil, sometimes because evil seems so appealing and other times because we simply lack the ability to discern. If we refuse to admit our utter dependence on God's Word, then we are left without any sure standard of what is really good and what is surely evil. Jesus demonstrated this Himself in His victory over the devil's temptations during forty days in the wilderness. In every case, Jesus responds to and overcomes the "pseudo" knowledge presented by the devil with the phrase, "It is written." The incarnate Word of God knows that there is no other source of truth and no other standard of good than God's wisdom, so He looks no where else for His defense. Paul urges Christians to remember this fact as they encounter temptations, knowing that the Word of God is THE means of escape that God always provides for us (1 Corinthians 10:13). The first and absolutely constant indicator of the health of relationships is the couple's (or family's) relationship with the Word of God.

Disobeying God's command meant rejecting His Word, losing His breath/Spirit, losing His life.

God's instructions to Adam were consistent with and an extension, if you will, of the breath of God that made him a living being. Living according to that Word and feeding freely from the tree of life would sustain life forever. Consider how the nature of the Son of God as His Word made it impossible for Him to remain dead after His crucifixion and even impossible for Him to see corruption. Union with the Word of God and conduct consistent with it means life! Knowing this means recognizing that Adam had already "lost his breath" when he was determined to contradict God's design. We also lose the breath of God when we consciously contradict His will. (Note the example of Ananias and Sapphira in Acts 5 and the severe warning in Hebrews 10.)

". . . It is not good for a man to be alone . . ."

As God the Father was not alone but begat the Son from eternity and as God was not alone but created man as an object of responsibility and care, so man was incomplete without an object of constant care and responsibility.

The expression, "It's not good for man to be alone," tells us something of great significance about God Himself. God's character—omnipotent, omniscient, omnipresent—and His nature to live and love means that life would proceed from Him. God has begotten His Son from all eternity and the Holy Spirit proceeds from Him. By way of extension there would be man. But man could not be in the image of God without extending that life to an object of love and through his role in procreation.

Now that Adam is in place, what is he supposed to do? How can he be in the image of God with no one in particular to take care of? What is more profoundly puzzling is how he should be fruitful and multiply when he is alone. He is not God. He cannot create out of nothing or out of the dust of the ground. Man will need help if his life is to have significance in the image of God. He will need someone who is an extension of his own person, someone to lay down his life for, someone to provide him with a means to participate in God's creative and redemptive work.

The observation of God remains true today. Proverbs 18:1 tells us that a fool isolates himself. We simply cannot know who we are or the life God intended us to know unless we are laying down our lives (loving) on behalf of others. A society that is self-centered and has no use for marriage or children is doomed. While both Jesus and Paul mention the advantage of not marrying, they are quick to remind us that the ability to do so is rare. In any case, life cannot be experienced unless we invest it in others, particularly in the raising of children (whether they are ours or others). Adults isolated from children are lonely and without significant purpose. The condition of elderly in nursing homes and of professional people is a clear witness to this truth.

"I will make him a helper to remain before him."

Man was created to be fruitful/multiply and to care for creation. Woman was made to be cared for and help man fulfill his purpose. Perfection requires man to concern himself with care for creation, and requires woman to remain before and help. God determines both the task and relationship of workers.

There are two key parts to this section: one has to do with the word "helper," and the other has to do with the phrase, "to remain before him." First, what does the text mean by "helper"? According to the image in which Adam was made, he needs to love and to be a part of God's creative work ("be fruitful and multiply"). But who is there for Adam to lay down his life for? To whom will he impart the counsel of God and protect from contradiction by steadfastness? How can Adam multiply by himself? Therefore God makes the perfect compliment to Adam. Not a similar, equal, or corresponding type of being (as many translations suggest), but a compliment. She will be of the very same nature as Adam. She must be, since God formed her from Adam's rib. In this respect, arguments over equality between men and women are absurd. Of course we are equal regarding our nature, but not according to our design and function. But this is only obvious in view of creation. An evolutionist has no such absolute and therefore must argue the point without any absolute criteria. The woman will help Adam by giving him a real person with an eternal soul to care for and by providing the means by which God creates the rest of the human race. The woman may also help the man in the rest of the enterprise of living, but not outside of this central purpose. In other words, no man is right in expecting a woman to help him do whatever he feels like he wants to do or in expecting her to do things he will not do because that is how HE defines "helpful."

Second, the phrase, "to remain before" is not as sophisticated as most translations, but it is clear and accurate. If it was not good for man to be alone, what good would come and what help would result from someone who remained apart from him? Historically, this was more obvious. Husband and wife worked together to raise a family and care for the land that provided for them. Consider what has happened to our culture since men left home and then women followed. Just as we are always in God's view for good, so also the woman was to always be in the presence of her husband in order that he might live according to his purpose. Anyone might object at this point, saying that such a life is no longer practical. Is it even possible for a family to be together unless we become Amish? There is always a way back to God's design. The first step on that way is to know and honor God's design in creation. The second step is to let His Word and Spirit move us to seek the design He has revealed. The third step is to believe that there is a way or many ways to approach the life He intended for us, if we only use the resources He puts at our disposal, especially our imagination. For example, many people establish their own businesses instead of working for someone else. This allows you to work out of your home and have much more control over the time that you work. You may also seek a career that allows you to work less and still maintain a reasonable income. Many couples found each other because they shared the same goals, so they became missionaries together, or physician and nurse, or ran a business together. When children come, these couples simply add them to the mix. The children have the benefit of their parents all the time and the added benefit of learning practical skills as they grow.

Example: I once knew a man who was a machinist. He changed jobs, moving from a local machine shop to one an hour away, because he was offered a substantial raise. For a while the whole family enjoyed the higher income. They bought all sorts of things with the extra money. However, in time the family realized that they really missed having the father around. The father missed the family as well. One day the father came home and said he had quit his job for precisely these reasons. He made a deep impression on wife and family because he believed absolutely that being with his family was the central purpose of his life and that the good Lord would surely help him find work in the area again. He was rehired by the local machine shop and was given a raise.

Every couple or family may not have such a simple story. There are plenty of cases where sickness or economic circumstances make family life very difficult. Yet in every case, there is always a way to manage the challenges when a family is convinced that their bond with each other, rather than bondage to the world, is where life is to be found.

Example: Many pastors have unhappy wives and children who grow to dislike the church because their father is never home. Many pastors' wives and children rightly feel jealous or hurt at the attention and responsiveness of their husband/father to the call of others, while he ignores their calls for attention. This is a failure in two ways. First, the pastor is undermining the very cause he is supposed to be upholding by contradicting God's design in his own life. How can he hope that the people he serves will approach God's will and know the joy of it if he is the first to abandon his family? Second, he is failing his family and that will cause damage, not only to his family's life but also among people who know his family. Paul makes clear that only when a man's life is consistent with God's counsel can he represent Christ in public as a pastor (1 Timothy 3). It is also clear that no man can represent Christ to his neighbor unless his life is being pursued according to the Word of God (Matthew 23). In contrast to the type of pastor described above, there was another pastor whose family loved and appreciated him and his work. This pastor made it clear, in kind but firm language that he could not at all serve as pastor unless he set the example of being Christ to his family. If doing so meant that the church would criticize him or threaten his position, so be it. What better way to confess truth and love before family and congregation than to remain firm in both, no matter what is threatened? This same husband never missed a doctor's appointment with his wife during her pregnancies. After one particularly difficult delivery, the husband made it clear to his wife again and again that he would stay with her and the other children as much as necessary in order for her to feel at ease about recovering. She could rest, not just because he was there to care for the home, but because she was at peace in his service on her behalf--just as Christians can be at peace knowing God's providence for us.

Genesis 2:21–25
". . . and He took one of his ribs . . . 'This is now bone of my bones . . .'"

God made woman from the man so he would know that she is an extension of his own person and nothing foreign—there is no mistake in her nature/creation. Therefore, if a man cares for his wife, he is caring for himself; if she helps, she is helping herself.

The fact that God created the woman from the rib of the man is of great significance. First of all, it contrasts the evolutionary theory. Evolution has no way of explaining why there is gender at all, not to mention a male and a female perfectly designed to compliment each other. If life develops by accident, then why not three or five different genders able to interact in different ways? Creation tells us that God made a woman, the female gender, in order to complete the creation of man in His image. (Remember from chapter one, "Male and female, He created them.") Interestingly, the Hebrew word for woman, "isha," is simply the word for man, "ish" with the feminine ending attached. In a similar way, in English the word "woman" is an extension of the word "man."

Second, God did not create the woman from the dust of the ground as He did the man. There is a relationship of origin between the woman and the man, just as there is between children and parents. Feelings and emotions are the least significant aspects of the union of man to woman and parents to family. There is no stability or certainty with emotions; they rise and fall. But the union based on common physical origin and common spiritual union with God is absolute and permanent. These unions are the solid, enduring foundation that we can build our lives upon and hang on to when situations make us feel like our lives are falling apart.

Third, God did not make the woman immediately after He made the man. God created a specific environment for Adam, gave him instructions on life and living, and demonstrated that no other created being was fit for union with him (hence the perverted and futile nature of bestiality). The timing would forever prove that woman is of the very same nature as man, that she is necessary to complete the image of God by providing an object of love for the man and the means by which every other human being/eternal soul would be created by God.

> " . . . Therefore a man shall leave his father . . . and be joined to his wife . . . "

According to creation there is no such thing as an "independent" woman. The man left his family to assume responsibility for another. The woman would remain under the care of her father until a young man *demonstrated* responsibility (see the stories of Ruth, Joseph, and Mary).

If you notice, the text does not say, ". . . OR a woman shall leave her father and mother." There is equality between genders in terms of their nature as human beings, but according to their gender they are complimentary. They are designed by God specifically to fulfill a purpose on behalf of each other. Similarly, we will see that the Bible never speaks of or expects a woman to love her husband. He loves her and she submits to that love (nevertheless, as Christians, in a general sense, they love each other and submit to each other).

A man leaves his father and mother because he has become a man. To be a man means to have matured physically and spiritually to the point that you are not only responsible for yourself but also ready to bear the responsibility of others. The man leaves his father and mother to stand on his own and to stand ready to provide for another. The woman, on the other hand, remains under the care and providence of her father, or related men in her family. Since the woman is to submit, she is at risk and depends on the men of her life to provide for that submission. For this reason it was, and should be, necessary for the intended husband to demonstrate his responsibility to the father of the intended bride before the father gives her over to the care of another man. Think how much less abuse there would be if fathers really did provide, closely and tenderly, for the care and well-being of their daughters so that the daughters were free to carefully assess the viability of a man who was interested.

The text also mentions that having found a wife, the man "clings" to his wife (in some translations "joined to"). This Hebrew word means to be connected or bound together in such a way that separating the two could not separate the part that was bound, but would mean ripping one or the other apart. Anyone who thinks that marriages can be created and dissolved like business partnerships has never witnessed a divorce. The union of man and woman in marriage was intended by God to be complete and enduring. In fact, because marriage is God's institution, it is impossible for a man and woman to unite without the bond setting in. "Casual sex" and "cohabitation" seem free and easy, but there is always great pain and cost when one denies the permanent nature such relationships were meant to have within a marriage.

Now we know why it is imperative for both a man and woman to know what they are doing before they marry. A man needs to be clearly and consistently responsible and capable of bearing the care of another. A woman needs to assess carefully whether the man interested in her is a model of Christ to whom she may freely submit. Careful and honest assessment helps assure a marriage that will endure to the joy and benefit of all—the couple, the extended family, and society as a whole.

" . . . and they were naked and not ashamed . . ."

They were not ashamed because they knew only that God's creation was very good and they were each within the purpose God had given. They had nothing to hide and no one to hide from.

First, "naked" physically is only appropriate and good within marriage. This is so very contrary to what the media and contemporary thinking impresses constantly on the minds of people. Television programs and movies constantly and consistently demand that we accept sexual intimacy as something to be expected, like introducing yourself to a person or going out for coffee. The problem with this reversal of order is that it works against the kind of openness and honesty ("nakedness," if you will) that is necessary if we are to know that a marriage is possible. As God's physical creation is very good because it is indicative of spiritual realities, so also physical intimacy is only good as an extension of or indication of the union of every other aspect of a couple's relationship and the public expression of that in marriage. Nine out of ten couples I have counseled admitted to being sexually active before they married. How does that relate to the fact that they are having problems now? It works this way: In our society, when a man and woman first notice each other, this "noticing" is usually physical. The physical attraction produces introductions and a conversation. If the conversation is enjoyable, and in the absence of hindrances, the couple finds themselves on a path to physical intimacy, usually concluding in sexual intercourse. If the sexual intercourse was enjoyable, then a "relationship" is born. The problem with the relationship that follows is that the sexual intimacy has severely constricted its boundaries. The man has already demonstrated that he is the opposite of God's intent. He is interested first in satisfying his own physical appetite and has little or no interest in providing for the eternal well-being (let alone the physical and immediate well-being) of any woman. Now that he has found a source of self-gratification, a willing woman, he instinctively orders his behavior in a way that will protect this gratification in the future. He will display interest, provide attention, and even show a host of care-taking activities in order to make the woman feel "safe" in continued sexual activity. The woman, on the other hand, will be bothered by a nagging sense that she has made a mistake. She has already given away that which is most precious about herself. What is most unique and private has been exposed to someone who is close to a stranger. Worst of all, often this exposure has happened because she was vulnerable in some other way—under the influence of alcohol, drugs, loneliness, rebellion, or simply swept away by emotions misinformed by our culture. The woman also has instincts that tell her to make sure her intimacy was not a mistake, so she works to insure that the man she had sex with is the man she will marry (see the example below). He will be maneuvering toward the next sexual encounter; she will be maneuvering to land a commitment from him. While they open wide their eyes to the nakedness of each other, they will keep closing their eyes to warning signs and to aspects of the other that they do not like. While they are taking their clothes off, they will be covering up whatever part of their personality they think will endanger the relationship—sexual for him and permanence for her. This is why serious marriage counseling is necessary today, which includes the cessation of physical intimacy in order to allow for honesty in all the other aspects of the relationship.

Second, "naked," meaning completely honest in order to know each other, in order to know if there will be a real union. In complete contrast to the above, the honesty of a man and woman always provides a clear view of the relationship and its potential for the future. Once again, a man and woman notice each other. What they wonder after recognizing a physical attraction is if there is anything else "attractive" about this person. Who is the person beneath the interesting exterior? So a conversation is pursued, but not as a necessary or expected prelude to sex. The conversation IS the goal, because it is the window to the other person's whole life and soul. Since the window is small and the life behind it is large, a great deal of time is spent in conversation, though the settings may very. Coffee, desserts, dinner together, walks, recreation, even shopping all provide different settings in which different aspects of the person become visible through that window of conversation. Note carefully that in all of these activities, there is never a need to repent of the relationship. Getting to know another person well in this way is never a mistake, for this is how friendships are discovered and sustained. Nothing secret or intimate has been given away that could be wanted back. In fact, where the physically intimate are forced to be overly optimistic, the truly honest couple can dare even to be pessimistic. "Do I really want to spend any more time with this person, given what I learned today? We already disagree about too many things. He doesn't want to do the things I like to do and I don't like the way he spends his time. Most importantly, do we have a common belief system, a worldview that determines all the rest of our lives?" This is the kind of "nakedness" that is very good between everyone. This is honesty. Honesty never asks anything of another person nor seeks to manipulate another person. Honesty provides for freedom and insures it. Honesty says, "This is who I am and what I am about. Who are you?" If the honest answer on both sides consistently reveals that a union in faith and purpose already exists, then first a public declaration of the same (marriage) and private expression of that (physical intimacy) is appropriate and need never be regretted.

The third issue is the distinction between honesty and trust. People consistently and loudly complain about an inability to trust their spouse or the person they are romantically inclined toward. "I can't trust you anymore" is usually the bomb that is dropped, followed by the massive destruction of the relationship. But who said trust should have any part in our relationships with one another? The Bible NEVER commands us to trust each other or even hints at this. On the contrary, the Bible makes it clear from Genesis to Revelation that human beings since the fall are utterly untrustworthy. Only God is worthy of trust because He alone is absolutely good and acts consistently with that good nature. What is essential in our relationships is honesty, since I cannot have a relationship with a shadow. God calls us to be honest before Him and provides regeneration and forgiveness as His response. God calls us to be His ambassadors, responding in the same way to others, thus encouraging such honesty.

However, once again physical intimacy is a commitment of one kind or another, either before or after marriage. Once the commitment is discerned by a man, he will often become critical of the woman, because the more he sees of her that isn't physical, the more he wonders if the sexual intimacy is worth it. The woman also becomes more critical, wanting to correct the flaws in this person she couldn't have made a mistake about. In response to more critical observation and criticism, both man and woman/husband and wife begin to make coverings for themselves or hide. They look for time apart from each other; they tell only part of what they are thinking, what they have been doing or what they are planning to do. Only an honesty modeled after the one Adam and Eve knew in Eden can sustain a good relationship. As Christians, we already know that grace and acceptance are required for relationships and love is commanded. We love each other because we trust God. We trust His revelation about our nature, His intent for us, and His providence. The beauty of starting with honesty rather than physical intimacy is that acceptance of others comes at a safe and manageable distance. We can do what is best for another person, we can be a friend without committing ourselves to a union that works against us or would be regrettable. Within a marriage produced by honesty, the presence of grace and love cover both spouses with the righteousness of Christ—nakedness covered with perfection. So the Bible often says, ". . . and no one who believes in Him will ever be ashamed" (Romans 9:33).

Exmaple: There were three girls who had been best friends since before kindergarten. Two of the three were members of my parish and had been active in every aspect of the parish ministry, especially youth classes that dealt very forthrightly about male/female relationships. As juniors in high school, they asked to meet with me. In that meeting they explained their concern for the third friend because she was withdrawing from their friendship. They were no longer bound together in friendship as before and worst of all, honesty was missing. At the same time they were distressed because she was "dating" a boy who was not a good choice in their estimation. The more they tried to express their concern about her boyfriend, the more the third friend avoided them and withdrew. This is what they could not understand. "How can she spend more time with such a bad person and cut us off?" they lamented. In response I simply asked, "Have they been sexually active?" They had and I went on to explain why that meant their friend had to convince herself that this boy was not a mistake. So she continued to have sex with him in order to keep him in the relationship. She continued to deny the obvious indications of bad character and avoided the warnings of her lifelong friends. The friends now understood but fell into deeper lament over what to do. There was nothing left to be done except to pray for her; to maintain a witness of love, concern, and truth to her; and to be ready—very ready— to "catch her" when the young man finally cast her aside.

Example: A woman came to see me because her third husband was an alcoholic and abusive to her. What was remarkable is that her previous two husbands were also alcoholic and abusive. What was no surprise is how she met her husbands. She met them at bars and agreed upon the first meeting to spend the night with them. She was lonely—so lonely that giving herself away sexually in what was bound to be a mistake was better than being alone, she thought. What was also remarkable is that over time I met all three of her husbands, and they even looked like each other. Providing a union for her with the Word of God and the Christian community at last provided a remedy for her loneliness and fears. This newly found freedom allowed her to discover a person who could really be a husband to her.

Example: A certain young lady was convinced from watching her own parents' marriage and from observing the general condition of humanity that she wanted nothing to do with dating or marriage. Nevertheless, there was a young man in her school who took an enduring interest in her. They were especially close friends through their school years and after graduation. However, they were only friends, as that was all she would allow and because he was not interested in having her for himself, but in being something for her. In the course of eight more years she realized that marriage was not the problem, but the absence of real union between men and women. She realized this, as knowing the young man so thoroughly over such a long time convinced her that they were indeed united as one without any romantic expressions. After they were married, the woman continued to confide in me that she appreciated her husband more and more every day. His character was what she had known through and through. Each day of their life together was an occasion for that character to find new expressions. The fact that honesty was all she would allow in her history with the young man meant that their honesty was of the highest degree. Honesty of the highest degree meant a marriage that continually affirmed the union that was already proven.

We hide behind excuses when we have rejected God's Word and will for us and when we have expected others to meet our expectations, rather than God's purpose.

Ever since Adam first replaced God's Word with his own will, there has been a corresponding displacement of expectations. On the one hand, we tend to adjust our expectations of our own conduct to match the conduct we display. This avoids guilt and allows us to feel justified in imposing our expectations upon others. On the other hand, we replace God's expectations of others, particularly of a spouse, with our own expectations and feel justified again in our disappointment and criticism. In both directions there is shame because of the dishonesty of displacing God's Word and of attempting to justify ourselves. If I first observe myself honestly before God, what I find is shame on my part, but grace on God's. Knowing my condition makes me careful not to impose expectations of my own invention that can only make my failure worse. Knowing God's remedy for my condition makes me ready to extend grace to others, especially my spouse. Jesus addressed this matter with his description of the log and speck in one's eye (Matthew 7:3–5) and in the parable of the unforgiving servant (Matthew 18:23–35).

III. John 8:42–47: ". . . You are of your father the devil. . . . He is a liar and the father of it . . ."

On to the bad news in Genesis 3. I prefaced this section with the John 8 passage because it exposes so plainly the nature of the fall of Adam. Jesus provided insurmountable arguments against the Pharisees who contended that they were Abraham's children and therefore without sin. Jesus did not timidly ask them to reconsider, nor did He use diplomacy to suggest a contrary perspective. Jesus was blunt and absolute, because there is no soft peddling our condition, nor can the truth be compromised. Jesus said to them, "You are of your father, the devil," and "He is a liar, and the father of it . . ." Lying and murder are at the root of the fall, and subsequently at the root of every fallen human nature. Lying and murder are opposite of the Truth and Life, which is the Word of God. This is a helpful vantage point from which to view the events of Genesis 3.

A. Genesis 3:1–8
". . . Has God indeed said . . ."

God's Word is the source and substance of all life. The devil attacks that source by leading one to doubt His word. If I don't believe God has already said something, I choose to believe other words in preference to His, but no other word has life; therefore, I begin to die in that choosing.

The serpent is described as cunning, which is the opposite of wisdom. The wisdom of God created the world and made man a living being. The cunning of the serpent (the devil) can only destroy and make man dead, even while he lives. The same is true today. People think they are clever or sophisticated when they mock the order and design evident in God's creation (homosexuality, for example). Yet the consequences are always destructive.

The fact that the serpent speaks to the woman rather than the man is also to be expected. The serpent may have already been aware that Adam had abandoned his responsibility to God and for Eve and attempted to reorder God's creation. Evidence of this will come in the next section. For now, simply note that the devil attacks at the most vulnerable place. Just as swindlers prey on the elderly, drug dealers prey on children, and cults prey on the lonely, so the devil puts the woman in a position of responding to deceptive speech by her own abilities.

Raising a question is the third point of interest. The question, "Did God really say?" is as fundamental to evil as the Word of God is to God's own nature. Ever since the devil first posed the question, fallen human beings have continued to recite it to their own ruin. Think of how many young people with good morals do things they regret later because of this insidious question. An opportunity came for sex, drugs, or alcohol. Their moral background warned them away but their human nature questioned, "Did God really say we have to deny our own instincts and desires?" The unhappy husband or wife says, "Did God really say I should endure the challenges my spouse presents?"

Any time that you find yourself dissatisfied or unhappy about something the selfish human nature is going to ask the devil's question. What is fascinating is that in Matthew 19, the Pharisees come to Jesus and pose an almost identical question: "Is it permissible for a man to divorce his wife for any reason at all?" These Pharisees were not looking for wisdom to apply to their marriages; they were looking for a way to justify abandoning them. Jesus' response to the Pharisees, as His response to the devil in the wilderness (Matthew 4), is definitive: "It is written . . ." In Matthew 19, notice that Jesus' appeal to the Bible recalls God's intent and design in creating man and woman. When God's Word has addressed a matter, the only good answer to the question is, "Yes, God has said, you shall not . . ."

". . . nor shall you touch it . . ."

Already, man has fallen. The woman is under attack by the devil's word, and man is not taking responsibility for correcting Eve and rejecting the devil. He has left his purpose knowingly, and death follows. Anytime a man rejects his purpose and creator, death follows in his own life and in the lives of all for whom he ought to be responsible for (see Romans 5:18 and I Timothy 2:11–15).

Two critical problems present themselves in this section: Adam is suddenly silent and Eve has a response that is not consistent with God's Word to Adam. Adam's silence is most noticeable because his purpose in Eve's life is to provide a constant witness to the truth, as the Word of God provides in our lives. The gospels reveal that Jesus always bore witness to the truth at all times, especially when that meant He would be hated, rejected, maligned, or suffer for it. Why Adam is silent cannot be known, but the significance of his silence is clear—Adam had abandoned God's design for him, following the temptation that says, "You'll have a better life if you do it your own way" (Deuteronomy 12:8).

Eve's response to the serpent provides more evidence for an earlier fall of Adam. God gave Adam instructions regarding life in His creation before Eve was created. The Bible makes it clear that this is central to the male gender: to be responsible for keeping one's family and community in the Word of life. We also know that adding or taking away from the Word of God is a function of the fall, since God forbids it in the strongest terms (Jeremiah 23, Revelation 22:18–19). The history of man's dominion further demonstrates that men subtract or add to the Word of God in order to create their own form of authority—to displace God, if you will. These observations suggest that Adam added the words, "nor shall you touch it" in order to establish his own idea or form of control over Eve. Husbands, fathers, religious leaders, and civil leaders throughout history have all commanded or forbidden things that God has not. Their efforts to control have not always been with evil intent, but the result is the same. We are arguing that we know better than God when we try to control others according to our own words. We endanger the lives of those who depend upon us for the truth when we displace it with our own ideas.

More evidence of this perspective on Adam's fall will come in the verses below, noting when he finally finds his voice and what he uses it for. For now, as you consider this history of our fall, consider also how much damage has and continues to be done because men do not fulfill their purpose of maintaining the Word of God in the life of the world. Also consider here how ignorant the suggestion is that the Bible is written from a patriarchal perspective and blames women for the fall. Nothing could be farther from the truth or from the entire witness of the Bible.

"You will not surely die, for God knows . . ."

Every temptation has this thought in common: "God is hiding a better life from you; you could do better if you would choose/act for yourself." Listening to that temptation has and is still killing everyone and every marriage.

Eve has just confirmed what the devil was counting on—Adam has abandoned his purpose according to God's design. Because there is already distance between what God said and what Eve believes to be true ("nor shall you touch it") there is nothing to stop the devil from driving in a wedge of complete separation. Now the devil is free to simply contradict the Word of God already compromised. The wedge has three parts:

flat contradiction, accusation against God as explanation, and half-truth. Related to these three parts is the fallacy of free will.

The flat contradiction comes in the words, "You will not die." Part of the reason so many people simply disregard the Word after challenging it ("Did God really say?") is that the consequences for doing so are realized by degrees. In other words, the first experience of contradicting God's design is often intensely pleasurable; fornication, adultery, substance abuse all provide the thrill of "eating the forbidden fruit." The negative consequences of these actions come later, sometimes much, much later—but they come. Contradiction is one of the first human experiences that feels like power. No wonder that one of the first signs of a maturing sinful human nature in toddlers is that they say, "NO!" The devil said and continues to say, "You will not die if you reject God's design and contradict His Word." But every day our world falls further into ruin because we refuse to hear God. Every single problem we experience is the result of replacing God's order with our own. Some of the problems are more immediate and such consequences teach us well. It hurts to hit ourselves with a hammer, so we stop. Other problems are further removed, so we ignore, forget, deny, or seek to avoid these consequences. Sexually transmitted diseases do not exist among men and women who are chaste before and within their marriage (understanding that disease can be spread by foreign means). Yet people insist on arguing that sexual gratification is a basic human right. This insistence means that millions of dollars are spent to find a way of "silencing" the consequences with a pseudo-cure and also means turning a deaf ear to the reports that sexual gratification is often taken from another against their will (rape, incest, manipulation, abuse).

The second aspect of the devil's wedge is accusation (the name "Satan" is Hebrew and means "accuser"). The devil offers an accusation against God as an explanation and reason to disobey. God is accused of making a commandment for no other reason than to protect his own supremacy. This accusation has continued to be raised against authorities ever since, legitimately and illegitimately. The pretended supremacy of usurpers has always rightly been challenged. The illegitimate nature of pretended supremacy is evident in the selfish, trivial, tyrannical, and abusive nature of the control imposed. Such evil is to be expected, since only the Lord can exercise genuine dominion according to His nature to love. The pretender lacks both the nature and means to provide dominion, so he takes what is not his and hates rather than loves (consider the example of Amnon and Tamar, 2 Samuel 13:11–15). So then, God's creatures fall like dominoes. First an angel would claim the godhead, even though he is plainly a creature and not the creator. Next, Adam falls in line, imposing new law upon Eve and rejecting the order of God's creation that makes him responsible for Eve. Now Eve will fall as well, lured by the idea of being in control, when in fact she will always be controlled, whether by good or evil—God or the devil. Popular thinking in society, media, and marketing still capitalizes on this dynamic today. The feeling of power and of having control over others provides intoxication against the steady witness of our existence that says we are not in control. If we can succeed in getting what we want from others, then not only can we get what we want from them, we can also tell ourselves that we can get what we want from God (or that we don't need Him at all). For example, Anthony Hopkins plays a wealthy businessman in the film *Meet Joe Black*. In the film, Hopkins is actually incensed that death would come for him. Hopkins feels fully justified in having a right over his own mortality because he has earned it. In a similar way, men and women today compete for control in their relationships, fuelling their egos and their carnal appetites while justifying their actions by their ability to do so.

The devil offers a half-truth in order to push Eve over the edge. It is true, God does know that in the day man or woman eats of the tree of knowledge of good and evil that they will be like Him, knowing good and evil. But the devil leaves something out. He didn't mention to them that knowing good and evil is not the same as having the capacity to tell the difference or always and absolutely making the right choice. One of the most unfathomable aspects of God's nature is His ability to know all things and to make them work for good (Romans 8:28). Within God's creation, Adam and Eve had the ability to make choices with a nature and within a creation that would always be good for them. Now they will know all that contradicts God's design and what is worse, they will be oriented by their initial disobedience to crave those things which are worst for them. Consider the effects of this in our lives and marriages today. We regularly prefer food, drink, and activities that rob us of life. We say what should not be said while helpful words stick in our throats. We think that getting rather than giving is what life is made of. When we sense the emptiness and futility of getting, we try to get more and faster, rather than repenting and turning to a life of giving. The whole history of broken families and marriages demonstrates this fact, yet people continue to leave one relationship in order to "get" what they were missing from someone else.

Finally, underlying all of the above is the fallacy of free will. First of all, I reject the premise that a life is meaningless without free will. Neither life itself nor the experiences of that life lose any value just because we are not in control of them. Second, consider what is required for a will to be genuinely free. First, one must possess absolute knowledge. How can I choose anything freely if I don't know what all of the choices are? So if I don't know everything, then I don't have free choice. Third, one must possess the power to always make the right choice. This requires absolute power. Fourth, one must be in all places at all times to know the choices and to affect them. So far, we have for the requirements what has been described as "omniscience, omnipotence, and omnipresence." Finally, one must exist in the absence of necessity, because if I have some sense of necessity, then I'm not making choices freely; I'm making them under the influence of necessities I feel. As contingent beings, our whole existence is one of necessity, whether genetic, societal, or circumstantial. If we did have free will, how would we account for a bad decision? Why wouldn't we live eternally and live according to our dreams?

Thus the solution to our dilemma is not to exercise our own will, but to recognize the consequences of acting against God's will. The whole Bible is a history of the contrast between the will of fallen and contradictory beings and the will of a loving and life giving Creator.

> "... then the eyes of both were opened ... and they were ashamed."

The knowledge of good and evil did not include the ability to judge rightly nor to choose the good. The choices I make for myself show my inability; God's choices for me demonstrate His goodness and Godhead.

The fruit that Eve ate was not poison. The suggestion that she was free to contradict the Word of God was the poison. God's creation is still good. Only contradicting His will within it brings suffering and death, in at least two ways. First, all of God's creation was meant to support life. But as we are determined to manipulate His creation and refashion it according to our own image, we transform it into problems. We turn natural resources into toxic fumes, radioactive waste, and rubbish for landfills. Even when we are not refashioning nature, we tend to relate to it in unhealthy ways. Food is good for us, but not in excessive quantities. Rest, exercise, and labor are all good for us, but not when they are pursued in contradiction to God's design. Using the beauty of God's creation as poison is particularly effective in regard to human sexuality. Start with the fallen desire for self-gratification. Add the chemistry of natural attraction of gender to support procreation. Add the enticement of presenting the human body seductively with a culture that treats sexual activity as if it was as essential as nutrition and you have a "practically" irresistible situation. The human body is exquisite. As the climax of God's creative work, why wouldn't it be? (Note how art and media never have anything to present that is more beautiful than nature—a magnificent landscape or a beautiful human subject. On the other hand, there is no end to the ugliness of human invention seen in horror movies and bad art.) The experience of sexual intimacy is also unparalleled. Again, why wouldn't the physical experience intended to be indicative of a spiritual union be so remarkable? Yet the real beauty and goodness is contradicted when God's will for experiencing such is contradicted. Hence the experience of shame.

Second, Eve recognized that the fruit was not only good for food, but also desirable to make one wise. Wisdom without the governance of God's character is only "worldly wisdom." Paul addresses the problem of worldly wisdom in 1 Corinthians 1. This wisdom shows you what to go after, but does not show you the self-destructive consequences of doing so. Knowing more of what God knows without being God is like turning children loose with inventions of adults. For example, scientific discovery does not include the wisdom to guide. New knowledge forces new issues that we don't have the wisdom to respond to. Attempts at cloning individuals have raised questions about the ethics of doing so. We don't know how to resolve these ethical questions because we have pushed ourselves into an aspect of human living that we weren't meant to know about or manipulate. What we can see in medicine as in other fields is the difference between thinking God's thoughts after Him and attempting to displace His design. There is a difference between learning that supports God's creation (care-taking) and learning that rejects His design.

Eve took the fruit and ate and gave to Adam and he ate. So Adam was there. Adam was there listening and watching while the devil led Eve out of paradise. Eve had not run away. She was not hiding from Adam while Adam was somewhere else doing God's will. Here is the root of feminism and a reason to sympathize with it. Adam abandoned his responsibility of Eve, leaving her to the wicked counsel of the devil. In the absence of Adam's leadership she made her own way forward. Ever since Adam's abandonment of responsibility, men have continued to abdicate and abandon women. Who can blame women for protecting themselves when the men are not or are doing the opposite? Norman Rockwell captured this reality vividly in one of his covers for the *Saturday Evening Post*. His painting shows a mother with several children following, all dressed in their fine clothes, walking out of the house to go to church while the father, in the foreground, slouches in his pajamas in his overstuffed chair, behind his newspaper.

After Adam and Eve ate the fruit, the text says that their eyes were opened. This cannot mean that their eyes were closed previously. It does mean that they now saw things that they could not see before. Now they had "critical" eyes, eyes that would pass judgment according to their own standards. Before this, Adam and Eve had eyes to see how great God's creation was. They could look in wonder while creation proved the power, wisdom, grace, and love of God. They could look at each other and always learn more about the union God had created them to fulfill with each other. The change in vision is obvious in the way human beings see nature and each other. Over time, men have looked more critically at women, no longer seeing the one they are responsible for but the one who is not what their fancy wants. Already at the time of Moses, the Lord had to protect women by legislating divorce (Deuteronomy 24:1–4). By the time of Christ, Jewish men had reversed the purpose of the certificate of divorce and were using that legislation as the very means by which they would abandon their responsibility toward women (Matthew 19:1ff). Since the 1940s, women's ability to conceive has been viewed as a problem for science to manage. In the last thirty years, more and more men have rejected their responsibility for women altogether in exchange for homosexuality. (Not surprisingly, Paul anticipated this growing perversion in Romans 1.) At the same time, man's eye has changed from learning about nature to overcoming it. Before the Enlightenment and modernism, people learned to live with and by means of the natural world that surrounds us. Since then man has left hardly a blade of grass undisturbed.

Genesis: Model of Paradise Created and Destroyed

All this means that husband and wife will need to be conscious of this critical perspective. Our mouths seem to be more attached to our eyes than our reason. Criticisms are voiced without any thought at all, while positive observations get stuck in our hearts or throats. Only honesty about our condition and God's remedy for the shame of it can restore our vision. Restored vision looks for the good in our situations and relationships. Instead of seeing our spouse as a mistake, by the grace and wisdom of God we can believe and know that our spouse is perfect for us!

Example: Eric Sloan wrote a book called *Sketches of America Past*. The book describes how Americans lived in the 1800s. In one part of the book, for example, he describes how one particular kind of chair was made of several different kinds of wood. The different woods were used because each kind had certain properties about it that made it work just right and the furniture maker understood that. So early Americans molded themselves around nature and let nature support them.

Finally, the text says that they were ashamed. Shame is experienced in two ways. First, Adam and Eve are ashamed because they now realize how they have contradicted the Lord, whose Word created and sustains their lives. Before the contradiction they could stand in the presence of God as His creation, perfect in form and function. Now their lives fall under their own critical eye, which cannot recognize the perfection of God's work nor ignore the ruin that has come about. Second, Adam and Eve are now different in each other's eyes. When God first brought the woman to the man he confessed the perfection of God's activity by saying, "This is now bone of my bone and flesh of my flesh." Woman was the means by which the man would realize the height of his purpose in God's creation. But now all that had been cast away. Instead of complimentary, man and woman would see each other as competitors. Instead of living harmoniously, hand in hand, man and woman would clash with clenched fists. And what to do with the shame? Since the fall, both men and women have exerted their life's effort in defense of themselves by accusing the other. In more than twenty years of marriage counseling, I have never had a husband or wife come to me for help correcting flaws they saw in their own life. What I have seen is men trying to justify their lives by finding fault with the women and vice versa. But seeking to hide our own shame by pointing to the shame of another only exposes more shame—leaving it exposed and unresolved.

> *". . . and made coverings for themselves . . . and hid . . ."*

The choice for the word of one other than God/the choice for self against God, is followed by endless other choices for self that only make matters worse. To hide from God is to hide from my life and the life giver. To hide from my spouse is to hide from my purpose and take away what I should have provided.

Both parts of this text deal with concealment. The problem with concealing a problem is that the problem is still there. If the problem is dynamic, then concealing it only postpones and increases the explosiveness of what has been hidden. Notice that while Adam and Eve are still alone, apart from the presence of God, they make coverings to hide from each other. We have our own sense of what we are ashamed of, so we try to cover that with image, excuses, or avoidance. If our spouse exposes some flaw in us we rationalize, deny, or argue in our own defense. Clothing, work, special interests, or just plain being "too busy" can be used to hide what we don't want others to see. Yet covering things prevents the very union we are trying to establish. Trying to glue two objects together that are covered with paint and dirt is futile. The very union the couple hopes to achieve by hiding their faults is prevented by the act of hiding. What is essential for a marriage is honesty about one's self and trust in the covering that God provides in Jesus Christ.

Adam and Eve hid from God as well. Trying to hide from God is more futile than trying to hide from each other, because nothing is hidden from God. Determination to hide from God is tragic because He alone has the means to save us from our self-destructive course. Hiding from God is like hiding from the sun. True, no one can see us as we are, but there is no life, warmth, purpose, or meaning in the darkness. Hiding from God and each other is not just a simple action; it is an insidious frame of mind. As the text continues, you will see just how desperate we are in our attempts to hide and how these attempts mount up the evidence of our wickedness.

Example: What is the fig leaf about? It is an attempt to use some natural argument to defend myself. In every case it means I make myself the victim. When my spouse complains, saying, "Why were you late today?"

I'm not going to say, "Because I was just indulging myself and having all sorts of conversations with people on the way out of the building because I like to do that and it was fun, and I thought more about that than I did about you wanting me to come home." What I'm going to say is, "All of these people kept coming up and talking to me, and I was trying to get home, and I couldn't, so what am I supposed to do? And why should I want to get home when all I find here is anger and accusations from you? And you're mad at me about it? *You* never talk to somebody when you're supposed to be somewhere?" Fig leaves (excuses and counter-accusations) don't help; they don't cover much or very well, they don't last and they are a visual reminder that something in fact is being hidden.

B. Genesis 3:9–19
" . . . God called to Adam, 'Where are you?'"

This is a question Adam never had to answer before. If we follow God, He is always with us and no one is lost. If we choose our own way, God is not with us. We walk alone; we are lost and have lost God.

The text continues, saying, "They heard the sound of the Lord God walking in the garden in the cool of the day." Before they contradicted God's design, the sound of God walking among them would have been natural and welcome. Now they feel compelled to run and hide from the presence of the Lord among the trees of the garden. When we are living in harmony with God's intent, then God's presence brings refreshment and peace (like the cool of the day). When we are contradicting God's will, His presence is like the oppressive heat of a noonday sun under the glaring eyes of disapproval (consider the account of Jesus and the woman at the well, John 4).

The fact that God calls to Adam and Eve does not mean that He could not find them. Throughout the Bible, God asks questions in order to expose the truth of a situation, not because He needs information. The first question God asks in the Bible is comprehensive and priceless for its framing of the problem: "Adam, where are you?" Notice that God does not call them both. Eve has disobeyed God as well as Adam, but Adam is responsible. Where is Adam? Where has Adam been? Where was Adam when he added to God's Word in order to create his own relationship of control over Eve? Where was Adam when the devil was seeking to control Eve in his own way? Where is Adam, what can he be thinking by trying to cover up the disintegration of God's creative work? The question is not about physical location but about spiritual and mental disposition. The same question penetrates to the heart of our troubles today. At any moment, we do well to ask ourselves where we are in relation to God's Word and His intent for our lives. The only solution to our troubles is to make the question unnecessary. If we remain in His Word, we all know where we are and where we are going (John 8:31–32; 1 John 1:6–7).

> " . . . I was afraid because I was naked, and I hid myself . . ."

Being naked before God brought neither shame nor fear until man rejected God's order of life. Man is the one who is now ashamed and hiding, because through his actions/lack of responsibility, he had contradicted God's conclusion that His creation was "very good."

Finally, Adam finds his voice. Choosing to know what is contrary to God's will for us is an act of contradiction in itself. Choosing to know evil has already clouded Adam's knowledge of good. It is right to fear God, but not because we are naked. We do have much to hide, but it cannot be hidden. God's will is that we should live, not die. That is why God gave Adam instruction in the way of life. Just as God is the creator of life, so also He has the power and will to restore it. Consider how Jesus' act of redemption was an exchange of lives. Jesus dies in the most shameful way possible, naked and exposed to public ridicule, and abandoned by His Father. Jesus endured this in order to cover us with His own righteousness.

Next, God asked Adam, "Who told you that you were naked?" God did not tell Adam he was naked, nor did God accuse Adam of anything. God simply wants Adam to consider where the cause of the trouble rests. Adam's own conscience has condemned him because he contradicted God's clear Word to him. What is really tragic is that the voice in Adam's head that is telling him he is guilty is also keeping him from the voice of his Creator. Why hide? Why not seek God when we are in trouble? The Bible is a whole history of why we should seek God, but two examples are particularly illustrative because they are offered within the male/female relationship. Ezekiel 16 describes Israel as a female infant discarded at birth, lying helpless in her own blood and waiting to die. God saw her struggle and commanded her to live. Then God clothed her in order to present her as beautiful and honorable. Ephesians 5 describes how Christ has done the same thing for us, presenting us holy and without spot or blemish. God provides a perfect covering for our shame and regeneration according to the image of Christ, so that every man may provide the very same in the life of his wife and family.

Finally God asks, "Have you eaten of the tree which I commanded you that you should not eat?" God's third question for Adam is really an invitation to recover, to do the right thing. He's giving Adam a chance to rebound, to be responsible and tell the truth. The problem for Adam is that he has died, as God warned. There is no part of his nature left that can respond according to God's design.

> " . . . the woman you gave to be with me . . . "

First man tries to hide himself behind fig leaves and among trees. When God exposes man in those hiding places, he tries to shift the shame—man accuses both God and his wife of guilt for his sin.

Adam responded to God's third question with accusation rather than confession. (Jesus described this change in image and creator in John 8, by noting the stark contrast between the Pharisees and Abraham, whom they claimed as their father. Their father was in fact the devil.) By contradicting God's design, Adam had refashioned himself in the image of Satan, the father of accusation and destruction. In this text we may note three accusations.

First, Adam accuses the woman of being the cause of their situation. Every human being, male and female, since Adam shares this orientation of blaming others. Yet Eve cannot be at fault because she was not created nor authorized to be responsible. In fact, Eve's vulnerability to deception was part of what made her perfect in union with Adam. But that perfection only existed as long as Adam was being responsible for her life in God's Word and will. Similarly today, when there is trouble in a marriage or family, the accusations fly. Each person is responsible for their own actions and suffers the consequences of them, but husbands and fathers are responsible for the whole. Here is the reason why this marriage counseling approach seems so heavily oriented toward the man. Adam is responsible for the fall of all creation. The Son of God, whom Paul calls the second Adam, is responsible for its restoration (Romans 5:12–21).

Second, Adam assigns the cause of the fall to God, turning from the woman who was given to the God who gave her. Human beings continue to follow this pattern as well. The world's history is filled with people who hate, renounce, or deny God because they blame Him for their miserable condition. Philosophers contend that this argument against the existence of an almighty benevolent God is insurmountable. God is either not powerful enough or not good. Is this true, or just more venom from the serpent? God created a universe that was perfect, where everything lived forever and nothing ever died. God provided a tree of life, from which people could eat freely. And, God commanded Adam not to eat from the tree of the knowledge of good and evil. How then is God responsible for the fall? I find it interesting that the same people who argue for free will also argue that God is at fault for our condition because He provided an alternative that would ruin us. But how can you have free will if there is no significance to the choices? On the contrary, I am arguing that human beings have never had a free will because we are contingent, not independent. We make choices according to the forces at work inside and outside of us. Before the fall, Adam had the right orientation and the command of God to keep him in the way of life, but he failed. Now human beings are oriented according to three forces; Adam's failure, the cumulative decline of the world, and the continued deception of the devil. But because we are contingent, God has also provided for our restoration. He has done so and affects that restoration in a person's life completely by His own effort (Ephesians 2:9–10). So what fault is there to find with God?

Third, Adam's response implies that there is a problem with "giving." Does Adam really think that if he had made the woman himself we would not be having this problem? This is on the mind of every man who finds himself dissatisfied with the woman he initially craved. The film *The Stepford Wives* entertains the possibility and consequences of men creating women according to their desire. The problem, however, is never with the woman nor with the giving, but with a man's refusal to live in the image of His creator. Consider the worst-case scenario. What if a man is married to a woman who is cruel, abusive, and in every way contrary to what God intended her to be? What if her husband suffers dreadfully in order to love her and even gives up his life in the process? That is precisely what Jesus Christ has done for us, and the image in which He has regenerated His people, especially the men. Because Adam's fallen nature is the source of ours, people think that "taking" is the way of life and do not know how to receive what is given. Atheists do not know what to make of the universal atonement, because the remedy for everything they complain about is simply given. People ignore the grace of God conveyed freely through His Word more than they ignore anything else. God pleads through the prophet Isaiah for people to see how life is given by Him, not taken from one another (Isaiah 55). Jesus had this very conversation with the crowd the day after He fed the five thousand (John 6:22–71). The absolute nature of God's goodness is finally and absolutely demonstrated by His self-sacrifice (Romans 5:8). God gave His only begotten Son to become a man born from a virgin, to fulfill all that the law requires for one to live and to suffer all that the law requires of one who contradicts God's design for life. The Son of God bore away the sin of the world, and by His Word and Spirit, provided the means of restoring life, now and forever. God then is not to blame and there is no peril in man accepting blame, since it is already forgiven. Men accepting responsibility, along with all that God gives to restore human life, is the way forward and the very course we are intending to follow.

> "... and the woman said, 'The serpent deceived me...'"

Eve follows the example of her husband—nothing is her fault, the serpent is to blame. The one problem that prevents all others from being solved is this hiding from truth and responsibility for one's own sin.

What can a physician do for a person who refuses to be examined? But Eve follows Adam's miserable lead by trying to hide her shame behind accusation. However, in contrast to Adam, there is a significant element of truth in Eve's words. The serpent did deceive her. She is vulnerable by nature and she was made even more vulnerable because Adam misinformed her. This, added to Adam's abandonment of responsibility, left her completely vulnerable. Paul refers to this vulnerability of Eve in an often misunderstood passage, 1 Timothy 2:14. Paul is not blaming the woman for the fall, nor is he arguing that women are not permitted to teach as a consequence of Eve's failure. Paul is recognizing realities of creation: Adam was not deceived, has no excuse, and is to blame for the fall. Eve, on the other hand, was deceived, since vulnerability is essential in her nature in relation to man. The significance of Eve's response it thus twofold. First, the fall of Adam infects everyone. As Adam accused Eve, so Eve accuses another in turn. We would rather accuse and blame others to our own ruin rather than confess our own faults and find a remedy. Second, there is no solution in Adam blaming Eve. Only when a man takes responsibility before God is there grace, restoration, and power to return towards the image of God we were created to enjoy and fulfill.

> ". . . He shall crush your head, and you shall crush His heel . . ."

Before God explains the consequences of man's sin, He provides a promise of forgiveness. The Seed of the woman, Jesus Christ, will re-establish God's authority over man, submission to His order of creation, and forgiveness for what is shameful.

There are three parts to God's response, and the order they come in is significant. First, God deals with the devil. He is the ultimate source for the fall, and God promises the means for overcoming him. Second, God describes the consequences of contradicting His design to Eve, then Adam. I say "consequences" not "punishment" because there is a significant difference between the two. Punishment is a permanent distress experienced as required by justice under the law. Consequences are simply the results of actions. If our actions contradict God's design for life, then we have a small taste of death. Yet consequences have a teaching quality; the intent is to turn us away from such actions so they will not be our ruin. Third, God provides a physical indication of the absolute remedy He provides through the life of His Son.

God deals with the devil summarily. The devil has already fallen from his proper domain and has now done his worst (Jude 6). Now God's justice will be executed against the devil, while at the same time His mercy will be accomplished toward His fallen creation. A man will be born of woman who will crush the head of the serpent. This man will be born of woman only, since God is His father. The "head" of the serpent refers to his power, and in this case refers specifically to his power to condemn people under the law (Revelation 12:9–11). The Son of God and Son of Man will destroy the serpent's power to accuse by taking upon Himself all of our guilt, full responsibility under the law, as Adam should have (Galatians 4:4, 2 Corinthians 5:21). This victory of the second Adam will not come easily. The serpent will crush the heel of the savior, which means that the savior would suffer greatly, as we witness during His passion and death. By His incarnation and life, this promised savior will not only redeem all people, He will also re-establish the model of male conduct and the means of re-creating men and women in the image God intended through the power of His Word and Spirit (Titus 3:4–5).

"... in pain you shall bring forth children ..."

Read verse 16 carefully.

The two things that woman was created to do in paradise were to bear children and help her husband. Since she was determined not to be content with God's order for paradise, she will have a span of life on earth to face the consequences of her own choice in contradiction to God's will.

Now, it will be hard for her to bear children and to submit to her husband. The only thing that will make child bearing and submission bearable (even enjoyable) will be a re-submission to God's Word and choice for her.

There are two main consequences for Eve. One has to do with child bearing; the other has to do with her relationship with Adam. What would have functioned perfectly for Eve before the fall will now come with great difficulty. First, in regard to bearing children, notice that the text says that her sorrow in conception will multiply. I suggest this means that before the fall, Eve would have ovulated only as often as God intended her to conceive. Just as there was no death or waste in God's perfect creation, so there would be no death or shedding of blood within Eve's physiology. When Eve would have conceived, her body would have responded perfectly and painlessly to the process of pregnancy and delivery. All of the pain and difficulties involved with women's reproductive physiology and the effect on their whole being are a constant reminder of what happens when God's design and intent for us is despised. Though these consequences are unavoidable, they are not insurmountable, especially for women of faith. Faith in the redemptive work of Christ relieves issues of guilt. Faith in God as redeemer and creator inspires women to consider their own experience from a different perspective. Christian women understand the pain associated with their ability to conceive as a consequence of the fall. This reminder urges them to attempt, as much as possible, to approach God's enduring purpose for them. In this way much good has been recovered in the last forty years or so. For most of history, women understood that bearing children demonstrated their essential role in life and the children they raised provided security for them. Children were wanted and welcomed because they gave permanent and absolute value to the woman's life. The modern period of history (1700–1950 AD), with its arrogance toward nature and its materialism devalued what was essential to the female gender. Children have been seen as unwanted and unpleasant by-products of sexual gratification. Careers in the production of trivial and disposable industry became exalted, while raising children with eternal souls was despised. Women's own natural instincts and abilities to bear, deliver, and raise children have been mocked, while modern medicine usurped the process of delivery: incapacitating the mother with drugs and forcibly delivering the baby in opposition to natural forces. Only since post World War II has medicine given credit to the wisdom of nature (by God's design). Lamaze and other natural approaches help women benefit from their innate ability in the whole process of pregnancy, delivery, and child rearing. I have known many Christian women who have a wonderful natural ability to bear children and their husbands are wonderful fathers. They approach parenthood in faith and it seems to come easy to them. But even for those who have great difficulties with bearing children, faith in God's creative intent and in His redemption imbues the suffering with value. A woman's life is still bound up in God's intent and design. Whether easy, difficult, or not at all, she realizes unique significance in her life in relation to God's continuing creation of new human lives. She may raise her own, she may help raise the children of others, she may support the process medically, educationally, or through any number of other arts—but the purpose remains bound up in the lives of children.

The second main consequence of the fall for Eve has to do with the relationship between woman and man. Since Eve rejected God's design that she thrive under the responsibility of her husband, the submission that once came naturally would now be fraught with difficulty. After the fall, a woman's desire will be for her husband, but he must rule over her. Most of the world believes that "desire" means some sort of physical or emotional attraction. This is simply not true. The meaning of the word "desire" in this text is made clear by its use in the very next chapter. In Genesis 4:7 the very same word is used when God told Cain that sin had its desire for him. Sin had no physical or emotional attraction to Cain. The meaning can only be that sin's desire meant control. Sin wanted to control and master Cain, and it did. Instead of finding submission to responsibility natural, Eve and every woman since find submission unwise, difficult, and even repulsive. Women do in fact desire to control their husbands in particular and other men in general. This desire has been determined and unrelenting in the modern period as well. Women's suffrage, women's independence, women in the labor force, and women's equality are all finding success in their respective agendas. In part these agendas and successes are understandable. If men are going to abandon their responsibility to women, what is left for the women to do? Many of the successes of the feminist agenda take place precisely because men simply stand aside. But God reminds us that the man "must" rule over her. Conviction of meaning here is provided, again, from the Genesis 4 text. God told Cain he must rule over sin if he would preserve his own life. In the same way, man must return to his role of caretaker and provider if life is to be experienced in a positive way. Remember here that "rule" means dominion according to the sense previously explained. Christ must rule over us if we are to live and thrive—but His rule is only one of giving and goodness toward us. So for the woman, faith is required in three directions. First, she cannot live apart from faith in the Lord Jesus, who promises to provide for her life in every respect. Through relationships with men and children, for better or worse, the Lord will surely and ultimately save her life. Second, she cannot know the significance of her ability in regard to children apart from confidence in God's creative intent for her gender. Third, she can have hope of knowing at least a part of what God intended in marriage by finding and submitting to the care of a man who also intends to fulfill God's design in his life toward her.

Example: One aspect of "control" that surfaces between husbands and wives is over money. One wife in particular was consistently frustrated with her husband because he would not allow her to spend as she saw fit. She wanted more control. On the other hand, the husband saw his control over money as a right which he should exercise as he saw fit. What to do? By faith, it would be possible for the wife to consider that one's life does not consist in the abundance of possessions (Luke 12:15). She might instead find her life and fulfillment in the pursuit of activities with her children and/or husband that were much more meaningful and gratifying. By faith it would also be possible for the husband to recognize that "rule" does not mean "control." To rule over his wife means to support and provide for her, just as God does for us. Perhaps the best way to bear witness to his love for her would be to relinquish control of the finances. Let the wife spend as she sees fit. What is the worst that could happen? What if she spent too much on what was not important and then there was no money left to pay the necessities? She would surely learn by consequence that her priorities were not good. Isn't that just what God did with Adam and Eve? On the other hand, she might just display prudence in her spending, in which case the husband would find the freedom to live without concern for the money. Either way, we realize our potential as God's creation by faith and by pursuing His will for us. Temporal and material things are always a good sacrifice (actually, little to sacrifice) in the interest of eternal life and well-being. Eternal and essential matters of life ought never to be sacrificed.

> "... Because you have heeded the voice of your wife ..."

Adam faces consequences for his choice as Eve did. Under God's order, Adam would have gladly cared for wife and creation while wife and creation would have willingly responded to that care. Now Adam will (and we too) have a constant reminder of the results of his choice. Care for the earth will be HARD work and responsibility for his wife is something he MUST (verse 16) do in the face of rebellion (as he rebelled against God).

The "buck" stops with Adam. Since he was responsible for Eve, the consequences of his failure conclude with him. God introduces the consequences with the cause—Adam heeded the voice of his wife. Actually,

Adam disobeyed God on two counts: first by hearing instead of speaking to and for Eve, and second by eating the fruit that God forbade. There is no wisdom or (good) counsel against God (Proverbs 21:30). That means any time we are heeding a voice that is not God's we are contradicting His design and will suffer for it (consider the good example of the Bereans, Acts 17:11). God's design for Adam and his failure explain why the New Testament forbids women to speak in the public assembly of Christians for worship. Men need to uphold and honor God's will by demonstrating responsibility for the well-being of women. This should be true above all in the visible body of Christ—the Christian congregation gathered for public worship. This does not mean that women have nothing worthwhile to say, nor does it mean that husbands may not or should not listen to their wives. What it does mean is that the only sure Word we have on life is from the Lord and that it is the man's responsibility to be a constant witness to that Word. If Adam had heeded God, he would not have eaten the fruit nor would he have allowed Eve to do so. Jesus demonstrates the fulfillment of God's intent by heeding only the voice of His Father (Matthew 4:1–11; John 8:38, 15:15) and by preventing His own faithful people from falling (Luke 22:32; John 10:27–28). God's Word and will for man means that man ought not and need not hear any other voice than God's, since no other voice can be trusted. Even a pagan husband can be converted without a word from his wife. Peter's counsel to women is thus consistent with the image of God men and women are to uphold. Peter says that even if a woman has an unbeliever for a husband, she may win him without a word by her chaste conduct accompanied with fear (1 Peter 3:1–2). Christian men listen to God and their wives, but differently. Christian men listen to God with absolute confidence in His Word and a critical awareness of their dependence on it. Christian men listen to their wives as caretakers, listening for a voice that is instructed and inspired by the Word of God or for a voice that expresses need for care and counsel.

After confirming the cause of the fall, God points out the effect for man. What would have been pure pleasure and come naturally before the fall now comes with difficulty. Just as pain and conception would increase for the woman, so pain and labor would now multiply for man's purpose of tending God's creation. First of all, the ground would no longer yield its strength. Just as human regeneration yields less and less of the perfection of our nature, so the ground is less productive. Instead of yielding fruit to sustain man, the ground produces thorns and weeds that work against him. What's more, man would find his labor difficult and painful. Sweat and aching muscles would replace harmony between the male body and the purpose it was to fulfill. Modern physicists bear witness to the reality of this curse by noting that our universe is "winding down." The energy present in our world to sustain life is being exhausted and cannot be recaptured. Consistent with the fall of Adam is the human response to this curse. On the one hand, many people refuse to change their self-indulgent habits in order to preserve our natural resources. Their selfish self-indulgence exactly parallels Adam's abandonment of responsibility. On the other hand, men continually idolize a life free from toil. Most men have found a way to liberate themselves from laboring in the soil, and the farmers that remain seek to eliminate the toil that remains. Chemicals combat the weeds, fertilizers replace the strength of the soil, and air-conditioned machinery prevents the sweat. But the witness of this consequence is not being lost. Instances of nature working against our lives instead of for them remind us that contradicting God's will has significant effects. The world around us can no longer support our lives, in time or in eternity. Comfort and over-eating have become the new gods of this world, but they hasten death, not life. Only the living bread that comes down from heaven (John 6) and the living water that Christ gives (John 4) can sustain our lives. Hard work in the Word of God and the essential aspects of human life remain the purpose and promise for men.

Example: Abraham and Job both provide excellent examples of the significance of God's Word to Adam. Sarah exercised her own will and lack of faith in God by compelling Abraham to take Hagar as a wife. Hagar bore Abraham a son, as Sarah had intended, but the plan was not God's and the relationship made trouble for Sarah. The text makes clear that Abraham only heeded Sarah's voice because God told him to—and this only to prove that we are always in error to replace God's wisdom with our own. Job's wife urged him to "curse God and die" as a solution to his suffering. Job did not heed the voice of his wife but responded, "Why do you speak as the foolish (unbelieving) women?" Job confesses and then in the end confirms that God's Word and will is trustworthy. Life is always found by clinging to it. Death and suffering without end are unavoidable if we abandon His Word.

C. Genesis 3:20–24

". . . God made tunics of skin and clothed them . . ."

Remember, within God's creation, no one and nothing was required to be sacrificed for life. Now that man is sacrificing others for himself, others must be sacrificed to remedy this. Animals (innocent) are killed to make coverings for Adam and Eve—as the Lamb of God will make the covering that takes away sin, guilt, and shame.

God's will for man is that we should always live and not die. He demonstrated that will by providing Adam to care for Eve, by instructing Adam to avoid that which would mean death, and by providing His own Son as a redeemer to provide universal atonement. Now God even provides a physical indication and confirmation of His grace by making a more substantial covering for Adam and Eve. Adam's disobedience brought death to his union with God and with Eve. In order to restore those relationships to life, God provides a substitute. God immediately sets His own Son in the place of Adam to provide an absolute covering for disobedience, shame, and guilt. God provides an indication of that by taking the life of innocent animals in order to make a covering for Adam and Eve's bodies. With these coverings in place, we can begin to recover a sense of life. We know that God does not deal with us according to our iniquities (Psalm 103:10). We know that God makes all things work together for good to those who love Him and are called according to His purpose (Romans 8:28). We know that his purpose for man is according to the image of His Son: to lay down our lives in order to convey the life-giving Word of God to others, that others might be covered by the atonement of Christ. We know that collectively, as Christians, we reflect the role of women as we submit to the gracious dominion of our Lord and savior. We know that women should take care to avoid relationships with men who are not seeking to live in the image of Christ. We know that if a woman is in such a state, the Lord Himself will provide for her life, and by the grace of God through her witness, even convert her husband.

> "... lest he put out his hand and eat and live forever..."

God did not choose to drive man out of the garden to punish man. God makes choices always for man's good. God puts man out so that he will not eat from the tree and live forever—AS HE IS.

Why did God drive Adam and Eve out of the Garden of Eden and put an angel at the entrance with a flaming sword? Was that Law or Gospel, a punishment or a gift? The text is quick and clear to answer that question. God is preventing the possibility that man could eat from the tree of life and live in this fallen state eternally. Consider, in the course of your life so far, how many experiences you have had that were bearable only because you knew there would be an end to them. What if there would never be any end to those times, no deliverance? God put man out of the garden, but not before giving the promise of a savior and not without confirmation of that in their coverings. Before the fall, Adam and Eve could learn of God from the circumstance of harmony. After the fall, we all learn of God by way of contrast. Not all of our experiences are negative. In as much as nature and our own lives are in harmony with God's original design, life is good. In fact, God purposely sustains life through nature as a witness to His will that we should live and not die (Romans 2:4). However, nature often wields destructive force. Whether quickly or slowly, nature testifies that we contradict God's design for us by returning us to the dust from which we came. Our consciences and experiences tell us that our lives are troubled and we trouble the lives of others. But God has given us a certain witness by which to understand our experiences. The Word of God bears witness to God's remedy for death and disaster. He has already provided universal atonement. His Word regenerates our souls according to the image of His Son. His Word is ever present and available as a tree of life. In this world, then, we live two lives: one according to the flesh and one according to the Spirit (Galatians 5:16–26). Our life in the flesh is passing away, but is doing so under the grace of God and not without the positive experiences of His influence. Our life in the Spirit is eternal and in perfect harmony with God's will. What we experience as Christians is the combination of the two.

4

The Ten Commandments in Marriage
The Model Revisited

IV. The Ten Commandments (Workbook p. 19)

> "... I have set before you life and death, blessing and cursing; therefore, choose life, that both you and your descendants may live; that you may love the Lord your God, that you may OBEY His voice, and that you may cling to him, for He is your LIFE ..."
>
> Deuteronomy 30:1–20

GOD IS not offering a collection of equally good choices before Israel in this passage. He is inspiring and commanding a particular choice. If you read the entire passage, you will see an insurmountable argument for choosing life. If you have read Genesis through Deuteronomy, you have seen an insurmountable argument for not choosing what is contrary to God's command. The arguments and commands of God are to affect our human nature; the promises and blessings associated with obedience inspire our regenerate soul. All together, God would surround us with a climate that would unite us inseparably with Him—for He is our life!

Obedience to God in our lives is also a powerful witness to others (Deuteronomy 4:6). A marriage according to the will of God is a witness that presents itself without creating fear or giving offence in any and every context of our lives. Counselors and friends are of little help to a marriage in trouble if we offer an unwelcome and unexpected diagnosis (however accurate it might be). It is not very appealing to say to someone, "Well, there's some problem with you that you probably didn't think you had, but I'm going to tell you that you have a problem, and then I'm going to tell you how to fix it." But a husband and wife each inspired to live and care for the other according to God's design does appeal to other men and women who are struggling. A husband in trouble may approach the witness with cynicism: "So, how long have you two been rehearsing?" or "I guess we know who wears the pants in your family." A wife in trouble may approach the witness with lament or longing: "Oh, I wish that was how my marriage worked." In either case, the witness has been observed. The witness of a marriage according to God's design and grace is strong, consistent, and appealing. The consistency of the witness allows time for a troubled husband or wife to make an honest inquiry and for the Christian to help. The help we offer is not just for their marriage, but for their whole lives. The witness is not only about what a marriage can be, but also a paradigm of what our relationship with God can be.

Example: I have regularly observed how a husband and wife will make jokes about each other in social settings. On the surface, the spouse is just being playful and sharing some good humor from his or her marriage. In reality, the husband or wife is making an attack. His or her frustration with the other is so great that it cannot be kept private. Disappointment, aggravation, anger, resentment, frustration, and all the other negative emotions accumulate and finally break the surface, even if a husband or wife would not intend for that to happen. That's why these emotions often surface in a poor disguise. In fact, the husband or wife is making a plea for help. The problem is that most of the time the others who hear the attack join in by agreeing or making a similar joke/attack against their own spouse. As Christians and especially as Christian spouses, we are free to confess our own failures, but not the failure of others. As Christ covers our shame before the Father, so we are called to protect the honor and life of those He has forgiven and redeemed. Self-effacing humor makes us approachable because it is the product of honesty and humility. These qualities invite others to abandon their bondage to maintaining an artificial image of themselves. Honesty and humility invite productive conversation and genuine union.

A. "Thou shalt have no other gods before Me."
Deuteronomy 6:4–12: "Hear O Israel, the Lord your God is One . . ."

Paradise was destroyed when man obeyed the authority and voice of another (his own and the devil's). Paradise is given back both eternally and in this lifetime when man returns to THE ONE GOD and diligently listens to HIS Word.

With the model of Genesis clearly in place and God's expression of the significance of His law, we consider the Ten Commandments. Paradise was destroyed when man obeyed another voice as another authority, but there is no other voice that speaks with genuine authority. God is alone; there is no other, so any other voice that seeks authority is deceptive. Therefore, to listen to any other voices, especially that compete with or contradict God's voice is to be following something that is taking us in another direction. Every voice that would displace God's will is speaking words that separate rather than unite. What is more, the competing voices do not have to be wicked or evil. They just need to call husband and wife in different directions. Marriage is only so elastic, and in time the union will break.

Example: One large contributing factor to divorce has to do with opinions of co-workers or friends. When people share what's going on in their lives in the workplace or with a friend, the opinion(s) shared usually favor the "easy way out." Since most people are divorced themselves, they are quick to give advice like, "Well, yeah, you don't want to put up with that. Just get a divorce." People feel better about their bad experiences if you end up sharing the same kind of bad experience.

Ephesians 4:4–16: ". . . one God and Father of all . . ."

Paul re-affirms Moses' word from Deuteronomy and explains that the purpose of the written Word, Church, and ministry is to restore UNITY in the knowledge of God.

"One God and Father" means that unity in reality, design, and purpose exists. The question is whether we will realize that unity in our lives or whether we will suffer needlessly by seeking to displace it with our own ideas. God unites us in many ways. Ephesians 4 talks about the "one Lord, one faith, one baptism; one God and father of us all" and so forth. The mention of one "God" is reaffirming the origin of authority in our lives. The Father reaffirms the origin of design and creation. There is absolute value in the work of the Creator, and this defines and shapes our relationships with each other. To think badly or negatively about our spouse or children is to pass judgment one way or another. I am either accusing God of fault or I am exposing my own failings.

One God, a man, and a woman create a triangle, with God at the top. If both man and woman are drawing nearer to God over the course of their lives, then they must also be drawing closer to each other. On the other hand, if one or the other or both are seeking something else, no matter how close to God it may be, there will be only greater separation over time. As children of one Father we have great optimism and confidence that He knows how to work union and harmony among us.

Jeremiah 8:8–12: "... they have rejected the Word of the Lord, so what wisdom do they have? ..."

If one God is the authority and His Word is in the lives of man and woman, they will draw closer to God and each other in a close bond. Any other word or authority will only offer opportunity for man/woman to choose for self against God and spouse and create a further separation between God and spouse.

In Jeremiah 8, God is talking about the false prophets, teachers, and leaders. He says, "They have rejected the Word of the Lord, so what wisdom do they have?" This brings us back again to the idea of competing voices. For example, if you go to most any bookstore and look in the self-help section or the spiritual section, you'll find hundreds of books about relationships. Any one of them may indeed offer insights or suggestions that could help a person or their relationship. But the possibility of help is uncertain. If an author is committed to renouncing God, then the question of Jeremiah is particularly relevant: "What wisdom do they have?" Even authors who claim to be Christian and use the Bible as a reference are often fundamentally at odds with basic teachings of God's Word. In such cases, any benefit depends on an author's partial recognition of truth and the reader's ability to recognize this. Why leave so much to chance when the Designer and Creator has given us His wisdom and Spirit in one single certain text? Life is too precious and time is too short to wade through the opinions of people who have displaced God with those things that are not. Only one text is without error, eternal, inspired, and powerful.

Note: I do not mean, at this point, to be understood as saying that there is no help to be found apart from the Bible or my interpretation of it. I am trying to make three points. First, only God can give us certain knowledge about ourselves and the creation we are a part of. Second, both the Bible and nature bear witness to God's design and may be recognized by anyone. Many people outside Christianity have observed truth in nature and have expressed it more powerfully and clearly than many Christians. Third, because of the fall, the further we are from the unified witness of the Bible, the more chance there is for fallen thinking to displace divine wisdom. In a similar way, anyone can learn truth and benefit from reading the Bible in their own language. But there is no substitute for studying the Bible in the original languages and testing every interpretation against the entire biblical witness. The fact that a multitude of conflicting interpretations of the Bible exist does not make void the clear biblical text that says the Bible is not of one's own interpretation (2 Peter 1:20–21). Such conflicting interpretations only exist because their authors refuse to subject themselves to examination. I understand and absolutely support the practice of listening to all voices with humility and charity. I have also seen the devastation that misinformation causes in the lives of people. Therefore, we listen prudently, charitably, but also critically.

Example: Secular counseling treats marriage like any other relationship, most often like a business partnership. Each person has a need; each has something to offer. Communication is about negotiating for equity and fulfillment with what is given and taken. This is a far cry from the biblical description of male and female purpose.

I have also met counselors who claim a Christian confession. Yet upon investigation, I discover that they reject creation as a myth and affirm evolution. From this perspective the counselor is only suggesting biblical principles as examples of history that may still work or may be antiquated or obsolete.

B. "Thou shalt not take the name of the Lord thy God in vain."

Philippians 4:4–9: ". . . let your requests be made known . . . if there is any virtue, meditate on these things."

God's command is to call upon His Name (Word) and forsake all others. When we refuse or forget to do this, we suffer needlessly. God's command includes holding His Name (Word) before us to the exclusion of the world and its images (words). When we refuse or forget to do this, we needlessly suffer and also cause suffering in others.

To begin with, understand that "Name" in the Bible is a term that means the substance of a person. In regard to God, His name conveys who He is, and more particularly refers to His Word. God's Word not only describes God but also affects the will and power of God, because it is inspired by His Spirit. The commandment itself is a negative prohibition. The text from Philippians offers a positive side of the commandment. Paul invites us to "let your requests be made know to God" and then he goes on to say, "If there is any virtue, meditate on these things." Accordingly, this section treats three aspects of the commandment: the negative prohibition, the positive invitation to prayer, and counsel regarding meditation.

Regarding negative prohibitions, our concern here is not about the kind of swearing in order to promote a lie or cursing in order to intimidate, which this commandment obviously forbids. I hope you are not in a bad relationship because the other person "swore to God" that he or she was a really good person or because the other person swore they would change for the better. What is a very common problem in the average relationship is that one person or the other will try to give the impression that their opinion is God's opinion. Right away, we think back to the First Commandment with a concern that my opinion has displaced God Himself. That thinking now makes me transgress this commandment, as I displace His Word with my own.

We also give false impressions if we claim a Christian confession but are not careful to keep the Word of God at the center of our lives. We are not Christians simply because we claim this title for ourselves. To claim the name of the Lord for ourselves but prevent His Word from providing dominion in our lives is to deceive ourselves and others. This is especially problematic, because most people who claim to be Christian were raised with good morals and are basically "good people." But to hold such an opinion of ourselves leads us to assume or take for granted that our thoughts, words, and conduct are naturally divine. Our fallen human nature is arrogant and selfish. As such, this nature in us quickly claims God as supporting our agenda in opposition to our spouse. This is claiming what is untrue and taking the Lord's name in vain. When couples call or come for counseling because their marriage is in trouble I always ask first, "What kind of life do you have together in the Word of God?" The answer is always, "Well actually none." No surprise in this. Claiming to be a living spouse without ever eating would produce the same effect—death to the relationship (only in this case it would be harder to deny).

Next, in the Philippians text Paul invites, even urges us to take refuge in God's providence and concern for us. On the surface, the New Testament might seem contradictory at this point. Paul says we should worry about nothing but always make our requests known to God. Jesus also said we should not worry, but He said we should not because God already knows what we need and provides for us (Matthew 6:25–34). Should we tell God what is on our mind or not? The solution comes in understanding which nature is being appealed to in the text. On the one hand, there is simply no need to worry, because God knows our needs and provides abundantly for us. This eliminates the thought that we might miss something if we don't remember to pray for it. On the other hand, there is no need to be afraid of expressing your concerns to God. God provides two remedies for worry: the Lord provides abundantly and the Lord hears sympathetically.

Even if you are not worried, prayer provides a means of "re-orientation." Obviously prayer is not getting God to do something that He wouldn't have done otherwise. How could it be? Thus, a purpose of prayer must be to provide a time for meditation and reflection on God's Word that would align our thoughts with His. If we believe God is wise, loving, and has created us according to His magnificent design, then it would make sense for us to orient our thoughts and actions accordingly. If we do pray according to His revealed will (this is what it means to pray "in My name"—John 14:13) we don't have to wonder what His response will be. Prayers are to be offered in faith with no doubting (James 1:6). Why add, "if you will," and pray in uncertainty when God has shown us His will and what He is eager to provide for us? So in a marriage, rather than pray for my own happiness or for God to change my spouse, I would pray for God to make me a good spouse for the happiness and fulfillment of my spouse. Instead of praying for God to deliver me from my spouse, I would pray for Him to deliver me to my spouse—to lay down my life in love according to the image of His Son.

Besides re-orientation, prayer provides a means of demonstrating love by advocating for each other. Our Lord prayed for those He loved, and continues to intercede for His bride, the church. His Word not only shows us this image in which we are regenerated, it also gives us the very words to pray (John 17). Praying as an advocate of spouse or family has several benefits. First and most obvious is the help that will come as God answers those prayers. Second, prayer for another has a way of helping us examine ourselves. Let's say your spouse or the both of you are struggling with a decision. If you pray for God to show you the way, it may occur to you that Christ is THE WAY and that His Word is the voice you have been praying to hear. The voice of God (via the Bible) will either tell you exactly what to do (for example, "Do not be conformed to the world" (Romans 12:2) or "Owe no one anything" (Romans 13:8)) or it will tell you that it doesn't matter what you do; God will work good. Consider God's intent for Paul to preach in Rome and the perilous means by which Paul made his own way there (Acts 19:21; 20:23; 21:4, 11ff). God actually offers tremendous relief from second guessing our decisions or those of our spouse by assuring us that He makes all things work together for good. Even when we do our best to make careful and considerate decisions, they may not be the best in hindsight. We need not lament over this, but in confidence see what God would have us learn or how we can support our spouse and family in a challenging context. What does it mean to say we "love" our spouse if we do not take the opportunity to demonstrate it by being supportive in situations we would not have chosen? Third, praying as an advocate exposes selfishness early. Let's say a man's wife does not keep house as well as his mother did. This husband is unhappy with the condition of his house and the disposition of his wife. What if he prayed about it before complaining to her about it? He might conclude in these preliminary thoughts that housekeeping is not worthy of bothering God about. If that is true, maybe it ought not to bother him either. If it still bothers him after some time, he might go ahead and pray. While he is praying for God to make his wife a better housekeeper, it might occur to him that his example would be the best way for her to become so. God's answer is clear: "If you love your wife and believe a clean house is essential to that relationship, then start cleaning. She will certainly recognize that you love her. She may recognize that living in a clean house is preferable. She may even be inspired to clean with you, and there you are! Man and wife in union of love, faith and purpose."

Fourth, and most importantly, is to pray as an advocate for your spouse's spiritual life. This prayer not only re-orients our thinking toward what really matters, it also conveys love in a particular way. Praying out loud for someone is clearly an act of love and concern. When a man prays a confession, expresses repentance, and seeks forgiveness, he sets an example and demonstrates humility in a powerful way. Having prayed thus for himself, he may continue and confess and advocate for grace for his wife without being misunderstood. Prayer for another is not criticism. Prayer for another is sympathizing, understanding, and believing that the other person is indeed struggling with their own conduct (2 Corinthians 5:20). Praying a confession for another and appealing to God's grace for them provides an unmistakable intent in the prayer. It shows that I want to take the log out of my own eye first (Matthew 7:3–5). It confesses that compared to my sin, yours is more like a speck. It demonstrates that I want to see clearly and be helpful in removing a struggle that I know you wrestle with. A wife or child may offer such prayers as well, especially in private. I suggest that the husband/father do so out loud in order to bear witness to his particular calling in the image of Christ (just as a male represents Christ in public worship, praying for His bride, the church).

The concept of advocacy will be treated in more detail in regard to Ephesians 5 and the second article of the Apostle's Creed. At this point, let me also comment that my concept of advocacy in marriage will probably appear radical—as radical as God sacrificing His own Son and as that Son explaining, "Greater love hath no one than this, than to lay down his life for another" (John 15:13). I will argue that in a Christian marriage, a husband or wife ought never to advocate for himself/herself against the other. I will explain that there is no need to do so and that attempting to causes great harm by contradicting the design of God and the vows that were made.

Last of all, the Philippians text speaks about the focus of our attention in life: ". . . if there is any virtue . . . meditate on these things." We surely take the Lord's name in vain if we confess to be His disciples but ignore His Word. Do we really concentrate on the witnesses God has given us concerning virtue, beauty, goodness, etc.? This is not a matter of pietism. We do not gain favor in God's sight because we don't look at or listen to what is vulgar or obscene. Paul's declaration is essential to maintain: "All things are lawful for me" (1 Corinthians 6:12; 10:23). But Paul continues, ". . . but not all things are helpful . . . but I will not be brought into bondage to any." It is indicative of a Christian spirit and essential to a Christian life to focus our senses on those things that support and inspire our lives according to God's design. We don't avoid what is vulgar or obscene because God will punish us if we see it. We focus on what is virtuous because it contributes to a healthy life and good relationships. What kinds of images will be in our minds, what kinds of thoughts will we have, what kind of words will we say to our spouse or family if our attention is fixed on images that are perverted? I don't know how young people who are dating or even married couples can have a wholesome approach to romantic interests if the images of the media are on their minds. Making sex the center of our lives, seeing sex as the purpose of every relationship, and quantifying one's ability to perform are the unrealistic, self-destructive images of people who are intoxicated with their own desire for gratification. How can anyone have a healthy romantic relationship if their minds are filled with pornography? How can we deal kindly and compassionately with each other on a steady diet of "thriller" movies? Relationships between men and women can only be genuinely gratifying, healthy, and sustainable if they are patterned after the design God intended. Physical intimacy can only be genuinely gratifying, healthy, and meaningful if it is an expression of love that is the composition of all the rest of the relationship. We surely take God's name (Word) in vain if we ignore it in favor of the images that the world surrounds us with (actually we are bombarded and flooded with them). Recognizing God's love and wisdom in the second commandment means keeping His Word; expressions of the virtues promoted means that we kept that Word and those images right before our eyes. We are not burying our heads in the sand, but we are consistently denying perverse images the chance to contaminate our beings.

Example: In the 1980s, a documentary film was made about life in the "projects" of south Chicago. Many young African American women were interviewed about their life there. One common and repeated experience of these teenagers was that they were raped. What was even more distressing than this report was that these young ladies had come to accept it as a way of life. What else could they do given their experience, their inability to escape, and the pop-culture that permits and even entices young men to take sexual gratification by force? How sad to think that these young offenders (men) and victims (women) are left with no better images of what life can be.

Example: Taking God's name in vain includes considering ourselves Christian but not conducting ourselves as such. This problem is even more pronounced among Christian leaders. I knew a young assistant pastor who was called to work with a senior pastor. This senior pastor treated his work like a businessperson, trying to overcome his personal insecurity by working long hours and expecting others to keep up with him. The assistant pastor had been married for two years and his wife had just delivered their first baby. Not surprisingly, the senior pastor expected the assistant to keep long hours away from home. Before long, the assistant pastor was in deep anxiety, caught between care for his family and meeting the senior pastor's expectations. During that year, the congregation was also served by a vicar who was pursuing his second career. As such he was older and in this case, wiser. When the assistant pastor expressed his distress to the vicar in confidence, the vicar replied, "The solution to your problem is simple. You have a command from God to love your wife. You have no such command to meet the expectations of your boss, especially when those expectations would contradict God's will for you." What a difference the clarity of God's name (Word) made for the young assistant pastor. From that day forward he stated clearly and acted consistently for the welfare of his wife and family first. He did not do this out of defiance, but out of love for all—love for his family and love for the senior pastor and congregation, which he provided by his clear witness in harmony with God's design. In one meeting, after being criticized by the senior pastor, he simply responded, "If I am not meeting your requirements as a pastor, you are free to terminate my call. But if I contradict the Word of God to meet your expectations, I would be defeating the very purpose of being called as your pastor." What a tremendous witness this made at that meeting and what a positive impact it made for every man and family that was witness to it! This was not about defiance; it was about faithfulness and love—about honoring the name of God in Word and deed.

C. "Remember the Sabbath, to keep it holy . . ."

Hebrews 3:12—4:16: ". . . since a promise remains of entering His rest, let us fear lest any come short of it."

God's Word grants rest from the demands of the Law. God commands rest, which makes time for His Word. His Word teaches us how to rest (to live under grace instead of law). As often as you remain in the Word, you have rest with God (forgiveness) and with others—you serve because you are pleasing/accepted, not in order to earn acceptance.

The third commandment is unique because it disappears from the other nine in the New Testament. Whenever Jesus or Paul recites the law in the New Testament, the third commandment is always absent. The commandment is not missing because Jesus rejected it, but because in fulfilling all the law, He established a permanent rest. The text from Hebrews and one from Galatians is illustrative.

Hebrews says that there is a rest for the people of God (Hebrews 4:9). The promise of entering that rest comes in two ways. First, God promises to give us rest from a contrary human nature by delivering us, through death, to paradise and by restoring our human nature to perfection in the resurrection. Second, because Jesus has fulfilled the law and has borne away the sins of the world, there is a rest even now for our consciences. Nothing in the life of a Christian is done out of necessity or obligation. Nothing is done to get something we want or don't have, because our union with God makes us heirs of all things. The promise of entering His rest, even now, depends on our connection with His Word/Spirit that bear constant witness to this rest and that inspires us to a life of love. Christians love because we are loved. We care for others because we are so abundantly cared for. We focus on others because God is already focused on us. We give because God gives us so much. Therefore, there is no such thing as "have to" in Christian life or marriage. Any time a person asks about what is required, they confess that they are not yet Christian and do not yet understand Christianity. Questions like, "What do I have to do to become a member?" or "How many confirmation classes can my child miss and still be confirmed?" or "Do we have to stay for Sunday school?" all betray an essential misunderstanding of Christianity. Jesus rested for three days after his suffering and death, setting an eternal rest into motion. Notice that Jesus was invulnerable after His resurrection. Notice that the apostles were the same after Pentecost. The apostles did not give their lives in service to the Lord to get something they lacked, but to give something they had, which is inexhaustible. When they were threatened and beaten, they praised God for the honor of suffering for His name (Acts 4:13–31). When they were imprisoned they advanced the gospel to those who were imprisoned also (Acts 16:25–34). You simply cannot threaten or take away the life of a person who has received eternal life from the Son of God, who has risen from the dead! This reality is what makes Christian marriage unique. This is why I ask the initial questions about being free to marry. Christian men and women do not seek a spouse to get something they lack, but to share something they have. The root of every trouble in marriage and for every troubled person comes from trying to live under the law instead of the gospel. The text from Galatians makes this clear:

Galatians 3

> (Verse 10) "For as many as are of the works of the law are under the curse; for it is written, 'Cursed is everyone who does not continue in all things which are written in the Book of the Law, to do them.'
>
> (Verse 11) But that no one is justified by the law in the sight of God is evident, for 'the just shall live by faith.'
>
> (Verse 12) Yet the law is not a faith, but 'the man who does them shall live by them.'
>
> (Verse 13) Christ has redeemed us from the curse of the law, having become a curse for us,
>
> (Verse 14) that the blessing of Abraham might come upon the Gentiles in Christ Jesus, that we might receive the promise of the Spirit through faith."

Ninety-nine out of one hundred people who get married believe that they will be able to change the things they don't like about their spouse after they take the vow. The man or the woman knows the other person isn't really what they were looking for, but time is passing and someone "not quite right" is better than no one at all. This thinking puts two deadly forces into motion; one is expectation, the other is the law. This is what Paul means by the curse of the law. If we have expectations of other people, we have made our own dreams, happiness, and fulfillment dependent on their performance. There are two significant problems with doing this. First, we have very little control over another person's performance. Second, expectations always breed dissatisfaction. As soon as one expectation or one set of expectations are met, our human nature, now feeling entitled, formulates more. The only expectations that are helpful are the ones a person knows God has for himself or herself. God's expectations are not whims, but integral to our lives. God provides wisdom, forgiveness, and inspiration to meet His expectations. No one is really ever stopping us from working on our own lives. We can do something positive about that at any time. Trying to get other people to do what we want is selfish, unhelpful, and destructive.

Law is the other force put in motion. The language of expectation is always law and the law always kills (2 Corinthians 3:6). It is deadly to be forever telling someone what you expect them to do or how they disappointed your expectations or how they fell short in their efforts to please. Solomon expressed this fact in Proverbs 14:1: "The wise woman builds her house, the foolish pulls it down with her own hands." As Christians and children of the New Testament, we know that the law makes way for the gospel to be effective, but the law can only make way. It is the gospel that regenerates and inspires the faith and love that move a person to love and serve others according to God's design—within a divine rest from the burden of expectations.

At this point, recall how Adam tried to establish an image and sense of control by adding to God's counsel. So now, it is human nature to seek control that is not ours, to make up new rules that other people have to keep, and then try to enforce them. Is there some command in the Bible that my kids are supposed to keep their rooms in a certain way, or that we're supposed to have dinner at a certain time? There are all kinds of things that go on in our lives that God hasn't said anything about. What He has said something about is what should be the substance of our life together as a family, which would be the nurture and care of one another according to His design, by the power of His Word and Spirit. So, this is where faith confronts unbelief. Unbelief says, "I don't see how that's going to run a household the way I want it. I think I'm going to have a messy house with kids who don't keep their rooms up and it's going to drive me crazy and I can't tolerate it! So I'm going to make sure that gets done. It is simply ridiculous to think that the Bible is going to make my family behave the way I think they should." Here is the curse of the law: Cursed is everyone who does not abide by everything in it. In contrast to this conviction, consider the blessing of Christ. He gave Abraham a son, which was entirely impossible. The blessing of Christ is that He accomplishes in our lives what He wills for us, and His will is that we know the fullness of life and of joy (John 20:30–31; 1 John 1:4). The blessing of Christ gives us rest from thinking we have to make a life for ourselves and from trying to make a life for ourselves on the backs of other people. We know that we are God's workmanship (Ephesians 2:10) and that our role in the lives of others is not to harvest but to nurture (plant and water, 1 Corinthians 3:6).

All this is not to say that we cannot have goals, or that we cannot explain to others how their way of living affects us, or that we cannot ask for their cooperation, or that we cannot urge high standards. We may do all of that, but we do so within the Sabbath rest that Christ has established for us. We refine our standards in light of God's will. We see ourselves as agents of that will—God's Spirit working in us to work with others toward a better life for them.

The Ten Commandments in Marriage: The Model Revisited

Example: There was a father of four sons who considered his connection with those boys to be more important than anything else in the world. He was so strongly oriented in this way because he was so close to his father and because of abuses he had suffered from his mother. He had a very good perspective on what really mattered in life and what did not. He provided a significant and consistent spiritual witness; he supported them in all their schoolwork, athletics, and other interests. He did not react negatively at all to things the boys tried that would make my parents' hair stand on end. His sons dyed their hair, had it cut in Mohawks; they tried earrings, tattoos, video games, and most other fads and crazes that were popular. I would not have dreamed of trying such things in my parents' house and I can't imagine allowing my own children such freedom—yet when I pondered all these things I realized that none of them were of any spiritual or eternal consequence. These sons felt free to see what the world around them was doing, without fear of condemnation and without a dependence or carelessness that would have done harm to their souls. This father never made them go to church; he never told them they couldn't do anything that was on the periphery of the essence of being a Christian. But he did let them know, always, that he loved them and cared about them and wanted the best for them. He kept a house that he thought would convey that witness to them. Once I spent a week with him and was amazed at how many times a day he called his wife or sons and how many times they called him—just to say hello, where they were, what they were doing, when they would be home, and most of all, that they loved each other. The boys never, ever, left the house without hugging their father and telling him that they loved him. While his boys did not go with him to every worship service he attended, they were still considering this aspect of their father's character. As they matured, they gravitated more and more away from the trends and pressures of the world around them toward the stable, godly life of their father. Since I spent that week I have tried to approach this father's perspective. When I first returned home, I tried to be exactly like him, but could not do it. Still, I believe he is fundamentally right in his approach, and I have slowly worked my way in that direction over the years. My friend's house was a Sabbath, a place of rest. God our Father calls us to enjoy the Sabbath He provides in the New Testament and to make our houses extensions of that testament/Sabbath.

D. "Honor your father and mother, that it may be well with thee . . ."

Deuteronomy 7:2–4: ". . . nor shall you make marriages with them . . . for they will turn your sons away from following me" (see also 1 Corinthians 7).

God has given parents the responsibility of raising and keeping their children in the faith. In order for parents to fulfill this service, God has given promises (Proverbs 22:6) and commands to children: "Honor father and mother." Honor for God our Father, for father and mother and for marriage is served when children obtain the consent of their parents for their engagement. Parents' consent ought not to be based on personal feelings, but on protecting faith and marriage by making sure that the two engaged are of the one true faith.

God commands children to honor their parents for several reasons. The first reason is because God has given parents to act as His agents to protect the life of the child(ren). No authority to whom we should submit is a free agent to do as they please. Authorities must answer to God for their administration of the responsibilities toward those whom He has commanded submission. Parents do well to remind their children that they are bound by God to be involved in their development, to guide, to correct, and to support. This guidance includes teaching the children why, what, how, and who to look for in their relationships. I am, in fact, in favor of arranged marriages. This always makes young people cringe with fear and howl with objections. In response I ask them to consider the following:

1) How successful is the practice of young people selecting their own spouses? The divorce rate answers that.

2) What are you afraid of? Your parents have brought you safely and abundantly this far in your life. Why would they do you harm now? They have everything to gain from you being happily married and stand to suffer with you if your marriage is bad.

3) Have you considered that we do much better at coming to realize the good that is given us by others than we are at choosing what is good for ourselves? Compare the decisions you made as a child that you regret with the decisions you parents

made, which only did you good. (You chose to eat candy until you were sick; your parents gave you broccoli, but never too much!)

4) The problem really comes with control and packaging issues. We learned in Genesis that we simply are not in control of our lives and that the trouble we experience as children of Adam comes from his attempt to take control that was not his. The best way for us is to appreciate God's control and honor the agents by which He would provide that for our benefit. What really terrifies young people is not that their parents would pick a "bad" person for them, but that they will not like the package. They are so afraid that an arranged marriage would stick them with an "ugly" spouse. What is truly fascinating is that marriages that are the result of physical attraction most often end in ugly divorces between two people who "can't stand the sight" of each other!

Now, I am not advocating the *imposition* of arranged marriage; that would be contrary to the nature of the very gospel the parents are trying to uphold. I am advocating the children's best interests by forming a strong sense of the parameters within which any person would make a good spouse (any package will do). I believe young people can both understand and invite this kind of cooperation. Consider a parallel example: car shopping. I am pleased to let my daughters choose any shape, style, and color car they want. They can keep it simple or get one fully loaded. What I care about is the make. Is it reliable, dependable, will it keep them safe and always deliver them to their destination? In my experience, children never benefit from rejecting the interest of their parents in their dating/search for a spouse and parents never benefit from seeking too much control, rather than measured guidance. The history of Israel is a study in the horrible and tragic consequences of parents abandoning their responsibility and children insisting on their own choices. The Old Testament consistently warned against making marriages with foreign, idolatrous nations that would turn children away from God (Deuteronomy 7:3–4; Psalm 106:34–39). Both Samson and Solomon dismissed the good their life might have done and known by despising the good counsel of their parents.

Example: I know of countless women who are unhappy in their marriages because getting married was more important in their young minds than being married. When I ask them, "What were you thinking when you saw him farming or bowling or playing with his high school buddies?" They always respond, "All I knew is that I wanted to be with him." They really just wanted to be with someone, but marrying such a man means that you will have to be with him, whatever that means. In another case, a wife was distraught by the way her husband only paid attention to her when he wanted sexual gratification. I asked her, "What was the first thing he wanted to do with you after he met you?" She answered, "He wanted me to have sex with him." She was at first shocked, then not surprised at all when I pointed out that his interest in her had not changed. She had given herself to him on his terms. She had joined herself physically to a man who was oriented only in the direction of his own interests. This is why good relations with parents and with Christian friends who can offer loving perspective are so important.

The second reason for children to honor their parents is because parents have a perspective that is more seasoned, objective, and broader than the child's. American dating practices are essentially undefined and terribly recent. Until very recent history, most cultures had established patterns or means of pursuing a permanent union with another person. "Courting" was done in public and everyone knew what to do and how to do it. Dancing, music, art, and writing were all disciplines that allowed young people freedom and provided confidence. Young people today struggle with their feelings because they lack the means of expressing them positively and effectively. I believe many young men are coarse in their language and treatment of young ladies because they simply don't know how to convey their feelings artfully. Parents need to teach and nurture these abilities in their children. Along with social and expressive abilities, parents help their children recognize what matters in a spouse. Being open and having conversations with our children while they are dating allows us to share our less passionate perspective, asking them to notice or consider what they might not have otherwise.

What, then, should we be looking for in a spouse? For better or worse, the saying is often validated: "You marry your parents." Positively speaking, this means that a daughter is looking for the good qualities and virtues of her father. She is looking for a man who will be as faithful to the image of Christ as possible. The good love of a father for his daughter gives her the setting of providence from which to safely assess the men who would be part of her life. The daughter will know whether she is prepared (or even cares) to assume the role of a wife from her experience with her own mother. A son will know well the good qualities of a woman from the example of his mother. He will also know whether he is fit to pursue responsibility for a woman by his relationship with his father. The benefit of family for young people dating comes according to God's design. Children ought to know that their parents' relationship to them is quite "one-sided." I don't want anything from my children except for them to live their lives to the fullest. They will not know if that is true of another person unless they have the freedom to assess and the measure to assess with. Every woman needs the same essential things from a man, and vice versa, according to God's design for their relationship. If those things are present, the union will endure joyfully, regardless of other challenges they face or how the "package" they were attracted to changes over time. If those essential things are not present, the "package" has little ability to make or sustain a union.

Example: "I didn't sign up for this!" Over the years I have known of many cases where a woman left her husband (and in some cases the children as well) because she did not like what her husband was becoming. Several cases involved men who decided to become pastors later in life, but whose wives simply could not cope with such a change. On the other hand, I know of a couple who pursued a marriage union because they came to realize that they were already united in their devotion to the Lord. When they met and married, he was an engineer with a very large income and prestigious position. They started a family and all was well. Then he decided that he wanted to do more with his life than just engineer the material world, so he quit his job and went to seminary. After seminary he decided he wanted to do more than just pastor a congregation, so he went to language school and became a Bible translator. His first assignment meant that they would be moving to a small island in the South Pacific—with whatever they needed being shipped to them in steel drums. This also meant that the wife would have to train in language and other supportive technologies as well as in medicine, so that she could act as family nurse, physician, and surgeon. What is remarkable is that the wife has continually risen to the challenges and thrived in the face of them. Her devotion to the Lord and desire to serve His kingdom was inspired before her marriage and was now being realized more and more because of her marriage. Her husband's devotion was giving her new and wonderful opportunities to pursue her own devotion to God in ways she had never dreamed of. The longer they are married, the more they both realize how their union to the Lord means that their union with each other will be something to discover and rejoice over throughout their lives.

Third, what does saying "I do" change about your relationship with your parents? For the man, maturity means leaving father and mother and seeking responsibility on behalf of others' well-being. This care for others should be the norm for every man on behalf of everyone else in general. But a young man may want to extend that care to one woman in particular. A young woman, in contrast, does not leave home in search of anything. She is enjoying the freedom of living, learning, and experiencing life under the protection of her father's care. Properly speaking, all of her male relatives and according to God's will, all men everywhere would watch out for her (Ruth 2:1—4:12). Sadly, because of the fall, too many men are predators instead of protectors. This truth makes the protection of trusted men in her life even more important. A young man from a position of mature responsibility and a young woman with the freedom to assess her life are in a condition to consider whether they wish to pursue the future as husband and wife. If they are determined to do so, the young man must obtain consent from the young woman's father. Just as the young man is exposed if he exerts any pressure for the woman to consent, so is he exposed again if he attempts to bypass or force the consent of the father. Time is needed and with the security of family support, time is available to gain a conviction that will not be disappointed in the future. When consent has been expressed, then both families need to understand that the young man and the young woman now have new priorities in their relationships. Mothers and fathers must understand that while the fourth commandment is still in place, God's design and the vows of marriage give priority to the married couple. The response of the couple to the parents comes next.

Example: Many parents work destructively in the lives of their children by trying to be too involved or too controlling. Usually the cause for this is a mother or father trying to get something they have been missing in their own lives. Mothers often covet the attention of their sons because their husbands do not give it. After their sons marry, they often resent the wife of their son and try to manipulate him, seeking his attention and affection for themselves. An especially challenging problem comes in family businesses. Parents of a family business can be particularly controlling, seeing their sons as assets, along with property and equipment. Wives of such sons quickly notice that they are welcome to labor in the business, but only as indentured servants. If the wife begins to express a sense of entitlement to her husband's attention and to a reward for the labor, the matriarch (mother-in-law) exerts herself and there is war in the kingdom. The son finds himself under intense pressure to please both sides, both of which feel entitled and resentful of the suggestion to compromise. This catastrophe is the result of the son never having really "left his father and mother." He has added a marriage to a union that already exerted priority in his life. The only solution is to clarify to whom the son will be bound: the parents or the wife. If he will not or cannot leave father and mother (and business, if that is involved) then he must admit that his vows of marriage were never valid.

In one instance, an older brother stayed in business with the father because the younger had made it clear that he was not interested. The older brother resented not being able to seek his own interests, but stayed out of devotion to the father. After experimenting with different vocations, the younger brother came home and expected to take up the option he had previously rejected. Again, the older brother was resentful but compliant. He left his position to his younger brother and went out on his own. For years, resentment plagued the older brother and his wife, but in time that resentment was replaced by a peace he had never known before. He was his own boss now. He approached the business as a vocation by which he could be a good steward of God's blessings. He rejected all temptations to make the business his life. He refused to let work be his master. He, his wife, and their children enjoyed the business, their income, and best of all, their freedom. The younger brother was no happier working with his father than in his earlier attempts to find a career on his own. In time, the conflict between his parents and his wife caused their divorce, and the unhappiness was complete.

Fourth, always advocate for your in-laws. Living according to God's design offers freedom from others, but also freedom toward others. The same will of God that protects a marriage from the tyranny of parents also protects the married couple as they seek to love and honor their parents. A husband or wife is especially free to increase their union by advocating for their parents-in-law. Many benefits are bound up in this approach. One benefit relates to the eighth commandment. As an advocate of my parents-in-law, I am careful to never criticize them, but to defend and speak well of them. At the same time, if I am the one frustrated with my own parents or critical of them, I have the benefit of a spouse who sympathizes (boy, can we sympathize!) but provides a godly inspiration toward honoring them. The second benefit is the spouse whom I love, who advocates for my parents, might even give me insights that allow me to appreciate my parents, rather than be frustrated with them. Three, parents will come to know, sooner or later, that their son or daughter-in-law is advocating for them, not against them. As in-laws draw closer together over time, the son or daughter cannot help but know a better union on both sides.

Four, practical benefits of this approach include resolving tensions over spending time together. Let's take Christmas for example. If both sets of parents want the family all together for Christmas, what should we do? Typically, this is the kind of situation that makes everyone resentful of everyone else, spoiling the holiday even when the family is all together. When we are each other's advocates, the scenario is much different. Both husband and wife offer to work out another time to be together with their family. One may offer to do so because his or her family is easier to work things out with. The other may offer because his or her family is just being difficult. In either case, the spouse that is determined to work out the schedule with his or her own family makes it clear that the other spouse was not making a problem here or insisting on his or her own way. The witness of love is strong—love that is determined to care for spouse, for in-laws, and for parents. Now the family that is all together for Christmas has even more to celebrate and the family that must wait or rearrange plans has more reason to do so. God is love and love is the most powerful of all forces. Challenges presented by parents and family are occasions to let that force work among us to inspire and to promote unions that are joyous and inseparable.

If an orthodox Christian is already married to someone who is not of the same faith, time must be taken to see if agreement can be reached in the faith and if parental consent can be obtained. If agreement in faith cannot be reached, the marriage may remain if the unbelieving spouse will live peaceably within the marriage. If the unbelieving spouse is making it impossible for the believing spouse to remain faithful to God, faith, and marriage, then he/she is free of that bond (1 Corinthians 7).

Here we simply note that honor for parents and the honorable conduct of parents is always worth working toward, from no matter where we are starting. Anxiety of parents or newlyweds over serious matters of faith and life will not be relieved by the pretension of conformity or the absence of interaction. Parents are responsible to God for providing a clear and steady witness to His Word and will. Parents' love for their children is still best served by such a witness. Patience, good care, and plenty of inspired explanation will nurture a union if there is one possible. If not, such care provides a setting in which a son or daughter can admit a mistake and obtain a divorce if there is no other way.

E. "Thou shalt not kill."
Galatians 3:10–14: ". . . for as many as are of the works of the Law are under a curse . . ."

The most serious form of killing takes place when one person imposes the law upon another without a view toward grace. Marriages are cursed and killed when spouses continually judge the performance of the other, while excusing or ignoring their own failures. Marriages are blessed in a context of grace and forgiveness where each is trying to give, not get—to meet God's expectations and not to invent their own.

The concern of this commandment for marriage is not that you are going to stab or poison your spouse when they least expect it (although we do read about such things in the news). The kind of murder that we are concerned with has to do with a careless use of the law. Paul wrote to Timothy that the law is good if someone uses it lawfully—". . . knowing this: that the law is not made for a righteous person, but for the lawless and insubordinate, for the ungodly and for sinners, for the unholy and profane, for murderers of fathers and murderers of mothers, manslayers, fornicators, sodomites . . ." (1 Timothy 1:9–10a). If we were quick to say, "The evils that Paul lists certainly do not apply to my life or my spouse's life," then the law would have no place in our life at all. Yet in Mark 7, Jesus lists what our hearts are full of by nature and the list is a very close match. How do we reconcile the two texts? According to our human nature, we are oriented toward all the perversions that the law condemns. According to our regenerate soul, we abhor and renounce these perversions. As individuals composed of both natures, we find ourselves guilty, more or less. Knowing this about ourselves, how then do we use the law lawfully? Consider a comparison between butcher and surgeon. Both require a clean work place, both wash their hands, put on special clothes, both use very sharp knives, and both cut flesh. The difference is small but crucial: the butcher cuts to destroy while the surgeon cuts in order to heal. The surgeon must distinguish what to protect and what to remove, what is vital to life and what is contrary to life. The surgeon must be careful not to cut what he cannot bind up again. So also spouses (and Christians in general) must be careful to take the surgeon's approach to using the law.

Using the law lawfully begins with knowing that the law always kills, because it is never satisfied. The first problem with misusing the law is this: if we have it in our heads that our life could be wonderful if we could just get our spouse (and family) to think, speak, and act as we would have them, we are putting a set of expectations upon them that they cannot sustain. Holding our "loved ones" under such a burden of law will result in the kind of cutting from which no one can ever recover, like a butcher. A spouse or child held under the law will either come to hate themselves for always failing or become defensive and combative. They will either feel condemned with no hope of ever being justified or they will justify themselves and repel even proper applications of the law.

Justifying ourselves over time produces a second problem. We have a conscience that knows the law and knows that the law is right (Romans 2:14–16). The more time we spend justifying ourselves to a spouse or parent, the more practiced we must also become at silencing our own consciences. This is similar to creating an illness that is resistant to medicine. Many individuals in a relationship come to feel no remorse or sensitivity toward the other person at all because they are so callused from the practice of self-defense against the condemnation of the law. The third problem is that the law works fear, and fear in turn misuses the law. Knowing that failure to keep the law makes death (or at least trouble with the spouse) leads us to concentrate all our efforts on satisfying the law. But our fear of what happens when the law is not satisfied makes us just as likely to impose the law on others, because we have adopted the supposition that getting everything right is what will make a life for us.

By way of comparison, using the law lawfully provides many solutions. First, the fact that Christ fulfilled the law for us means that we can distinguish the essence of our life from the lawless human nature in which we live. We are already justified from all those things which the law and spouse would accuse us of. Three important questions need to be

The Ten Commandments in Marriage: The Model Revisited

reviewed in the face of these truths. One, did you know that your spouse had a fallen human nature when you committed to this relationship? Two, did you know that their human nature and the law had no capacity to change the character of that nature? Three, did you commit to dealing with your spouse as Christ has done, not dealing with them according to their failure in relation to the law, but according to the redemption that Christ accomplished (Psalm 103:6–14)? If you know these things but insist on dealing with your spouse by your own justice, then you are no Christian and your partner is counseled to question the future of the marriage (Matthew 18:21–35; 1 Corinthians 7:15). On the other hand, if you know these things and depend on them in your own life, then you know how essential it is for you to deal with others accordingly. Here is the beginning of a good surgeon. A good surgeon is not surprised or offended by the condition of the person on the operating table. The good surgeon sees the value and eternal soul of this person, regardless of how hideous or terrifying the outward appearance may be. The good surgeon knows that this life was created and will be sustained by God, whether in this life or the next. Therefore, we use the law carefully, in order to relieve another of that which hinders life and to make room for the Word and Spirit of God, which promotes life—all of this taking place under the canopy of God's redemptive act in Christ.

The second solution provided by Christ is fearlessness based on invulnerability. Christ has redeemed us from the curse of the law, having been made a curse for us. We are justified in the eyes of God, and no amount of accusation can change that. We have a regenerate soul that lives eternally—so no amount of bad cutting by the law can take that away. This means that we need not react to someone using the law badly against us, but are free to respond. Responding is not self-defense; responding is thinking about how the law is being used badly and explaining that to our spouse when they are doing so. We can say, "What you are doing or saying is killing me" without the desperation of a person afraid of dying.

The third solution is a monumental confidence inspired by a gospel that is powerful and effective (Romans 1:16–17). Having no fear of the condemning property of the law is enhanced and complimented by having absolute conviction about the gospel's ability to work good and bring life. If our spouse is using the law badly, not only can we disarm them with humility and truth, but we can also liberate them by the grace of God as demonstrated in His Son and the forgiveness He provides. No one can take the life God has given us, so we are at peace even under attack. The life God has given us can be shared with anyone, so we are advocates even of our attacker.

Finally, using the law lawfully and clinging to the grace of God for our life keeps us focused on the things that matter. Fear of losing something we want tempts us to misuse the law. Displacing God's content of life for our own, we use the law for our own purposes to force a manner of compliance which is counter-productive. For example, we can spend all of our time directing, correcting, and warning our spouse and children about their habits that bother us (since I am convinced that what bothers me ruins my life). So I spend my time doing what I want, unless you are doing something I don't want, at which time I criticize and/or condemn you for it. On the other hand, if my life and the lives of the people I love are safe from the law under the grace of God, then I am free to spend my time contributing to a life in my family that endures. Every day that we feed, clothe, read with, walk with, play with, and nurture our family is another investment in their lives. Those investments seem small at any moment, but over the years they build a relationship that cannot be broken. Consideration, doing what is good and pleasing to the other, will come, not from fear or criticism, but from inspiration to love in return. Not killing our spouse means applying the law according to the needs of our human nature and in the service of the Word of God's grace that creates and keeps recreating life.

Example: One of the most commonly used and effective weapons between spouses is the "cold war." This refers to the practice of dealing with anger or differences by not speaking to each other. The silent treatment is popular because it is both painfully effective in killing the one we love and seemingly non-violent, so as not to upset our self-righteousness. Many Christian couples of the World War II generation kept their marriages intact by this method. One husband I knew was very good at giving his wife and family the silent treatment when he was displeased. His ability produced some children who resented this burden and rebelled against it, while the wife and other children did their best to "stay out of trouble," but lived in anxiety over the penalty of making a mistake. Either way, the grace of God and joy of loving others was traded for living with minimal annoyances. Even since this husband died, the wife and children still struggle to rid themselves of the burden of the law. What is worse, some of the children have their own children and are horrified to see themselves making the very mistake their father did. Only the abundance and persistence of the grace of God has been able to keep hope alive and gradually remake a family where law and gospel are used well in the interest of life.

F. "Thou shalt not commit adultery."
Psalm 106:34–38: ". . . they mingled with the Gentiles and learned their works . . . they even sacrificed their sons . . ."

Life for man is bearing responsibility for his wife and children. Life for woman is to help man in the bearing of life while submitting to that responsibility. Responsibility rejects self-indulgence; love rejects the sacrificing of others. When men and women choose to be self-indulgent, children are sacrificed, along with the means and purpose of life.

"Thou shalt not commit adultery." My goodness, that seems simple enough, doesn't it? Experience throughout history and especially today argues to the contrary. Psalm 106 explains that the reason for such failure among Christians in this regard comes from adopting the practices of the nations who do not know God. Gratification that can be purchased with money and especially sexual gratification are the gods of today that too many people have learned to serve. Money and sex have become the currency of life, the "be all and end all" of human existence. We have come to this because in the absence of design and Designer, there are no absolutes and no enduring purpose for living. The only arguable point of living apart from God's design is to satisfy one's appetites. Notice how right that must seem to human nature. How can it be wrong to obtain the things our own nature tells us we need? The problem here is not only the depression of life without enduring purpose. When one lives contrary to design, gratification is elusive. In fact, the more we try to gratify ourselves, the less gratification we experience. God forbids adultery because it is self-destructive and self-defeating.

Thus, we are not going to learn from the nations. We're not going to take our concepts of romantic interaction from the world around us, nor from film, nor television, nor magazines, nor paperback books. We are going to learn about an emotional, physical, mental, and spiritual bond between man and woman from the biblical texts. The Bible uses language like, "Speak to the heart" (Ruth 2:13; Isaiah 40:2; Hosea 2:16). Speaking to the heart of a person is entirely different than trying to have your way with someone by talking them into it. Real romance is speaking to the heart of a person. The heart of the person is the expression of a person's soul that has a need to be connected with its Creator, along with the fulfillment that would bring. So when a man speaks to the heart of a woman, he's saying the sort of things to her that God would say to her: "You are loved, you are valued, you are the image of your creator, you have potential that knows no bounds."

What kind of life and love can be experienced with this sort of orientation? A Christian husband is always thinking about the well-being and potential of his wife. He begins with the necessities: "Is she eating? Yes, she's eating." Then he thinks about her mental well-being, the context in which she eats. If it's been a tough week for her, and if the kids have been making a lot of demands on her, he would like to provide her with affirmation, support, encouragement, a sympathetic ear, and most of all relief—some time to herself. He encourages her to go for a walk with a good friend or a neighbor. He might offer to cook dinner or take her out somewhere to dinner. Next, he thinks about how to speak to her heart over dinner; what kinds of things does she need to hear to re-orient, to be inspired, or to come back to peace? He also thinks carefully about how to provide physical support and affection without making her wonder what is being expected of her. He takes her hand, he looks her in the eye, he gives her a hug or sits beside her on the sofa. He is there for her and she knows this. All these examples parallel language that the Scriptures use to describe how God makes Himself available to us.

Physical affection that leads to intimacy should still be consistent with God's intent and should still "speak to the heart." In this aspect, as in most others, the dynamics are different for a woman than for a man. The capacity for and interest in physical intimacy for men is like water; water is always there, looking for someplace to go. Women are more like the soil. There are many conditions or circumstances in which the soil will not receive the rain; it will simply run off. Men are always ready to pursue the next level of intimacy, but struggle with restraint. Women are more restrained, which often puts them in a struggle with men. How do we make these dynamics work together? For the man, the energy that wants more intimacy needs to be channeled in the opposite direction. Instead of wanting more, the man needs to invest more in what there already is. Notice how this makes the more common and less intimate physical aspects more meaningful. How does he hold her hand in a way that says, "Holding your hand means a lot to me"? How does he hug her or kiss her in a way that says, "This hug or kiss is to assure you that I care for you. It is a destination all of itself."

It is not a means to some other, selfish destination? The woman rightly considers the advances of a man or her husband. She needs to know if his conduct is dismissing her concerns or creating new ones. Women want attention from men. Consistent restraint in the display of that attention by the man demonstrates a character of love that will never do the woman wrong, never put her at risk, but rather prevent risk. As much as a woman may crave the attention of a man, to allow a predator to make advances is to destroy the very condition of safety and peace that attention is meant to provide. If a man wants something from her, he is not the man for her. If he offers affection in order to get something else, then there is nothing good for her in this relationship.

So then, even within marriage, I am proposing something uncommon about intimacy. I am proposing that a man never advance beyond what is invited, first according to God's command, then according to the disposition of the woman. Before marriage, men do well to restrict their affection to what might normally be displayed in public. If it can be done in public, then there will never be cause for regret or shame. After marriage, the husband's focus is on the entire person of his wife. Consider levels of physical intimacy as the shape of a pyramid. The more basic the contact, the more of it there is. Just being physically in the same place is the base (remember Genesis 2, the woman was made to "remain before" her husband). In the same place, he pays attention to his wife—seeing her, listening to her, working "hand in hand" with her through the fundamentals of living. The more secure and consistent the base, the more appropriate and inviting it is to build upon that foundation. Over time, she will invite more contact and more intimacy. Eventually she will acquire the conviction that his character is Christ-like and true. With this conviction, she will welcome intimacy that is complete and climaxes with physical union. She can make this invitation for three reasons. First, she is free and not expected to offer it. Second, she knows that the union of body, soul, and spirit with her husband is real. Third, she knows that if she should conceive a child that would be wonderful (contrast that with the underlying fear of almost all men and most women when it comes to intercourse).

This does not mean that you have a "stop" sign and "go" sign. It does mean that two people who genuinely love each other are sensitive and can hear each other, even without words. Why should you "know" a person carnally before knowing them well enough to do only what is appropriate and welcome? Physical intimacy can only have real meaning to the extent that it is a reflection of and is supported by love at all other times and in every other way. The singularity of the experience can only be supported by the pyramid of care beneath.

Malachi 2:13–17: ". . . He seeks godly offspring . . ."

When man indulges his passion with a woman but prevents the possibility of conception, he deals treacherously (Genesis 38:1–10).

God has great respect for sacrifice, especially that which is offered with a broken and contrite spirit. So why does he refuse the sacrifices of Israel as described in this text? Because the lament of Hebrew men was not over their contradiction of God's will but over God's refusal to accept their offerings as a substitute for repentance. What are Hebrew men doing that is so wicked that God will have nothing to do with them? God calls it "dealing treacherously." This term "dealing treacherously" occurs both in Malachi 2:14 and in 2:15 with a definition of the term placed between. Hebrew men have been indulging their sexual desire with their wives while preventing them from conceiving. We do well to remember at this point that until very recently, women wanted to conceive children. Conception meant several important things to women. First, conception meant that womanhood was validated; a real woman held the capacity to bear children. Second, conception meant that there was significance to sexual union besides the personal experience. Third, conception meant children, which were the only means of security for the woman's future. There was no "social security," no public welfare, no retirement plans or pensions; there were only the children. Please be clear at this point that God is not so angry because these men did not want children, nor that they did not want to be responsible for the well-being of another. The account of Onan in Genesis 38 makes clear that self-gratification through sexual intercourse while denying a woman the significance of that union is what God calls "treachery." This is not to say that men or women are required by God to want children or to have as many children as possible (see discussion of below). It is the pretense and hypocrisy that God hates. If a man would avoid responsibility for others, then let him keep clear of women altogether. If a man declares publicly that he is a husband, then let him be one to her. In the case of Onan, some have argued that God killed him, not because he prevented conception, but because he did not want to raise children for his dead brother. However, the Old Testament makes clear that a man was not doomed if he did not want to raise children for his brother or provide for his dead brother's wife (Deuteronomy 25:9). The penalty was public humiliation, but not death. Clearly the issue with Onan (and perhaps with his elder brother who was killed by God) was that he took the privilege of sexual indulgence while preventing that from providing anything meaningful for the woman.

Accordingly, men need to be careful in examining their motives for seeking the company of a woman. Men want to be particularly careful to show responsibility and care for a woman by providing a context in which physical union is consistent with a character that "provides for" rather than "takes from" a wife. If a man is not capable of this responsibility or if he would avoid it, let him take Paul's advice and avoid physical contact with women altogether (1 Corinthians 7:1).

God's express purpose for the union of man and woman is godly offspring.

Providing for offspring is not the same as demanding, requiring, or being careless about conception. The responsibility of men for women in general and of a husband for his wife in particular is to provide for the woman's entire well-being. Within that context, the love of a husband considers what the woman's disposition is toward bearing children. A husband who would force a fearful wife to bear children is no better than a husband who would deny her the opportunity. A loving husband also confesses the sovereignty of God by recognizing that only God can provide for conception. Therefore, a husband provides the loving context within which a wife may come (whether quickly or slowly or never) to a place of confidence that would allow her to welcome a pregnancy if it were to be granted by the Lord. That confidence might be present from the first day or it may take years. What matters is that the husband is caring for the woman as a whole person. He is caring for her and not his own sexual appetite. He is caring for her and not just her ability to bear children. This sense of caretaking endures after children come as it had before. Most women need time, after having their first baby, to gain confidence, to recover from the pregnancy and delivery, and to feel comfortable enough with the first child that they might welcome a second. This pattern will remain true no matter how many children come. The consistent care of the husband protects the well-being of the wife, whether she is content with the children she already has or whether she would be open to more.

A second point to consider is that offspring can mean anyone's, not just your own. There is a profound difference between a husband who selfishly prevents his wife from conceiving because he would be irresponsible and the husband and wife who do not seek conception because they have devoted their lives to the care of children who are already in the world. Here I anticipate objections from both ends of the spectrum. I can understand the alarm of someone who thinks that a couple can only have intercourse if they want conception and that they must have as many children as possible. I can also understand the objection of those who strongly believe that God will not grant conception unless He intends it, therefore to be faithful means to have as many children as possible. In both cases I would point out that such an opinion contradicts the very nature of the gospel by which God deals with us. God has commanded husbands to love their wives. This means supporting them in their reluctance to have children just the same as in their interest in having many children. The gospel does not demand what a person cannot provide. The gospel provides the context within which and the means whereby we might at least approach life as God intended us to live.

Man's rejection of responsibility for the sake of self-indulgence results in sacrifice of children and women. His irresponsibility and self-indulgence leads to violence, abuse, and divorce.

The third time God uses the word "treacherous" has to do with further consequences of a husband's wicked self-indulgence. In Malachi 2:16, God addresses two more abuses: divorce and violence. What do these problems have to do with preventing a woman from conceiving? Consider the pattern of a man indulging and gratifying his desires by taking advantage of a woman. He takes a privilege but refuses any responsibility and denies the woman any meaning or benefit. Why would such an attitude and practice of a man remain restricted to sexual intercourse? The fact is that such an attitude reveals itself in the rest of his conduct. If a woman is no longer enticing to her husband, why not embrace another who is? And if he would avoid the consequences of being judged an adulterer, then he will just put the first wife away with divorce. This is just the problem underlying the Pharisees' question of Jesus and this is exactly why Moses required Hebrew men to give a certificate of divorce (Matthew 19:1–9; Deuteronomy 24:1–4).

Consider further that if a man is allowed to feel legitimate in sexual gratification and in divorce, what would keep him from violence? He feels like satisfying his sexual appetite and she is expected to oblige while he bears no responsibility. He feels nothing toward her anymore, so he indulges himself with another woman and bears no consequences. If he feels frustration or anger or any other emotion that sought expression, why not strike out against his wife? He has been taught by society that he has every right to indulge his passions without ever realizing consequences for his actions. Recent experience in American society confirms the truth of the Lord as reported by Malachi. Until 1940, every major Christian denomination was publicly opposed to contraception. At about that time, a woman named Margaret Sanger ignited a movement that promoted sexual gratification without responsibility, provided for mainly by artificial contraception (please consult recommended reading for more information about Margaret Sanger, her intentions and the enduring effects of her movement). Following 1940 every mainline denomination came to approve artificial contraception except the Roman Catholic Church. Not surprisingly, the use of artificial contraception by married couples became almost universal within a few years, and why not? It certainly appealed to the selfish orientation of most men and it offered many women relief from bearing children of an irresponsible man. What is also no surprise is that the incidence of divorce also began to increase, and right behind that was an increase in domestic violence. Even men who intended to be responsible and loving had difficulty escaping the temptation of indulging themselves sexually and of asserting this privilege in other aspects of their marriage, since they were free from any responsibility or consequences. Consider as further evidence the history of King David and his sons, particularly Amnon. David's determination to indulge his sexual appetite and to avoid any consequences not only led to the death of a noble and faithful warrior, Uriah (2 Samuel 11:1–25), but also established the pattern of his son's conduct. Like his father, Amnon also felt entitled to indulge his passion and raped his sister, Tamar (2 Samuel 13:1ff). What is so revealing in the case of Amnon is that he hated her after the rape as intensely as he "felt" he loved her before (see *Has Joab Foiled David*, listed in recommended reading, for a more complete treatment of this example).

Example: An interesting parallel is found in the behavior of alligators in the United States. Historically, alligators were afraid of people and would flee from them. However, in the recent past people thought it was interesting or fun to feed them. The problem with the alligator is that he does not know where the food ends and the feeder begins—so the alligator sees the person as just as much a part of the meal as the chicken bone. In the same way, selfish indulgence knows no limits and cares nothing for the damage it inflicts upon others.

> *Romans 13:8–14: ". . . make no provision for the flesh to gratify its desires . . ."*

Lives are sacrificed any time arrangements are made to prevent or avoid the consequences of my actions. Careless words, thoughts, spending habits, sexual behavior, etc. all work against the life of individuals and marriages.

This section from Romans begins and ends with imperatives that relate to each other: "Owe no one anything" and "Make no provision for the flesh to gratify its desires." Seeking to gratify the desires of our flesh make us needy for what can never satisfy us. Trying to find satisfaction from what cannot do so makes people try even harder to get what they do not possess, which leads them to debt. Being in debt binds a person in two respects: they are bound to the debt (they have to pay it back) and they are still bound (and even more encumbered) to their intent to satisfy the appetite of their human nature. Paul provides a list of human desires that he urges us to put away. Interestingly, this list describes a situation very much like the one Malachi was responding to. While human nature seeks material things more and more, real satisfaction is always sought in something that can be consumed: food, drinking, sexual gratification. Just as Malachi revealed the connection between self-gratification, divorce and violence, so also today we can see that over eating, alcoholism, and sexual immorality all share a common cause. The solution to these problems begins with responding to Paul's first imperative: "Owe no one anything" (beware of how most English translations neutralize this imperative, for example "leave no debt outstanding"). To live a life free of debt is possible because God provides all things for us. He gave His Son to insure our eternal life. This gift provides confidence in all God's other promises to provide for us, especially when that looks the most unlikely (John 6:5–11; Romans 8:32). In as much as our souls are reunited with God through the presence of His Word and Spirit, we are fulfilled and relieved of our sense of need/want. We see our lives in terms of how we can give ourselves away to others, rather than in how we can get from others what we feel we need.

Paul's imperatives are general and universal, as such they also apply to the issue of adultery. God has already clearly forbidden the acts of fornication and adultery. Here Paul offers wisdom by forbidding that we even make provision to satisfy those self-defeating desires. "Making no provision for the flesh" means that we think ahead in a way that keeps us from situations that would compromise our Christian convictions. For the unmarried, this means keeping a relationship public, out in the open where the company of others keeps their selfish appetites in check. Contrast this with schools that provide contraceptives to students, "just in case." Watching movies that arouse sexual emotions while drinking alcohol when there is no one else at home except your girlfriend is a recipe for disaster. Similarly, married men and women do well to be careful that their relationships with co-workers or clients do not become private and self-gratifying in nature. Artificial contraception is manufactured expressly for the purpose of making a provision for our flesh to indulge itself as the opportunity presents itself. Knowing that the provision is in place even heightens the interest and changes us into predators instead of providers. Living responsibly depends to a large extent on keeping consequences close to actions. Experiencing the truth that selfish behavior is self-defeating helps small children learn to share and treat others with kindness. Knowing that approaching another person for sexual gratification will ruin many other essential relationships will keep us from the intoxication of deception.

Marriage and the Counsel of God

> *I Thessalonians 4:1–8: ". . . each should know how to possess his own vessel in sanctification and honor, not in passion of lust . . ."*

Man was created to bear responsibility for the life and well-being of woman. That means keeping himself chaste and abstaining from passion when a woman would not welcome conception. It also means loving physically with a view toward conception, which is the life and honor of the woman (Song of Solomon 3:5).

The text in Thessalonians stands behind the argument of Paul in Romans 13. Paul begins by reminding us that God's will is our sanctification (verse 3). Sanctification means to be set apart for another purpose. Since the fall, humanity apart from God ruins its own life by obstinately contradicting His design. Sanctification means that God would separate a person from that mass in order to restore life. A large part of that "being set apart" has to do with "abstaining from sexual immorality," as Paul goes on to explain. But in the next few verses it becomes obvious that Paul is speaking directly to men. What does it mean to "possess his vessel in sanctification and honor" and why would not doing that "take advantage of and defraud a brother"? Since Paul is addressing sexual immorality, clearly "his vessel" refers to the man's genitalia. According to Paul, a man may either possess that vessel or be possessed by it. That is to say, a man's sexual organs were intended to serve a function within the whole person and whole relationships, in contrast to "passion and lust" of sexual appetite dominating the life of the man and all his relationships. The folly and irony of passion and lust, as described earlier, is that they are self-defeating. The physical act of sexual intercourse has very little meaning in itself. The truth of this observation is proven constantly by the sense of emptiness that sexually active people complain about (and Hollywood even makes a movie about this from time to time—*An Officer and A Gentleman*, for example). The more a man lets his sexual appetite drive him, the more often he seeks sex and the less meaningful that sex is. With the frequency of sex comes a conscience that says his conduct is perverse and reprehensible. The relationships he has apart from sexual activity are also unsatisfying, since he is either trying to impose his desire upon another or he is dealing with the consequences of having done so.

Paul adds that such conduct not only dishonors women, but also defrauds "his brother." To "defraud" means to take something from someone under false pretenses. There are two possible explanations for Paul's intent. The first is that "brother" is generic, referring to fellow Christians. In this case, Paul would be saying that a man should not take sexual gratification from a woman. The other and more likely possibility is that "brothers" refers to the men in a woman's life who are responsible for her well-being. Biological as well as spiritual "fathers" and "brothers" care for their women in order to protect them from having to use their bodies to get what they are lacking or from giving their bodies to a man who would dishonor them. In this regard, Song of Solomon includes a refrain that warns young women not to excite the sexual appetite of men until a relationship exists in which that can have positive expression (Song 2:7; 3:5; 8:4).

Finally, Paul concludes this section with a very strong warning which echoes the intensity of God's disposition in Malachi. Any person who rejects this teaching on proper relationships between men and women is not rejecting some prudish, puritanical thinking, but is rejecting God. The real force of this warning is not that God will somehow get even with a person who despises Him. The force of the warning comes in realizing that contradicting God's will brings destruction. Everyone suffers when a person or people act selfishly. When a man seeks to satisfy himself sexually, he finds that the activity was not satisfying at all. There is also now a woman or many women whose lives are disturbed by him. There is also his family and her family that may suffer anxiety, heartache, and the distressing task of trying to restore to the woman what the man has taken. In contrast, God has called us to honor and has sanctified us. Thus, our relationships are not passionless, but full of a greater passion that builds as selfish desires are denied. This passion is thoughtful, enduring, virtuous, inspiring, and spends itself freely yet carefully so that others can come to a similar sense of fullness in their lives. This is a passion that orders relationships between men and women according to the image of God and therefore need never be denied, hidden, or regretted.

ON NATURAL FAMILY PLANNING VERSUS ARTIFICIAL CONTRACEPTION
There is a natural means for dealing with concerns about conception. This natural means seeks to honor God's wisdom in creation and serve the husband's responsibility to care for his wife according to the gospel.

Before entering a consideration of contraception, we need to confirm the nature of our relationship with God. Remember at this point that we are justified before God through the life, death, and resurrection of the Lord Jesus. Faith in His atoning sacrifice worked in us by His Spirit is what redeems us to God. The question for our life is no longer, "Can I make a life for myself that God will accept?" The work of Christ means that the question is now, "What can I make of my life because God has already accepted me?" Nothing we can do, except despising the Holy Spirit, can keep us from the justification Christ provides. But if we recognize what Christ saves us from and where life is to be found, why would we want to do anything except make the most of this life (Romans 6)? In short, the issue with contraception is not whether it will condemn us before God. The issue has to do with approaching God's design in our lives in order to know the fullness of it. Now that God has saved our lives, what is the best we can do with it?

The intent of natural family planning is to be faithful to and benefit from God's design in nature. This care takes into account the consequences of the fall. Man was created to be responsible but now has great difficulty doing so. Women were created to bear children, but now that is complicated and laborious. Nevertheless, "being fruitful and multiplying" is still a blessing from the Lord and He still supports that blessing through nature. Our lives can only find real meaning as we devote them to the care of other eternal souls and to good stewardship of the world that supports us. This is in contrast to artificial contraception, which seeks to overrule and displace nature. Even here, when considering the differences between the two approaches, the gospel must orient our thinking. If a wife is so concerned about a pregnancy that she only feels relieved using artificial contraception, then her husband should consent. His consent, however, does not mean that he abandons the kind of care that would provide the setting by which her anxiety would be dismissed. On the other hand, if a husband would force his wife to use artificial contraception because he wants the greatest sexual privilege with the least amount of responsibility, this is a disposition that opposes love, and the woman ought not to submit to it. This is an occasion for her to seek an advocate.

How does natural family planning work? Many people who hear this term assume we are talking about the "rhythm method." There are at least three problems with that assumption. First, the rhythm method has a reputation for being used because a pregnancy is not wanted, just as the case is for artificial contraception. Second, natural family planning considers all the symptoms that a woman's physiology provides to monitor her cycle, while the rhythm method depends on only one symptom. Third, every one I have ever asked about the rhythm method had reversed its application. As they explained it to me, they thought that the best time to have intercourse was precisely when the woman was most likely to conceive and they abstained while she was infertile. This clearly accounts for the poor reputation this method suffers from.

Natural family planning begins with a couple's devotion to God and respect for His design in creation. Husbands are devoted to care for their wives and wives are devoted to helping their husbands, both according to the revealed will of God for their good. The husband's care for his wife means that he is already interested in her physical well-being, including her disposition toward conception. Accordingly, it is the husband who bears responsibility for monitoring and recording his wife's symptoms. Five different symptoms provide a means for crosschecking indications and recognizing cycles, especially when women's cycles are very irregular. This care of the husband serves as a consistent witness alongside the rest of his care for her. In this context the wife is free of anxiety about a husband whose sexual appetite is unwelcome and anxiety over pregnancy concerns.

At this point, many object that natural family planning is no different than artificial contraception since the purpose of both is to prevent pregnancy. This objection cannot be sustained. The two methods are, in fact, opposite in every way. First, almost all methods of artificial contraception put the burden of implementation and consequences on the woman. She is the one who will suffer the side effects. Natural family planning requires the husband to bear responsibility. Second, there are always side effects with artificial contraception and they are always negative and often very dangerous. There are only positive effects of natural family planning. For example, the practice and enduring witness of care the husband provides for the wife. Along with that witness is a conviction about the husband's fidelity. If he practices self-control and abstinence regularly for the benefit of his wife, what reason does she have to worry about his conduct while they are apart? Third, artificial contraception is used only for the purpose of preventing conception—consider how their effectiveness is measured. (The exception to this would be to provide medical relief for a woman struggling with other physiological problems, yet even in these cases, women ought to consider if there are not other means that are safer and more effective.) Natural family planning is practiced for precisely the other reason—because a couple wants to allow for the possibility of conception, even though they are thinking that now would not be the best time for them. This approach honors the dignity of conception and respects it as a gift of God, while confessing in humility that we know very little about what is really best for us. Fourth, unmarried adults and young people rightly argue that they are entitled to the benefits of artificial contraception. Marriage does not legitimate selfish indulgence. If a husband will not practice chaste conduct for the benefit of his wife, why should anyone else? Natural family planning makes the opposite witness. Chaste conduct is always good, and faithful husbands make a clear and constant witness that physical intimacy can only be enduring and meaningful within an enduring and complete commitment between a husband and wife. Fifth, artificial contraception tends to make sexual intercourse the object of the relationship. Even when contraception removes concerns about pregnancy, a woman still has other concerns for her relationship. While a man will do as much as he has to for the woman in order to satisfy his sexual yearning, the woman will satisfy the man in negotiation for care that will satisfy her yearning for commitment.

This kind of relationship is like an inverted pyramid, where sex is the controlling factor but ill-equipped to support the whole—making a very unstable relationship. (How many movies are about unstable relationships between a man and woman who are sexually active? Most of them! Contrast *Rumor Has It* or *Bridget Jones: The Edge of Reason* with *Miracle on 34th Street*.) Natural family planning promotes the opposite approach between men and women—the normal pyramid. The base of the relational pyramid is broad and least intimate; we share a world with many other people. We see and talk to each other, we share a community, and that is essential for our lives. We are closely related to fewer people and we are more intimate with them; we hug and kiss our relatives and closest friends. We share our thoughts and concerns with each other. If we find one person with whom we share all these things so completely that we are united as one, then marriage declares that truth to the world, and physical union of the greatest intimacy is a natural peak to its expression. Such absolute intimacy has depth of meaning and freedom from anxiety because it rests upon the immovable foundation of the preceding and complete union of the man and woman.

So what does a couple practicing natural family planning do if they are not engaged in intercourse? Such a couple is free from a vulgar sexual drive to invest themselves in all the other aspects of living that our world provides. Walking, talking, cooking, painting, traveling, shopping, dancing, sailing, reading, and a thousand other activities are waiting for them to explore together. Physical tenderness and romance is also available, and their passion provides inspiration to show this long and well. For example, providing a wonderful evening at home by creating a romantic setting, cooking a special meal, and watching a favorite film or concert is wonderful all in itself. Giving a massage to your spouse is an opportunity to care for them intimately and for as long as you like (I have never known the spouse receiving the massage to say, "How soon will you be finished?" unless it is an especially poor massage). The wholeness of natural family planning inspires and excites us to explore aspects of our life together that a narrow focus on sexual intercourse makes us blind to and disinterested in pursuing.

Let me say again that the concern with artificial contraception is not that it is sinful or condemns a person before God. The concern is that it is such a contradiction to God's intent for relations between people. A Christian couple may have many good reasons for using artificial contraception and need not carry any burden of guilt. But in doing so they also trade the benefits of natural family planning for the challenges and dangers of contraception.

G. "Thou shalt not steal."

Matthew 6:19–24: " . . . For where your treasure is, there your heart will be also."

A marriage cannot remain when spouses are taking from each other to satisfy themselves. It is not the getting or taking of things that makes for life, but taking CARE OF others. You cannot serve the world's idea of wealth (taking all I want from everyone around me, including God, and returning only as much as I feel comfortable with) and have God's true riches. Only caring for and giving of myself protects what God has given me (marriage) and whom He has given me (spouse, children).

As with murder, so also with stealing, the concern is not about taking cash out of each other's wallets, although that happens too. The problem with stealing in most marriages is how subtle and seemingly justified it seems to be. This kind of stealing can only be recognized by connecting this commandment with the first and by comparing lifestyles with God's design/intent for marriage. Every commandment relates to God since the laws of creation are His. Stealing is wrong because all things belong to God. Stealing is futile because all things belong to God and we lack the capacity to own anything. Stealing is a mistake because it only makes our lust for things worse. The New Testament word translated "lust" really means "the desire for more." A desire for more cannot be satisfied because as soon as we get something it's not "more" anymore. The desire for more means we are bound to continually grasp for material things that are limited, giving us less rather than more. We were created to be united to God, who is infinite. When Adam disconnected humanity from God, the human soul that was left suffered from an infinite lack. The soul knows its desire to be filled, but our human natures are inclined to use only finite, material things to fill that void. Worse still, because materialism takes us further from God, the harder we try to fill our own lives by our own means the more emptiness we feel. (How many films are made with the theme of depressing emptiness suffered by the wealthy? Try *Meet Joe Black* or *Bruce Almighty*.) On the other hand, a regenerate soul reunited with its Creator through His inspired Word provides a fulfillment that gives a completely different perspective on the material world (Colossians 3:1ff). Men and women can now see each other as possessing an eternal soul instead of something to possess (like a trophy to add to his or her collection). If a man has matured, he has already found his equilibrium with the material world. He knows God provides, he knows how to provide, he knows how material things can take more than they provide. If a woman has men in her life that provide for her, she can mature in the same way. She knows to value the provider more than what is provided. She knows above all that God will provide and that trading Him for the immediate material offerings of a predator is a dire mistake.

What about the more subtle and justified threats? What happens when a spouse takes care, time, and support for academic or career advancement, personal ego, competition with the world around? This kind of stealing is subtle because it is only part of a relationship that is otherwise mutual. The husband and wife care for each other . . . but the wife cares a little more while the husband is out with friends or the husband cares a little more because the wife wants to keep pace with her friends. Then the subtle stealing can be justified by the thief. The husband explains that he has to be out evenings with co-workers or clients in order to succeed in his career—for the good of the family. The wife complains of her need to keep pace with her friends or she will sink into depression. There is always an argument ready to justify taking more than we give in a relationship, but the argument never provides anything; it only creates resentment toward the thief. Bearing the image of God grants conviction about the ability of God to provide for us. Sometimes that providence comes precisely because of what we lack! The solution to a sense that we lack something is often the conclusion that we are better off without something we don't have and/or a new appreciation for what we do have.

So, we begin with a conviction about God's abundant provision for our life. Next, we consider how the real substance of life comes more from relationships with people than with things. Finally, both husband and wife concentrate on what they can do for the other. For example, a husband may expect his wife to take care of meals because he is tired from working all day. Has he considered that she has been working too? Has he considered that preparing a meal and cleaning up afterwards can be great therapy for stress and precious time to think over the day? If the wife shares in this task there is the added benefit of her company, which was the point of committing to a life together in the first place.

The biggest obstacle for the "thief" to get past is the fear of being "low income." Most people I know dread a lack of material resources more than anything else in their life. How about using a little imagination and creativity under God's providence? Confidence in God's providence inspires creativity and enhances vision—the ability to see a better way. Choosing to give ourselves to each other according to the image of God does not mean we must live in poverty or despair. Consider the young college graduates who are going into teaching. Most of them are leaving college with formidable loans to repay and they are going to teach for a relatively low income. What will they do for housing, transportation, entertainment, recreation?

Consider housing with a little imagination. On the one hand, there are often elderly people or widows still living in large homes who would love to have someone else in the house. On the other hand, a teaching job in the right climate (southern California, for example) means that a small home would be fine because one need never be there except to sleep—the weather is too nice and there is too much to do outside! Public transportation is very inexpensive and can offer time for reading, thinking, or meditating. New cars are expensive but I have seen restored classic cars sell for one quarter of the cost of a new model. As a pastor I drove a 1965 Mustang convertible. It cost less than a quarter of the cost of a new one and was a great conversation starter with the youth and many others. Entertainment is often free if you know where to look. My first year of marriage was spent in Washington, D.C.—not an inexpensive place to live. But every night there were several free concerts or exhibitions that we could choose from and bus fare was fifty cents each way. Our nation provides public parks, libraries, and a host of other places to enjoy recreation. Bicycles make good transportation and are very inexpensive.

Not stealing means we approach others with a mindset of giving and being given to (not give and take!). Knowing how and how abundantly God gives life to us orients us to give our lives to others in the same way, especially a spouse. This kind of giving can't be purchased at a store. In fact, trying to transfer love to material packages hardly does justice. When we give our lives to those around us and others are giving their lives on our behalf as well, we are giving and being given to. Giving and being given to does so much more for us than taking what we think we don't have.

Example: I know of many cases where a couple marries, knowing that the wife is going to work while the husband finishes his education. In one case, on the day that her husband finished the last of his exams, the wife came home early from work and found him in bed with another woman. Things don't always turn out this way nor do they have to, but there is risk involved when a man asks a woman to be responsible for him instead of him for her.

Example; I also know of many cases where employers compete, sometimes purposely, for a husband or wife's devotion. In one case it was a congregation that was competing with a pastor's wife. A few members who felt the need to exercise control sought to extend that control over the pastor by contending with him over vacation time. The pastor explained to these members that before he accepted the call to be their pastor they had spoken expressly about this issue. The pastor had said that he would be devoted to their care and they, in turn, could be devoted to his. That approach meant that the pastor had no set amount of vacation time, just as he kept no record of how much time he spent, after normal hours, taking care of the congregation. The pastor was with the members when they needed him and he was with his family and away with his family as much as he needed to be. After a time the controlling members raised the issue of utility bills from the parsonage that were higher than they thought was appropriate. The pastor responded by offering to be taken out of the congregation's budget altogether and live on donations that members would designate for his support. In an effort to support the pastor, the church council acted to set an amount in the budget called "living expenses" that would be provided for the pastor so that he might be protected from such private scrutiny and attack. Eventually, the pastor and his wife found a home of their own and made plans to move out of the parsonage. Some members objected that he could not do this or that if he did, the church would not provide him a housing allowance but they would keep the rent on the parsonage for themselves. The pastor explained that the issue of living in a private home was also discussed before he accepted that call but it mattered not, he would move in the best interest of his family and in doing so act in the best interest of his congregation by his witness to the freedom that Christ has provided to love and live (Galatians 5:1). If the pastor had retaliated somehow, or succumbed to the attempts of others to control him against the well-being of his family, he would have been stealing the devotion that God intended them to benefit by.

Example: During my last year of seminary I purchased a restored 1965 Mustang convertible. That whole year I worried about the well-being of that car, even hesitating to let my wife drive it. She plainly recognized that I had misplaced my loyalties but was patient with an American man and his driving machine. When we made the long move to my first parish I paid to have the car moved in the moving van to keep it safe. When the moving truck arrived I watched placidly as the car was driven off, only to see that the tie-down straps had put deep creases in all four fenders. After an embarrassing bout with grief, I spent some time assessing my priorities and considering whether God had cursed or blessed me. He had blessed me indeed, reminding me of what matters and what does not. I didn't bother getting the fenders fixed, since the car was more fun to drive when I didn't have to worry about it getting hurt and now my wife could enjoy driving it as well. I had been stealing priority of concern from my wife and spending it on a collection of metal and plastic. It is hard to steal in the light. By exposing the truth of a situation, the Good Lord reformed a thief and made him give back what was taken.

H. "Thou shalt not bear false witness against . . ."
Matthew 12:31–37: ". . . for the mouth speaks what the heart is full of . . ."

The heart we are born with by human nature is evil above all things and desperately wicked. This heart of mine would always see things so that I am right and everyone else is wrong. I can by my own thinking see my spouse as such a horrible person that a loving marriage is impossible even to suggest (2 Samuel 13:15).

The Eighth Commandment is essential because of the condition of our heart since the fall and because of the relationship between our heart and our mouth. Have you ever noticed that no effort is required to think negatively about the world around you? We are critical, resentful, condescending, hateful, selfish, proud, and egotistical. These and other evil properties of our hearts not only put the worst construction on what we see, they also generate ideas—we imagine things about others. Since the ideas were generated in our own hearts we tend to act upon them assuming they are true. After all, they are our ideas!

For example, let's say the husband and wife are out running errands and shopping. The husband drops off the wife and they agree to meet in the same place at a certain time. When the husband returns the wife is not there, but he does not worry, assuming she will come in a few minutes. After ten minutes or so the husband begins to think about all the things that could be keeping her: long lines, trouble finding sales people, remembering an errand that would be great to get out of the way. Another ten minutes pass and the husband's thinking shifts to what might be wrong; she has been mugged, she is in a place that is being held up, she has been taken hostage, whisked away into a rented van by terrorists like you see in movies. More time passes, but he doesn't hear sirens. If she were hit by a car, if she collapsed with a massive heart attack would there be sirens? More time passes with no sirens. Now he is thinking that she is just plain inconsiderate. "Doesn't she know I'm waiting? What's wrong with her, how can she do this to me, make me worry and wait and wait?" From worried to angry—so the heart goes. Then, suddenly he sees her coming. At first he feels a huge sense of relief but then, instead of expressing his relief and joy at her return he says, "Where have you been? Didn't you know or care how long I have been waiting and worrying?" Then, instead of knowing his concern for her well being she is confronted with an assault on her character. She responds as any human nature would with defense and counter attack. She argues that it was his errands she was trying to take care of and why hadn't he done this himself when he was here the day before? Then the battle escalates as each draws from the past; offenses and aggravations that had not been resolved are lobbed like grenades at the other. Where is love and the image of God in this?

What if he had been honest? What if he had prayed, recalling promises of God that never fail instead of listening to the evil imagination of his own heart? What if he had simply said, "I am so glad to see you, so relieved! I was worried and fearful, then I overcame that uncomfortable feeling with anger and resentment"? Then, first of all, she could appreciate his thoughtfulness, honesty and humility. She knows he cares but couldn't do anything about it. Now she is free and encouraged to be honest and helpful in return. She would be free to explain how she was sorry to worry him but had found opportunities to save them time and/or money later. She was wise and prudent, giving him cause to be grateful along with being glad to have her back. Or, she might actually have been careless. Understanding his care, she would find encouragement to apologize. She might consider that in the future she needs to be careful about their plans because he does care for her so. He, on the other hand, might conclude that staying together works better than splitting up. Saving time is not nearly as rewarding as sharing the company of his spouse and giving no opportunity for worry or fear to set in.

In view of the inclination of our hearts to construct evil thoughts, consider a counter strategy. First, if we are aware of the inclination of our heart to generate worst case scenarios we can be more prepared to fight them off as they come. Second, know that even if you succeed in fighting off evil thoughts, they can spring to the surface before you know what happened. Just when you are feeling good about yourself for overcoming negative thoughts and putting the best construction on everything, something else will trigger some sense of injustice and all the buried thoughts will come flowing out. Paul warns of this, saying, "I find it to be a law then, that when I desire to do good, evil lies close at hand" (Romans 7:21). Third, be ready to think the best of your spouse when they are thinking the worst of you. If you are late or have forgotten something, be ready for a storm. The best way to weather a storm is to lean into it. If you know that fear is causing your spouse to feel angry or frustrated—calm the fear and dismiss the anger with the same demonstration of humility and spirit of reconciliation, especially if it is not your fault. You can always start with, "I am so sorry that I am late, that I made you worry, and that I frustrated you." Let that soak in a minute. Then you can go on to tell the story (if there is one) of how or why you were late. The explanation will give your spouse a chance to sympathize. Fourth, if there are still issues that you want to deal with, do it later, when there is calm and conditions for productive conversation. When you describe what made you angry do it as a narrative rather than as prosecution, something like, "First, I was not thinking too much about this and then I got really scared that something terrible happened to you and then I started getting really angry about why you would be so late." The narrative reminds you of distinguishing between natures. We have human natures that are often worthy of suspicion or anger. At the same time this nature seeks power through prosecution of faults and failings. But it is our soul, a regenerate soul inspired by the Spirit of God, that is the essence of who we are. This soul is not insensitive, forgetful, distracted, frustrated or angry. Expressing our feelings in narrative form reminds us to make these distinctions by stepping outside of the situation. If we look more objectively at what happened we will find it easier to reconcile and to build a better strategy for the future.

God's Word has provided and continues to provide a new heart (Ezekiel 36). This heart does not seek a way to justify its wrong doing by accusing others. This heart knows that as God has determined to love and think well of me, so I am to love and think well of others. God will expose and avenge if I am being taken advantage of. Everyone is served well if I speak helpful words. These words can only be provided by God.

On the positive side of the equation, the promises and faithfulness of God make a way for us to think well of others. According to Ezekiel, we have a new heart from God. This heart, like God, is oriented toward seeing others in the best possible light. Then the heart of God moves Him to act in the lives of people so they begin to approach His vision for them. This heart and gracious ability in us flows from the Lord Jesus Himself. Paul describes how the Son of God lowered Himself, even made Himself of no reputation, so that He could redeem us before the Father (Philippians 2:5–11). When Jesus had accomplished our salvation God raised Him up and seated Him at His own right hand. Consider what that means for us, especially in our marriages. We can always see people in the best possible light because that is how God sees them. They are still God's creation, and the regenerative power of His Word and Spirit is limitless. Next, we can put aside our concerns about protecting ourselves because God will protect our life. Think again of the situation where someone is late. On the one hand, I need not fear at all for my spouse's well being because God watches over our lives. On the other hand, I need not indulge a sense of frustration or anger because I am not my spouse's judge. I am God's agent to love and care for my spouse. While I am waiting then I may think of all the good qualities of my spouse that make we worry about her. I may also turn my energy in a positive direction by praying for her and for lots of others who are in similar situations. When my spouse returns I will be in a positive frame of mind, grateful for who she is, and refreshed by prayer during the wait.

But what if my spouse or others take advantage of me because I think well of them? Thinking well of someone is not the same as being careless or deceived. There is no reason to put ourselves in harm's way by thinking no harm can ever come to us, even though that may be true in the long run. Thinking well of others begins by considering them a living soul of God's creation instead of despising them as unworthy of my care. As God's creation, my spouse or any other person has potential that God has called me to help him or her realize. Within a safe and prudent context, I will set aside my ego and sense of entitlement (as Jesus set aside His garments to wash the disciple's feet, John 13:4–5) and take good care of my loved one. Loving care can teach and inspire a spouse to be on time. Active service can teach and inspire a selfish lazy person to realize that life is found in giving it away rather than taking it from others.

What is there to lose, then, in this approach? If we think the best of others we may find out they are quite good, someone to be grateful for. If we think better of them than is accurate, we may inspire them to be better than they are. If we love them because God has loved us we may become better than we were. If we are completely wrong about them, so what? Jesus is no less the King of kings and Lord of lords because some people refuse to honor Him. We will be no less His children if we think too well of a person who ends up proving us wrong.

In all our relationships, but especially in marriage and family, this commandment rests firmly on the conviction that with God there is always a positive way forward. God makes His wisdom and Spirit abundantly available in the Word so that we might make the most of this potential!

Example: Transient people often come knocking at the door of parsonages. They always have a story about the straits they are in which will all be better for a few dollars assistance. I have tried to believe these stories and have offered the assistance only to find out that the person went directly to the liquor store. But who is the worse off for thinking too well of this person? The liar always makes his life worse through the lie but the generous person is still justified in his or her generosity. However, prudence taught me to offer assistance to such people in a way that is more difficult to abuse. I made arrangements with a gas station, a restaurant, and a hotel to provide for people's needs without giving them cash.

Example: A young woman called looking for a church to have her wedding in. It would have been easy and justifiable to simply refuse her inquiry since she was apparently interested only in His house and not in God. Yet how could I be sure she would not respond eagerly to an invitation to consider marriage according to the counsel of God? Instead of a refusal an invitation could be extended: "We are a Christian congregation that provides for and supports loving marriages. When would you and your intended like to come by so we can talk about this?"

I. "Thou shalt not covet thy neighbor's house, nor wife . . ."

Proverbs 15:16–17: "Better is a little with the fear of the Lord, than great treasure with trouble . . ."

To covet is to want something so much that it changes the way you live your life. Remember the fall of Adam. Paradise was being satisfied/content to take care of God's creation in one place, Eden, and in one person, Eve. Satisfaction/contentment does not come from things we can get, but from taking care of what God gives us.

I have combined the ninth and tenth commandment because they both deal with covetousness. Consider the irony of human disposition with regard to material things; the more people have the more they want. Wealth breeds covetousness. For most of the world's history and for many nations still, having very little makes them grateful for what little they have and significantly affected by a gift. On the contrary, for people of wealth a gift has little or no meaning because they have never known need.

The fear of the Lord is a function of a person's awareness of their need before God. We are utterly dependent upon Him. He is the creator. He sustains the universe that sustains us—sun, earth, wind, water. He sustains the biological processes that science calls "involuntary." But they are not involuntary, God wills them. What is more, we have offended God with our contradictions and rebellion. There is great reason to fear God because we are needy in every way before Him. From a sense of our need before God's justice we turn in awe to His providence for us. He loves us still and has reconciled us to Himself through His Son. Reconciliation means eternal life and a heartbeat that begins to mean so much more. What could we possibly covet when we already have three lives from God? One life is forgiven, one life is regenerated for time and that life is destined for eternity. He gives us the lives of others to care for, so really He gives us innumerable lives to make ours all the more meaningful. In as much as we see our life this way, every act, even the smallest act of kindness is king size in our estimation. We have the best of both worlds. We need not covet because all things are ours through our union with Christ (1 Corinthians 3:21–23). We need not covet because we are constantly aware of the abundance of good gifts from God and from the people around us. Consider how wonderful it is to breathe, to swallow, to see color and nature, to shower, to eat, to have a day and all that comes with it.

Next, in regard to covetousness, consider the reverse economy of God. Our idea of economy is the result of everyone getting what they can for themselves. God's economy means finding the fulfillment of your desires in providing the very things you want for others. Let's say a husband sees things in other women he likes better than what he sees in his wife. He could covet another woman and either be consumed with desire he cannot fulfill or he could commit adultery. There is another way according to God's economy. Instead of seeing other women, he might consider qualities of men who are better husbands than he is. He can spend his energy, vanquish covetousness, and love his wife all by taking better care of the wife that is his to care for. Similarly for a wife, instead of seeing what other wives have that she does not, she might use the gifts God has given her to make a home that is more substantial than interior design can provide. She can use imagination, prudence, and determination to excel in a way that will inspire her husband to do the same.

Making people and care-taking the focus of my life brings still more benefits. First of all, if people are what I'm interested in taking care of, and if that's where I see the focus of my life, then my life immediately becomes less fragile. In other words, life is no longer bound up with cars that can get crushed or stock markets that can crash or a home that can lose its value, burn down, or be broken into. Second, the tangible aspect of your life is more enduring because that aspect has to do with people. You are making an investment in time. Let's say you're working with an older person who never really knew God, but now because their life is drawing to a close they'll open a door to you. Or you work with a student that's having all kinds of difficulties. You work with her several times a week or even every day for years. The progress is slow at first but then you begin to see the difference, not only better grades but inspiration, a different perspective on life, a sense of purpose. You make a huge investment of time but you saved a life for now and for eternity. Third, since you are concerned for people and not merchandise you are no longer competing with the rest of society. In fact, you are moving against the flow on the other side of the street. There are no lines to visit the elderly in homes or the lonely in hospitals. There is no waiting list to become a mentor or tutor for school children. There is no expense to you except the exercise of love and a fatigue full of contentment. When you come home from this kind of work you don't need to "get away from it all" or feel a sense of power by spending something (many people spending what they do not have). You are spent but not in debt. You have labored but not against frustration in trying to get where you are not or in competition with others.

Finally, some suspect that the solution for covetousness is living in ignorance. Is it better not to know at all than to be tormented by temptations you cannot satisfy? There is something to be said for living in ignorance. In other words, I suspect that Amish children are happier than my children because they have a really interesting, fun life. They're very much family oriented, they're active and they're busy, and they're not thinking about what they don't have because they don't know what they don't have. My kids struggle because they're always seeing what else there could be but they don't have any of. On the other hand, ignorance is a dangerous thing because a lot of people grow up to feel betrayed. They may in fact fall prey, as Eve did, to the poison of suspicion: "I knew there was a whole world full of wonderful things out there and you are keeping me from them only so you can keep me a prisoner here." Neither ignorance nor liberty to know the material world solve the problem. Both are dangerous and self-defeating. Ignorance can be discovered and resented. Knowing the material world breeds lust that cannot be fulfilled because it is selfish and depends on finite things that are passing away.

Example: Think of the difference between being a guest or an employee at a resort. Would you want the resort to own more or less property? Would you want larger or smaller rooms? In every consideration, would you want more or less? A guest, of course, wants more of everything but may have to wait for service and eventually become bored, no matter how much there was to do. The employee would prefer less because that is less to take care of. The employee never has to wait in line, has the satisfaction of providing for others, and during free time enjoys the setting of the resort. So, as Christians in God's creation, are we guests or servants?

Luke 12:13–21: ". . . for one's life does not consist in the abundance of things he possesses . . ."

If my life consists of what I get from my spouse, from God, from the world around me, nothing will ever be enough and I will continually cast aside what I have in search of more.

The truth of Jesus' words depends on two underlying realities. First, we were created to live in communion with an infinite God. Material things are hard to come by; they cost money and we must compete with other people to get them. Material things are finite and disintegrating so they cannot ever fill the void left if God is absent. Second, we do not possess material things, they possess us. Material things depend on us to keep them as our own (from being stolen), to keep them from disintegrating, to keep getting rid of them when they are junk or obsolete, to keep replacing them with the latest. Material things don't give life to us, they take it from us. How can I think that I possess things when I cannot keep them because I am aging and will die? Material things can provide a way of expressing ourselves, but at what cost? How much of my life is required to earn the price of a jet ski, to maintain it, to get it to where I can ride, etc? Is the experience of riding it really worth all the life it took to obtain that? Rather than say, "This is my . . ." or "I own this . . ." we would be more accurate in saying, "This home and its contents and the car in the garage own me." If we were more honest with ourselves we might find more liberty in avoiding material things that take our life.

If my life consists in the study and care taking of what God has given me, then I will always have an abundance of life in the care I provide and in observing the good results of that care.

Life can either be about getting what we don't have and can't keep or it can be about giving away what God continually gives to us. If we turn our back on God and presume to gather a life by our own efforts for ourselves then we must do that alone. We have left no room for God to provide. Even what God still does provide we would take for granted (consider how God sustains the physical life of the person who blasphemes Him). After a lifetime of gathering for ourselves, what will we do as it slips away when our life slips away from us? On the other hand, if we seek God we have a perspective from which to see how and what He provides. We have time to explore and develop the talents and interests that God has already given us. We will find deep delight in learning about God's creation and great joy in refining our ability to be a part of His providence. What is more fun than doing what God has given us the ability to do well? When people excel at their work they are appreciated and provided for. Physicians, teachers, public servants, international volunteers have all found that they had great support from people who recognized their gifts and devotion.

5

The Creed
The Nature of God Related to Marriage

V. The Creed (Workbook p. 27)

> *". . . He gives to all life, breath, and all things. And He has made from one blood every nation of men . . . so that they should seek the Lord."*
>
> Acts 17:24–31

PAUL'S SERMON on Mars Hill is invaluable for the truths it conveys and the Christian apologetic it provides. First of all, Paul reminds us that our lives are in no way independent. We depend on God for our being and all that is required to sustain it. Second, Paul levels the playing field among all human beings by confirming the fact that we are all the creation of God through a single set of parents. There is no issue of equality among people from a creationist perspective. This reality also dismisses the idea that there is only one right person for each of us—and what happens if I married the wrong person? Third, there is an organic relationship between God's design and His law (a witness to that design). Finally, as we consider these three aspects in more detail, remember Paul's overall point: God has made all things as they are so that people should seek Him, though He is not far from each of us. Knowing God fundamentally changes the way we live our lives. The question for a Christian is NOT, "Can I keep myself alive for another day?" since God has provided for our lives in this time and in eternity. The question for a Christian is, "How can I make the most of the abundance of life that God provides for me?" The First Article of the Creed gives us an occasion to consider how dramatically these two perspectives affect a man and woman who intend to be married. According to Paul, there is no way that God would create us and sacrifice His only begotten

Son whom He loves for us, only to let us perish because He doesn't care or wasn't paying attention. No experience we have in our human nature can change the truth that God loves us and gives us life (consider Romans 8:38–39; Daniel 3:16–18). It is precisely in the situation of death and impossibility that God demonstrates both His power and His love for us! This is no less true in a union between man and woman.

A. "I believe in God the Father Almighty, Maker of heaven and earth . . ."

First, this article about God the Father points us to the witness of nature and redemption. We are invited to make a comparison from the greater to the lesser. Even in cloudy, cold weather there is still a sun in the sky that keeps us from freezing. We still have homes with heat and light that compensate. Sometimes there is more rain than convenient and sometimes it is so dry that grass withers, but there remains a balance in nature that returns so that plants continue to grow and thrive. If we are lacking for something is it because God is not providing, or because we are absenting ourselves from what and how He provides? If we are fearful because of what we think we lack, could it really be possible that after the cost of redeeming us God just quit caring about us? If we recognize the witness of nature and the means available for compensating for its challenges, then we can apply that wisdom for our spouse's benefit as well as our own. In fact, compensating for our spouse is much more therapeutic than just compensating for ourselves. Is the cloudy weather getting to you? Send a bouquet of yellow, orange, and red carnations to your wife at work or come home from work before she does, turn up the thermostat a little, turn on all the lights and put together a picnic in the living room. If there has been plenty of sun and too much heat, you can go out for a vanilla malt or get the ingredients and figure out how to make them at home. If life has been just too demanding, you can escape to a quiet corner booth somewhere for a long dinner and conversation or you can spend a late afternoon and evening walking at a public beach or park. If we are not worried about God being willing or able to provide abundantly for our lives, why shouldn't we enjoy taking part in His work by providing as we are able? The challenges of life and marriage come whether we like it or not, but there is no rule that says we can't respond to them positively, creatively, energetically, and even humorously.

Second, what if managing daily challenges becomes too difficult because of an underlying challenge that says, "This is not the right spouse for me"? The benefit of comparison helps here as well. Would God create and redeem your life only to let you marry the wrong person or miss the fact that your marriage is making you languish in misery? The notion that there is only one right spouse for each of us is mistaken. According to God's design, there are essential qualities that must be in place for every husband and every wife. The "package" that those qualities come in varies. We may have found a person whose non-essential characteristics make this easier or harder, but there must be something in God's providence to be gained here as well. As a couple matures in faith, their perception of what matters centers more on what is essential and becomes more accepting of what is not. If we really believe that God has provided our spouse for us, we can even appreciate the challenges of our spouse as the very means by which God refines our own character. A husband's demanding career may challenge the wife to become more capable of managing the home and/or of using her insight to serve as a sounding board or counselor for him. A husband may find his artistic or imaginative abilities in responding to his wife's depression. In short, God's providence means that I need not second-guess my marriage (except in those circumstances that do call a marriage into question: abuse, adultery, unbelief). Divorce is not an option, so I do not need to torment my soul or cripple my life by agonizing over it. Rather than dwell on what bothers me about my spouse, I am free as a Christian to repent of my own reluctance to change what bothers her about me. My life is no longer about what I want, but about discovering how God has equipped me to provide my family with what they need. The first article of the Creed lays a foundation of incredible potential and optimism that never fails, but always inspires.

Example: I have worked through any number of marriages with spouses who are at odds with each other—so far at odds that they could not say a peaceable word to each other. They avoided each other, and yet they were still married somehow. In one case, I talked at length with a wife about all the sorts of issues between her husband and her. When we had all the issues on the table and broke them down, we discovered that the real issue was: "Will you trust for God to provide a life for you, with or without your husband, through him or in spite of him?" In other words, she had an opinion about every single aspect of her marriage and act of her husband. She could not let anything happen other than how she wanted it and felt it necessary to argue her cause. Once in December, he came home from Christmas shopping for their three children. His feeling was that the children would only be these ages for a little while, so he wanted to enjoy giving the kinds of toys that young children enjoy. She was unhappy and critical that he should buy so many gifts. He responded by getting right back in the car and buying even more gifts for the children. His feeling was, "The more she is critical about things that are not wrong to do, the more I am going to do them." She resented his generosity and he resented her criticism. The really sad part was that she could see what I was explaining. She understood that having faith in God would relieve her of her stress, dismiss her need to criticize, open a door for unity with her husband, and make her marriage a joy—but for all that she could not give away her opinion or attempts to control the people around her.

Third, there is an organic relationship between our behavior and the consequences in our lives. Many people have the impression that God arbitrarily imposes hardship in our lives when He doesn't like us or doesn't like what we are doing. Furthermore, some people think that God does this in order to control or modify our behavior. This thinking is contrary to the truth and very detrimental when people import it into their family life. It is not unusual to discover that husbands and wives "get even" with each other by doing what they know the other doesn't like or approve of. The worst case of this I have ever seen was that of a professional counselor who told a wife that the best way to respond to her husband's adultery was to have affairs of her own. To a lesser degree, I have found it common for a frustrated wife to buy something for herself against her husband's wishes. Then the husband will respond by buying something even more expensive that he knows she does not approve of. But this is not God's way.

There is a profound difference between natural consequences of actions and retaliation out of selfishness. If a wife is frustrated with her husband because he is acting badly, frustration is the consequence, not her own expression of bad behavior. If a husband is fearful because of his wife's spending, fear is the consequence, not anger or his own irrational purchase. Being honest with each other as husband and wife means that we share the natural consequences with each other and avoid the imposition of our own retaliation. Why not simply say, "I feel so frustrated and bound because of our disagreement over spending," or "I am so frustrated and disappointed by your need to spend"? With the truth before us, we can apply faith and mercy as a remedy.

Christianity is completely opposed to behavior modification—simple physical means of controlling other people's behavior to suit our standards. Christianity recognizes opposing natures in body and soul. We understand that our human natures are always going to be contrary in their actions and responses to the actions of others. We also live in the conviction that regeneration by Word and Spirit is the means by which God transforms us into loving, caring, giving people. I love my wife, especially when her conduct distresses me and I orient my care for her accordingly. If a wife is materialistic, then the husband makes the real riches of God's kingdom more evident and more abundant in her life. Instead of taking away the only things she finds refuge in, he gives her a better refuge, so she is free to relinquish the other (this is precisely what Paul describes in his own life; see Philippians 3:7–11). Similarly, if the husband is overly concerned with finances, the wife can help him transcend those fears by showing him the family's ability to live well at little or no expense. The important thing is that the behavior of the flesh is recognized for what it is and the gospel is allowed to make real and positive changes. It is not God's will that we suffer, die, or endure miserable relationships. He makes that clear by defining good relationships and forbidding the conduct that ruins them. He does will that we learn from the consequences of our actions, turn away from them, and live according to His providence and image (Ezekiel 18:19–32).

Romans 1:16—2:6: ". . . for the wrath of God is revealed against all who suppress the truth . . ."

God is our Creator. God has created us within a gender and with a personal identity to fulfill His purpose in our lives. Any time we choose to suppress this truth in thought, word, or behavior we will meet God's wrath.

We live in an age that is deeply opposed to creation, design, and divine intent. Most people assume evolution, and by accepting a universe of accident, they have eliminated any possibility of purpose. If nature is accidental, then gender is as accidental as our appetite or leisure time interests. Certainly in the past, men abused and dishonored their gender by claiming privileges over and against women. But the solution is not for women to improve their ability to compete selfishly for a material world that is passing away. Ignoring the Bible for our own conception of role and relationship is not freedom, but bondage to our very limited vision. The Bible provides the vision and explanation of the Creator so that we can have confidence regarding the path to fulfillment. Who are we? What were we created to be and do? How should we relate to each other in order to recapture, as much as we can in the flesh, the life that God intended? These are the questions that matter and the Bible is the authoritative answer.

> "... therefore, God also gave them up..." (Romans 1:24, 26, 28)

Not only do we suffer direct consequences for refusing God's order/purpose for our lives, we also run the risk of becoming completely blind to that order. Only when we are given completely to God's Word/order are we safe from being given over to the devil and his order (Romans 1:29–32).

Submission to the Word of God is not "blind faith." In fact, faith is not blind at all, but sees what we could not see otherwise (2 Corinthians 5:7; 2 Kings 6:15–17). Blindness comes from human nature's determination to throw off God's dominion. The drive to do so is evidence that we are under the control of the devil. What could be worse than being blind and driven by a lying and murderous taskmaster? Even if we are amiable to most of God's will, any determination contrary to God's design that we preserve will only infect the rest of our thinking over time (1 Corinthians 5:6).

> "... or do you despise the riches of His goodness ... not knowing that the goodness of God leads you to repentance?" (Romans 2:4ff)

God is neither good to us nor patient so that we might assume He is pleased with our behavior that is contrary to His created order. He is good in order that we might remember how well He cares for us, even when we care so poorly for one another and ourselves. Repentance would lead us to conform our lives to His order so that we might be a part of His goodness, rather than those who oppose it.

People are generally blind to the graciousness of God. We are smug in our own opinions and justify our actions by our own standards. Then, because our lives sort of work out, we assume that God approves. But God's goodness is not intended to confirm us in our contradiction, but to reveal a patient and gracious God who provides for us in spite of ourselves. If we consider how magnificent nature is and how good our life is in spite of our carelessness and mistakes, we would discover a powerful witness to the goodness and wisdom of the Creator. If we incline our attention to His Word, we find warnings to keep us from folly and wisdom/inspiration to pursue a better course. For example, many married people sought marriage for the wrong reasons and, having realized this, seek a divorce for equally mistaken reasons. They think that what pleasure they have known is due to their own genius and the pain is the other person's fault. In fact, God still gives life and provides joy as an appeal to hear Him. More joy and life can be known in a marriage if the husband and wife live for each other. Repentance and reconciliation are infinitely more bearable and rewarding than divorce and the delusion that we can simply walk away from a relationship.

> *Philippians 3:7–21: ". . . but indeed I also count all things loss for the excellence of the knowledge of Christ Jesus my Lord, . . . that I may gain Christ . . . and be found in Him . . . that I may know Him . . ."*

Notice that Paul does not say he counted all things sacrifice or trade for the knowledge of Christ. Like the pearl of great price, Paul found that absolute wealth in Christ has made all other created things insignificant by comparison (Matthew 13:45–46). The first article of the Creed confirms the reality that faith is not blind nor is it a leap. Without God, we are like people falling down a cliff, grasping for anything to hang on to along the way. God does not ask or demand that we simply let go as a test of our devotion. God "brings a mountain of stone" up underneath us, which makes clinging to grass and branches seem ridiculous (Daniel 2:35, 44–45). With our feet firmly planted upon God's truth and mercy, we let go of that which can never support us. Having our feet firmly planted in the Word and having let go of the world, we have two hands free to reach out to others.

B. "And in Jesus Christ, His only Son, our Lord..."

The second article of the Creed introduces us to the second main watershed of Scripture that deals with marriage. Genesis gave us the model, Ephesians gives us the restored version. Genesis gives us a glimpse or sample of God's creative ability. Ephesians gives us a grand look at His re-creative ability. The fact that God wills to recreate us (love) and is able to do so (power) proves that His Word is true, "... for with God nothing shall be impossible" (Matthew 19:26). The fact that the Son of God emptied Himself first, then sacrificed Himself under the burden of universal condemnation, then endured the accursed crucifixion and burial, but was raised from the dead by the Father without having seen corruption reveals limitless potential. What kind of challenge could make us shrink from loving our spouse or family? If our spouse seems to be the enemy, we are especially prepared to love them all the more (Matthew 5:38–48).

The section from Ephesians 5 that we are concentrating on suffers from being mistranslated and disconnected from the text that precedes it. Paul does not command wives to submit, but describes this as their conduct. This conduct is the gender specific expression of what he describes in 5:21 regarding all Christians who are "submitting to one another out of the fear of Christ." Notice that there is no question about submitting for either gender. Human beings are contingent and therefore will submit to greater powers, either to God or the devil. That submission will determine what our relationship is to everything else around us. If we submit to God, then our submission to creation is according to His design for the life and well-being of all. If we submit to the devil, then we spend our lives self-destructing and abusing the world all around us in order to claim that we are free. The question is not whether humans will be submissive; we always are. The question is: to whom will we submit and what will that submission mean?

So where is the imperative upon which all this submitting depends? The string of descriptive language flows from imperative language that begins chapter 5: "Be imitators of God" (5:1); "Walk in love" (5:2); "Do not let fornication (including pornography) or any unclean lust even be named among you" (5:3); "Walk as children of Light" (5:8); "Have nothing to do with unfruitful works of darkness" (5:11); "See that you walk circumspectly" (5:15); "Do not be unwise, but understand the will of the

Lord" (5:17). These imperatives, especially the repeated imperative to "walk" in certain ways, are the defining feature and motivation for Paul's description of gender roles and the proper conduct of wives and husbands. Thus, we will want to keep all of Ephesians in mind as we move ahead with our consideration of the later part of chapter five.

(Note: I did not include all imperatives in the list above, but enough to give the flow of Paul's thought. Actually, imperatives to walk in certain ways begin at 4:1—"I exhort you . . . to walk in a way that is consistent with the calling with which you were called." But even that imperative is based on the foundation Paul has laid since chapter one's description of divine election and chapter two's description of our salvation.)

Ephesians 5:22–33 (Read verses 1–21 for fuller appreciation): "Wives, submit to your own husbands, as to the Lord . . ."

Wives are to submit to their husbands because life depends on submission to God's order. Wives are able to submit by faith in God, who will always husband them perfectly.

Just as God addressed first Eve, then Adam after the fall, so Paul also begins with the woman and then deals with the man. Paul also parallels Genesis by firmly establishing our salvation as the product of God's grace and surrounding these instructions on conduct with promises that flow from that grace, just as God does in Genesis. We are never expected to act in isolation. God does not simply command us to do something in the absence of a system of support and inspiration that would accomplish this in us. Wives are to submit to their husbands AS to the Lord. This means that wives submit on the basis of Christ's submission and that wives ultimately submit to Christ, who will never fail them, regardless of how well or poorly the men in their life conduct themselves. So then, consider the overlapping relationship of support/protection and submission that exists in all relationships. Paul teaches that the head of woman is man, the head of man is Christ, and the head of Christ is God (1 Corinthians 11:3). In the biblical text "head" means to be responsible for those in your care. In biblical times, the "head" of the nation was first to go into battle as protector (remember how David's neglect in this respect foreshadows his entire collapse, 2 Samuel 11:1ff). Headship includes both the idea of protection from assault and support that enables those under that headship to accomplish their purpose according to God's design. The Son of God is submissive to the Father. This means that the support and protection of the Father supplied the means by which the Son of God would give His life for the world. The Son of God was free to love us completely with His whole life because He knew that His well-being was safe in the care of His Father. Similarly, men can only provide support and protection for their wives if they are supported and protected by Christ. No man can love his wife if he suffers under the delusion that he is making a life for himself in this world and that he can justify his worthiness to live in eternity. Such a man will sacrifice a woman rather than himself in order to fulfill his self-deception. But a man who is regenerated and filled with the Spirit of Christ is free to spend his life for the good of another. Women in turn submit to the support and protection of their husbands so that they are free to discover and fulfill their potential as the means by which God continues to create and nurture life.

Second, remember that the woman's submission to her husband is still defined by God's purpose in creating her. There is nothing more dishonorable or perverse than a man who uses a woman to shield himself from harm, as criminals often do by taking a woman hostage. But men are equally reprehensible when they use women to support themselves. Prostitution is the most public example of this, but far more men do this privately by expecting their wives to work inside and outside the home while the husband indulges his own interests, or does nothing at all. Submission "as to the Lord" then includes the essential element of design. God commands our submission to him only so that our lives have significant and enduring purpose. Similarly, wives are commanded to submit to their husbands, as to the Lord, who would have their lives consist of eternal significance. Living as the object of her husband's care, bearing children as the Lord gives them, and pursuing the nurture of these eternal souls is as uniquely significant as the Lord is uniquely our creator and savior. The focus on her well-being and her life of caring for others, especially children, is the rule by which she may evaluate her relationship with her husband (or men in general). The farther a man's expectations would take a woman from this focus, the more concerned she rightly is about the propriety of her submission (this will be discussed in more detail below). A wife would rightly question and object to a husband who would, by his will, force her away from the life of her family. On the other hand, a wife rightly embraces the freedom and opportunity to raise lives within the support and protection that her husband provides (whether as mother, homemaker, or in a career that nurtures life outside of the home).

Third, our particular focus on this submission has to do with "redeeming the time, because the days are evil" as Paul said in 5:16. Submitting to a husband *as* to the Lord provides the additional benefit of streamlining a woman's pursuit of her most virtuous and valuable purposes. Regardless of her husband's ability to support or protect, a woman may always depend on the Lord. She need not delay, pass up opportunities, nor subdue her inspiration because she fears for her own life. The faithfulness of Christ allows both wife and husband to "redeem the time"; that is, to make up for lost time by their concentration on their central purpose. For example, many women and men feel like they require and are entitled to time that is just their own, time "to do what I want to do without anyone bothering me." This kind of time may indeed have benefits in reducing stress or avoiding depression, etc. Nevertheless, a person may also realize that making the well-being of others their life's work is a work they do not want a break from. Why not be a husband who wants to spend every minute he can with wife and children? Why not be a husband who has devoted his life to real service to others and has found a way to include his wife (and even family) in that service? There is always the potential of finding work that is a labor we may rest from, but need not break from. The right purpose for our life is one we never want to retire from, which we can still fulfill in some meaningful way even as our physical ability declines in old age. We all know and appreciate women who mother, teach, and nurse to their last breath. We know how they have thrived and how we have benefited because their lives were about living.

Submitting to husband as to the Lord also includes obeying God rather than men (Acts 5:29) and testing the spirits to see if they are of God (Acts 17:11; I John 4:1).

"As to the Lord" includes the safeguards that Scripture affords those who are submitting themselves by the will of God. We obey God rather than men and we test the spirits to see whether they are of God. Paul provides the test of headship by adding that Christ is ". . . Himself the savior of the body." God commands all people to submit to the governing authorities (Romans 13:1), yet Peter and the apostles disobeyed governing authorities by continuing to preach the gospel. Children are commanded to obey their parents, yet Jonathan disobeyed Saul on order to protect David's life (1 Samuel 20:30–34). Civil authorities, husbands, and parents act on God's behalf, and because of that purpose, submission is required for the benefit to be realized. But when a ruler, husband, or parent contradicts God's will, they prove themselves to be unworthy of submission. Submission can tolerate inadequacies and a multitude of shortcomings in the one who is head, but contradicting God's design cannot ever be tolerated. Therefore, women and children want to maintain a life in God's Word by which His Spirit will make them discerning about the spirit of the husband and father. That same Word will give them grace to endure shortcomings, patience to support a husband/father who is trying, and courage to seek help when a man would dishonor God's intent by abusing his family.

Wives are commanded to submit to their husbands as Christians are to Christ, because the husband bears responsibility for the life and well-being of his wife.

Responsibility for others requires authority as well. How could someone hold a baby-sitter responsible for the well-being of the children in her care if they were not required to submit to her authority? Just as God safeguards the lives of those who submit by requiring faithfulness of the head, God is safeguarding those same lives by requiring submission in all other cases. In other words, it is just as important for wife and children not to refuse submission carelessly as it is for them to not endure carelessness. Here, the most important indicator is the husband's relationship to the Word. He must have enduring contact with the Word if God's Spirit is to inspire him to faithfulness and care. He must live in submission to that Word and not abuse it as a means of justifying the abuse of his family. A husband will also want to keep his family in the Word so they all have the spirit of faithfulness in submission, the inspiration to thrive within the support and protection provided, and the discernment to prevent abuse.

The Creed: The Nature of God Related to Marriage

"Husbands, love your wives, as Christ loved the Church and gave Himself for it . . ."

We are powerless to live before or love God unless He loves us first (He made us alive when we were dead and enemies of His, Romans 5:10; Ephesians 1). So also a woman is unable, even unwilling to submit until she is loved by her husband. That is why his love for her cannot depend in any way upon her response/behavior.

Paul describes the role of the husband in terms that are perfectly complimentary to those of the wife. This relationship is as radical in terms of selflessness as our culture is in its idolization of selfish material gratification. The entire life of the husband is devoted to the life of his wife. There is no career, no pursuits, and no hobbies that are distinct or unrelated to her well-being. This kind of focus and devotion requires an invulnerability that our society can't even imagine. Invulnerability means that no one can take my life away from me because it is eternal, given and sustained by God who raised Jesus from the dead (1 Peter 1:3–9). If a husband should perish physically in the service of his family, he would only realize the fullness of his life earlier than he expected. Acts provides the history of Christians who could not be overcome in their devotion to advancing the gospel for the life of the world. They were arrested, threatened, beaten, stoned, imprisoned, and shipwrecked—yet in every moment they realized opportunity to bear witness to Christ, who delivers us, whether we are aggressor or victim. They did all this by the power of the Holy Spirit in the conviction of the life, sacrifice, and resurrection of Jesus. This is the love that regenerates and inspires the submission that leads to more and more life.

Love is all-encompassing. When Paul commands husbands to love their wives, this means nothing is left undone. The old arguments and expectations over who is supposed to do what in a marriage are expelled. A Christian husband does well to accept that everything in the life he shares with his wife is his responsibility, with one obvious exception: the bearing of children. Husbands love their wives as Christ loves the church. What part of our lives would we like Christ to throw back in our laps? From diapers to dishes, from laundry to lawn, from toilet training to driver's training, there is nothing that a Christian husband would cast off on his wife, for two reasons. First, his life is realized in these very things; the more his human nature resents a task the more likely that task is to define his love. Second, his responsibility for these things is the setting by which his wife finds her way of expressing love for him, and the two come to equilibrium. The all-encompassing nature of love means that the husband also keeps perspective on what matters. The book *Don't Sweat the Small Stuff—And It's All Small Stuff* intends to help us keep our perspective. Much of what troubles marriages from day to day is small, but small things can also mount up in time or worse, they can be indicators of serious, underlying problems that need to be addressed. In either case, love maintains the big picture and endures in faith that God makes all things work together for good to those who love Him, who are called according to His purpose (Romans 8:28).

Invulnerability leads to a second radical Christian notion—that of never being your own advocate. You will note from the Gospels that Jesus never defended Himself nor acted on His own behalf, except for remaining perfectly faithful to the will of the Father. When He responded to the accusations of the Jewish leaders, it was in defense of the truth for the sake of everyone else, even His enemies. He refused to respond at all in His own defense when He was on trial, except to bear witness to the truth when asked a direct question. Why then shouldn't we, who bear His name, approach our lives in the same way? What would happen if we never advocated for ourselves, but only and always for others, our spouse and family especially?

Before pursuing that question, consider two essential clarifications. First, being a person's advocate does not mean giving them whatever they want. Being an advocate means providing what is best according to God's design. This may mean saying someone can't have something or do something just as much as saying that they will do something whether they like it or not. The crucial nature of the Word of God is evident here in order that we might be faithful in distinguishing what matters from what does not. Second, being an advocate does not mean we cannot raise an issue or correct an abuse. Advocacy of others is not suicide; it is the submission of our entire being to what is always best for those around us. Neither does advocacy mean that we submit to abuses needlessly. Jesus told His apostles that they need not fear for their lives, but He also told them to flee if they were persecuted. The combination of these two principles accounts for the rapid spread of Christianity from the apostolic period even to this day. If husbands are to love their wives as Christ loves the church, then we have everything to gain by giving ourselves to the mission without reservation.

How does always advocating for the other actually work? There are five components to this system of advocacy:

1. Maintain God's perspective of role and relationship according to His image and design
2. Take time to consider and evaluate apparent contradictions
3. Take time in prayer and reading to test your observations
4. Act and speak for the good of the other person
5. If a problem endures, seek the advocacy of others

First of all, we will be forever muddled in our thinking and at odds with each other unless God's clear Word provides the model that we compare every issue with. Only the grace of God in our own life can give us any hope of being objective in our relationships with others. Only the truth of God can provide the means by which we know what we are to do for each other. The models from Genesis and Ephesians provide principles that can help us navigate through all the particulars of our daily life.

Second, we need to develop our ability to take time before reacting. We do know well from the Scriptures what our actions ought to be. Knowing what to do is usually not the problem. We make trouble for ourselves when we let our emotions displace what we should do with a reaction to what has been done. If only we could just be matter of fact when someone's questions are frustrating us. If only we could just go ahead and clean up the mess or postpone our plans when our spouse is being inconsiderate. Then we could have time to consider whether the offence is against God or just against our pride. There is much to be gained by holding our tongue, by giving ourselves time to evaluate what is happening and has happened. But we must beware also of letting things go if they are brewing just below the surface. Jesus loved others in every instance because He is love, through and through. We are a regenerate soul, but that soul is covered with flesh and blood. We can only be as gracious, patient, and fair-minded as the presence of His Spirit makes us.

Third, we must beware of the temptation to displace God's thoughts with our own. This is a special temptation for people who are particularly devoted to God or "naturally" pious. The time we have spent in "religious education" in the past may allow us to assume that our thinking is now consistent with God's will. We can afford to make no such assumptions, as Paul warned: "Keep on testing yourselves to see whether you are in the faith" (2 Corinthians 13:5). Prayer and meditation on the Word of God soothes our anxieties and relaxes our frustrations. Prayer allows us to hear our own thoughts, and meditation allows us to reorient those thoughts according to God's truth and mercy. Time in the Word provides the Spirit of Christ, who alone can keep us true to our desire to be gracious and an advocate of the other.

Fourth, the union of husband and wife (just like parents to children, Christians to one another, and God to us) means that acting for yourself selfishly, is to act against yourself. Only by denying ourselves can we be of real service to others, and by so doing find the life that God has for us (Matthew 10:39, 16:25; 2 Corinthians 5:14–15). So you have determined that there is an issue you need to deal with, but not as your own advocate. This is not about getting your wife to keep a neater house because that's the way you like it. Nor is this about the wife getting you to spend more time at home because she is lonely. This is about recognizing a significant pattern in the life of a loved one that is contrary to God's will. My life is safe with God, whether anyone else ever does what I want them to or not. My life is even made clearer to me in the challenges of advocating for another in difficult times. How else could we know that we love each other unless we actually lay that life down? Now we are talking about a wife whose fear of losing loved ones makes her overprotective and critical. The husband does not advocate for her by complaining that he doesn't like how she makes the family tense and irritable with her micromanaging. He advocates for her by spending the time to learn the reasons for her fear, which produces behavior that she probably doesn't like any better than the rest of the family. A wife will appeal to her husband to reflect on the purpose of his life and how his time away from family affects that, rather than complain that he is neglecting her.

Fifth, by the grace of God, the issues of our lives will be resolved long before this step. Yet the support system God has established for us is just as much a function of His grace and of His wisdom to foresee our needs. If a husband or wife should fail in their attempts to resolve issues by advocating for the other, there is a final system of advocacy. A husband or wife has many other people in their lives who bear responsibility for them. The pastor is an obvious example. In pre-marriage counseling, I make it clear that the couple is welcome to call for assistance at any time in the future. Calling upon the one who has done the pre-marital counseling streamlines the advocacy, because all three know what was discussed and how advocacy works. However, a family member or a trusted mutual friend can serve this role well if they understand it. If then, the wife is exasperated with the husband's absence: she may call me to express her dismay. She may find, upon our conversation, that she would prefer to work on the issue herself. She may, on the other hand, feel even more convinced that she cannot resolve this issue and remain true to God's design for her. Knowing the issue, I would call the husband and make a date for a time to meet. I can inquire of his perspective, try to reconcile the two outlooks if necessary, and review the principles of marriage that we had talked about (in the case of a couple I did not counsel before the marriage, I would be introducing this material to him). The same would be true if a husband contacted me about his wife. In either case, a husband or wife examining their life with a faithful pastor, family member, or friend works much differently than fielding the same observations from a spouse, especially if the observations come as criticism in the heat of a disagreement. In my experience, this advocacy works well. In most cases, the couple responded well to an outside perspective and to the re-orientation that the Word and Spirit of God provide. If progress is resisted, then the process of church discipline comes into play in order to protect the aggrieved spouse from abuse. In any event, we have protected husband and wife in their God-given relationship and have taken the best possible course for the future of both, by reconciliation or by divorce if advocacy is resisted in impenitence.

It is love/sacrifice of the husband that allows for the proper behavior of the wife, not the demand of the husband for submission; the Law always kills.

Getting someone to behave in a certain way is a very easy thing to do. Our human nature knows two great forces: fear and appetite. If we appeal to either, or better yet to both at the same time, we can get people to do most anything. Recall that many people pursue relationships out of fear or appetite in the first place. A young woman craves attention or liberation from her parents or she is afraid of being lonely. A young man may also be afraid of loneliness, and at the same time have intense sexual cravings.

These forces are not left behind at the wedding ceremony. Both individuals are still subject to these forces, and their human natures know it. Consider, for example, the gross misuse of the word "love" in our culture. If you want a definition that makes sense as people use it, the word means, "To want for myself, to consume." When a young man and woman are dating, their emotions well up and they say, "I love you." They do not mean to say, "I would do anything to protect you and provide for your well-being." What they mean is, "I would do anything to perpetuate the pleasure I am experiencing at this time." The proper definition of "love" is selflessness—sacrificing myself for another for their benefit alone. The common use of "love" is selfish—I am willing for anything else to be sacrificed for my benefit alone.

Within a marriage, this force means that a husband may easily and even unconsciously let selfish manipulation displace selfless care-taking. A husband may use Christian stewardship as a pretence for criticizing his wife's spending habits. He lets himself fly into a rage when he disapproves of something she buys with the intent that fear will prevent her from shopping. But this is not Christian stewardship. Christian stewardship begins with handling the Word of God rightly—letting truth expose error and letting grace regenerate and inspire a heart that is set on things above. Such care does not demand immediate results nor does it contradict itself with anger (James 1:19–20).

For example, a husband may appreciate the moral character of his wife, yet when his sexual appetite gets the best of him, he will manipulate her for his own gratification. He makes advances toward intimacy, but she is not so inclined. So he becomes sullen, silent, and pouts. She feels sorry for him, pays attention to him, and even gives him a hug. While they hug he begins making the advances again. Now she is in a bind. If she resists he will become even more sullen or maybe even resentful, if she lets him have his way, both of them will feel compromised afterwards. The fact that manipulation works does not mean that it does not also work against us. Our human nature does know how to get its own way, but nothing but devastation ever comes of it (consider the success of Jewish leadership at the time of Christ; they cast off the salvation of the Messiah and brought upon themselves the wrath of the Roman Empire). Men were designed by God to be care providers, to use their lives in service of women. Manipulating women, regardless of the intended outcome, is utterly contrary to the principle of love.

The Creed: The Nature of God Related to Marriage

Example: A young husband discovered over some years that his wife was both alcoholic and adulterous. In this time she had given birth to several children. The young man was determined to remain a devoted husband and father, in spite of his wife's conduct. Eventually, she moved in with a man she was having an affair with and sued for divorce. Everyone assumed that the husband would find a lawyer and fight for his children and his possessions, but he did not. He explained, "I vowed before God and man that I would love this woman until death parts us. I will love her still, whether she honors that love or not." The husband represented himself in the divorce court. When it was his turn to address the court, he made his confession again: "Your Honor, I love my wife and am devoted to her well-being. I cannot make her respond to that love nor appreciate it; neither can I contradict my devotion to her by consenting to an action that is detrimental to her life and the lives of our children." The judge granted the divorce and a property settlement was imposed. The husband was grieved over his wife's actions, but never regretted being true to his commitment. What a profound witness he made to the power of God's love for us. His faithfulness is a powerful cause for us to examine the reasons for and ways in which we relate to God and family (Shel Silverstein wrote a children's book that makes this point called *The Giving Tree*). Consider how the landscape of American family might be so very different if men consistently bore this determination to love selflessly. Not only would enormous amounts of money be saved by not requiring divorce attorneys, but we might not need the divorce at all!

> " . . . that He might present it to Himself a glorious church . . ."

We are the primary focus of God's loving attention. God makes all things serve our well-being. Because He loves us, He bears the responsibility of presenting us to Himself in a splendid and holy manner. When we are so presented, we are HIS glory because we are His workmanship (see I Corinthians 1:18–30). Thus, a husband's honor does not come from how he makes himself look in comparison to his wife or in the company of his peers. Rather, his glory is in how well he presents his wife, by taking good care of her spiritually and physically.

This expression of result is set between the two supporting principles. One, husbands are to love their wives as Christ loves the church. Two, whoever loves his wife loves himself. The purpose of a wife is not to make her husband look good, any more than the purpose of the church is to make Christ look good. Only what is false, like idols and lies, require the support of people to exist (Psalm 135:15–18; Proverbs 26:20). God exists by His own nature and is without necessity or dependence of any kind; so is the truth that flows from Him (Acts 17:24–25). Consequently, men who live in the image of God need nothing for themselves that God does not provide. Equipped by God, Christian men live to support and protect others, especially a wife. In particular, a husband is to be an extension of Christ as he applies the grace of God to her life. Worldly men (and the human nature of all men) boast and compete in their ability to take life from women. Some men live off the labor of women and some men gratify their selfish sexual appetites with women while refusing any responsibility for this. Other men, many of them claiming to be Christian, try to prove their value by belittling their wives in private and public. But this is their shame, not their glory. They are brutes and bullies, too lazy, weak, or mean-spirited to do any good for another. These men are despicable and ugly, and whatever beauty of glory their wives maintain is in spite of them, not because of them. No, God designed men to realize their character in supporting and providing for others. When a wife lives and thrives according to her God-given abilities because she is free to, then her husband knows real satisfaction. Even more, when a man humbles himself in confession so that he can lead his wife and family in the path of honesty to grace, then he begins to realize an everlasting satisfaction (1 John 1:6—2:6). Men who love their wives and see them as glorious accordingly have a fourfold benefit. First, they have the joy that comes from living according to God's design. Second, they have the eternal joy of being a part in God's work of providing eternal life to their family. Third, they have the constant joy of watching the beauty and talent of their family every day. Fourth, they have their eye on the challenges that matter. These challenges refine the character of our family members and have consequences of eternal significance.

Example: I see this frequently, but will give one particular example of a husband and wife who would tease each other in social settings. Much of the time the teasing was good natured and comical. However, as time passed and unresolved grievances brewed under the surface, the teasing became more like taunting. The husband would make jokes about how the

The Creed: The Nature of God Related to Marriage

wife looked or mistakes she had made. The wife would respond with jokes about the husband, about things he did that frustrated or angered her. Three problems resulted. First, the other people quickly became uncomfortable as they realized what they were listening to. No one likes to be in the middle of a fight. Second, often other husbands and their wives would join in, finding a setting for relieving their own pent-up frustration. Third, the husband completely undermined his own life and joy by demolishing rather than justifying his wife. How funny would we think it was if the Lord Jesus joked with the Father about our failings? We depend on Him to always remain true to His nature of love and grace. If anything, the husband should humble himself in social settings in order to bear witness to the justification of Christ that we all depend on and to protect the honor of his spouse. It is much better for a wife to say, "You are really not as bad as you make yourself out to be. In fact, you are so much more." Then the husband can respond with Paul, who gloried in his weaknesses because they kept him solidly in the strength of Christ (2 Corinthians 12:5–10; Philippians 3:4–7). Social settings and especially gatherings of men are an unparalleled opportunity for Christian men to lead by their example of loving as Christ loves the church.

When a husband hates his wife (sacrifices her instead of himself), he is ultimately the one who suffers for it in eternity and also in this life—in a cursed relationship.

The truth of God is inescapable. Marriage binds a man and woman together such that their lives become inseparable. I know of men who hate their wives and feel no remorse. They do not in fact have a marriage but a public charade to mask their abuse. I also know men who claim to be Christian but deny it by the way they treat their wives. On the outside they feel smug, as though they are stealing and getting away with it. But I have seen them in private and know that they are afraid, insecure, and miserable. Hating your wife does not only mean abusing her. "Hate" as the opposite of "love" means to "sacrifice nothing for the good of another." Not only the abusive, but also the neglectful husband does himself wrong by refusing to do what God has designed and called him to do. The majority of Christian husbands I know will not read the Bible with or pray with their wives. What is worse, if they try, many wives resent it because it seems to them like a sham, another trick by which they would look like they are loving, only to get their way in some other area. The problem with men is that since the fall of Adam we hate our own lives first. We renounce God as if He were a spoilsport and indulge our physical appetites as if they were our eternal guarantee for bliss. We cannot love a wife until we are loved by God and know that love in our souls. Only our union with God will allow a healthy union with a wife (which is what makes dating and pre-marital counseling so important as a means of discovering the condition of the man). With God, we come to know someone who has only loved and never hated us (Hebrews 12:1–11). If we are regenerated in the image of Christ, then we share a nature that knows love, how to love, and possesses the determination to do so for the good of the wife we have joined ourselves to.

C. "I believe in the Holy Ghost . . ."

The first article of the Creed confirms that God is the One who creates and sustains life. Therefore we are free from concerns for our physical life so that we may give priority to spiritual concerns (Matthew 6:25–34). The second article of the Creed confirms that Christ is the One who recreates and sustains our spiritual life. Therefore we are free from concerns about justifying ourselves before God so that we may give priority to the physical and spiritual welfare of others. The third article of the Creed confirms that we do not provide the energy or motivation for this life's work. There is no aspect of our life that God does not provide for, since leaving even the smallest detail to depend on us would be disastrous. Consider the difference in the apostles before and after Pentecost. We are formed by God but are not yet living beings until His breath dwells in us and animates us. In this section we concentrate on the necessity of the Holy Spirit for a blessed union of man and woman.

> *John 14:26–27 and 16:14–15: ". . . but the Helper, the Holy Spirit will . . . bring to your remembrance all things that I said to you. He will glorify Me, for He will take of what is mine and declare it to you."*

If we use computers as a parallel, God the Father provides the hardware, God the Son provides the software, and the Holy Spirit is the electricity. The best computer equipment will just sit there and do nothing unless there is a power source. Christianity has suffered from the beginning because human nature assumes that faith is an intellectual property of our own making. But faith is to the soul as energy is to the body; both require fuel. We are not well fed because we know what good food is. It is the food ingested that makes energy. Similarly, it is the Word of God regularly ingested that creates faith that is active in love.

Jesus provides a beautiful and long discourse about the Holy Spirit and the necessity of staying connected to Christ through Him in John 14–16. We will focus on two main activities of the Holy Spirit: to bring to remembrance and to make declarations. First, just as Jesus is faithful to the will of the Father, so the Holy Spirit has no new or novel information to provide. He is the agent by which the Word of God returns again and again to the consciousness of the apostles. That agency allowed the apostles to speak and write with authority on behalf of Christ (Mark 16:16–20; 2 Timothy 3:16). Today the Holy Spirit still brings the Word of Christ to remembrance in three ways. One, the Lord continues to provide us with those who precede us in the faith, who urge us always to maintain a life in the Word. Two, the Bible is the very remembrance of the Word of God, preserved with remarkable fidelity even to this day. Three, if we remain in the Word, the Holy Spirit is faithful to bring that Word to mind as we have need of it. Proverbs 16:1 says, "The preparations of the heart belong to man, but the answer of the tongue belongs to God." That proverb explains Jesus' imperative not to worry about what to say in the time of trial and Peter's imperative to always be ready to make a defense. So we are dependent on the Word, which makes it necessary to maintain a life in it, but we are free from anxiety over how to respond with that Word because the Holy Spirit will bring to mind that Word which is particularly applicable. For both husband and wife, but especially the husband, who is to be Christ to his wife, there is no escaping the essential nature of this truth—but who would want to escape it? God provides a continual feast for us in the Word. That feast in our consciousness gives the perspective, will, motivation, and articulation that love requires. Our union as husband and wife is as healthy as our union with the Word.

Second, the Holy Spirit will glorify Christ by taking what belongs to Him and declaring it to us. This is the origin of both the purpose of a husband and his ability to accomplish that purpose. To begin, consider the meaning of "glorify." The root "glory" means to do what no one else can or would do. To "glorify" then means to bear witness to or give expression to what has been done. The Holy Spirit bears witness to the singular nature and work of the Son of God by declaring His accomplishments to the credit of all people (universal atonement). By contrast, in our culture, "glory" means the opposite. The glory of people today is to take more than they give and to keep what they have taken. All kinds of security systems are employed by the wealthy to make sure no one takes what belongs to them. But the glory of the only begotten Son of God is to give all His life to us and take our death instead. Next, the declarations that the Holy Spirit makes are not empty words, but as God's Word created the universe, so it still is powerful to accomplish what it describes. The words "You are forgiven" make that forgiveness so. The Word of God recreates men and women in the very image of God that Word is describing. Next, as said above, knowing that God provides a man with all things required to sustain his life makes the man free to give his life on behalf of his wife. Finally, the relationship of Christ and the Spirit to the husband are a constant inspiration and reminder of his purpose. The husband's first priority is to convey the Word of God to his wife. God's Words become his words, God's breath becomes his breath (1 Peter 4:11). The Holy Spirit conveys the life of the Son to the husband, which he in turn conveys to the wife. Husband and wife together share that life with their family and the world. This activity is the center of marriage and is the discriminating feature for everything else that life entails. What kind of work to do, how much time to spend at it, how much time to play and how we play, what we buy and what we have no use for—these things all find their place and meaning in relation to the eternal life of our souls.

Example: Two examples demonstrate our dependence on the Spirit of God to bring what we need to our remembrance and our role in declaring it to others.

I knew a graduate student who was also holding down a full time job. He had decided to make the effort to earn a doctorate in order to serve the Lord more effectively as a professor. It was during his studies for comprehensive exams and again in preparation to defend his dissertation that he had a most unsettling sensation. As he tried to think randomly about the material he had studied, nothing came to mind. His mind was blank, as if he had no knowledge whatsoever about his discipline. Yet when a particular question was before him, all the applicable data came to mind. At first this was indeed unsettling, but in time this young man found a way of understanding and appreciating what was happening. His perspective was that God kept him from arrogance by reminding him that his knowledge was not a function of his own abilities, but was a gift of God. When a need called upon the man's learning, the learning was there with which to serve. In the absence of need, the man was left with his need for faith in God.

I also knew a young pastor who lost his ability to remember, but for a slightly different reason. This pastor had learned well during seminary that his spiritual abilities depended completely on his life in the Word of God. While he studied, he was amazed at the clarity with which he saw issues and at how the appropriate scriptural texts presented themselves in his memory. However, in the "busyness" of his first months in the parish, he forsook his daily studies in order to "fix" the problems at hand more rapidly. It wasn't long before the young pastor was shocked when no answers or texts came to mind in the face of questions or issues. What had come so easily before, so clearly and quickly, now completely eluded him. Thankfully he realized his mistake right away. He gave his studies priority again and as he did his ability to recall the necessary scriptures returned. He made the same mistake several more times over the course of his parish ministry until the cumulative effect of the lessons made him very steadfast in his contact with the Word. He enjoys being of service to people according to the Word of God and is at peace knowing his dependence on that same Word.

Romans 10:1–17: ". . . faith comes by hearing, and hearing by the Word of God."

Anyone can bring ruin to his own life by deceiving himself concerning faith. To tell myself I am acting faithfully when I am not puts me in peril of hell and does harm to everyone around me. True faith, godly faith, requires five things:

1. KNOWLEDGE—You cannot believe what you know nothing about.
2. ASSENT—To know it is true; there is no benefit in believing falsehood.
3. OBEDIENCE—Faith means dependence; faith orders behavior and thinking. (e.g.—I believe in gravity; it affects me constantly and I order my life accordingly.)
4. MEMORY—I cannot believe what I cannot remember.

5. ARTICULATION—I cannot obey or act upon what is unclear. Obedience and assurance (comfort) require clear expression in word and thought.

Where does this faith come from? Martin Luther confessed that it was NOT "by my own reason or strength." Sadly, most Lutherans have forgotten this part of their memory work, and even if they remember they have difficulty explaining where faith comes from. Still fewer Christians know what Romans 10:17 says: "So then, faith comes by hearing, and hearing by the Word of God." The one thing that I required catechumens to know above all else was Romans 10:17. Consider how different Christianity today might be if everyone knew that passage instead of John 3:16. If you know the necessity of the Word, then you will be well familiar with John 3:16 as well. But it appears that knowing about John 3:16 too often leaves you just there—knowing about but not united with Christ in faith, something that only the Word can sustain.

Paul's discussion about faith in Romans 10 maps out the components of faith. Faith includes knowledge, because Paul talks about the Jews having a zeal for God, but not according to knowledge.

Example: Most men and women assume that they "know" how to live their lives. They carry that assumption into marriage without realizing that the orientation of their human nature is contrary to God's design and will surely clash with their spouse's ideas of what marriage should be. This problem is even worse among people who claim to be Christian and assume that their thoughts are God's thoughts (Isaiah 55). "Good" people are generally convinced that their ideas are good, Christian people assume that their ideas are Christian. Most people are not interested, or are even resentful of the suggestion that they need marriage counseling, before or after the wedding. But our knowledge of God's will for us was lost with Adam and replaced by contradiction. Contradiction includes justifying our own thoughts and ignoring God's. How can a union exist between man and woman unless they are united in the inspired, inerrant, infallible Word of God?

Faith includes the idea of assent. If you don't believe something is true, it doesn't matter if you know about it or not. It doesn't affect your life.

Example: Most people know about the Bible and its teaching about creation and moral conduct. Nevertheless, the majority of those people have renounced the assertion that the Bible is true. Many, perhaps even most Christians today do not believe in the literal six-day creation as recorded in Genesis. Whether people consider Genesis figurative or fable, that disposition denies any absolute truth-value to all the rest of Scripture—which is where the modern world rests its case. So, many husbands and wives may seek marriage in a church and may even be active in a congregation, but at the same time give no assent whatsoever to the biblical teaching on gender, design, or sexuality. Assent in the Bible is necessary if our study of marriage is to yield real benefits by affecting regeneration in our lives.

Faith includes obedience. The children of Israel were disobedient to the gospel, so it didn't do them any good, even though they knew about it and knew it was true (John 3:2; Acts 2:22–24; Romans 1:18–19; 1 Corinthians 10:1–13). The book of Hebrews is devoted entirely to this subject; consider especially 3:16–19. Paul and James both make this point (Romans 1:5; James 2:19–22). Faith is not just "what" is believed; faith is also the "energy" that believes and so controls our life (1 Peter 1:5; 2 Corinthians 5:14).

Example: One day I was reading Judges 2, which describes Israel's failure to complete the conquest of the promised land according to God's command. The chapter concludes with God's response—He will leave the nations in place to test His people, to see if they will be faithful. But the test is actually for the benefit of the people; they may contrast their relationship with their neighbors to their relationship with God. Whose ways will they follow? Israel's history provides a witness to centuries of the unchanging truth that our human nature has no capacity to obey God. We are no different today. We too are surrounded by the "nations" (secular society and culture) and the Christian church is practically indistinguishable from them. We pursue the same standard of living, we compete in all their categories, and we adopt their practices (even in worship) in order to be "relevant" and "popular," as if the bride of Christ were some teenage girl in middle school. Our marriages and families revolve around making and spending money, but Jesus said clearly, "One's life doe not consist in the abundance of possessions" (Luke 12:15). We carry enormous loads of debt. Christian churches even borrow money to build their structures, but Paul clearly said, "Owe no one anything except love" (Romans 13:8). Is divorce any less common among Christians than non-Christians? Faith depends upon a connection with the Word and Spirit of God that not only informs us but also reforms us in the image of God and performs in and through us.

Faith includes memory. The commands to remember and to not forget are repeated over and over again in the Bible. The disasters that the children of Israel brought upon themselves are explained in terms of their forgetting and not remembering (any concordance will give you numerous examples). We cannot benefit from what we do not remember. Remembering means having something in your consciousness—in the front of your mind, not the back.

Example: Sometimes we do what we shouldn't because we don't know what we should. The component of knowledge addresses that problem. The rest of the time we do wrong because we forgot to do right. If we took a test on what we should and shouldn't do, we might well score 100%. But in most moments of our lives it is our contrary human nature that is doing our thinking for us, and our consciousness is assuming that all is well. This is why the letter to the Hebrews warns us to "give the more earnest heed to the things we have learned, lest we drift away" (Hebrews 2:1). I have never heard a confession of fornication from a young person who did not know very well that doing so was both contrary to God's design and self-destructive. I have never heard an adulterer or abusive spouse claim that they didn't know this was a mistake. The mistake is the assumption that we will automatically live as God intends, simply because we like the idea. This is why the Bible thoroughly rejects such an assumption with language like Jesus': "If you remain in My Word, you are my disciples indeed. And you will know the truth, and the truth will make you free" (John 8:31–32), "My sheep keep hearing My voice, and I know them, and they keep following me, and I give them eternal life" (John 10:27–28) and like Paul's: "Let the Word of Christ dwell in you richly . . ." (Colossians 3:16).

Faith includes articulation. Articulation means that we are able to put what we believe into concrete language. Articulation comes from knowing something so well, from such a union to it, that it becomes part of you. Such a union means that you are not only ready and willing to speak, but that you can use terms that will be understood by the other person. Jesus did this consistently with parables and with the simplicity of His language.

Example: Consider our experience with accidents and emergency rooms. Usually someone will try to offer help or comfort by saying, "Well, God makes all things work together for good." In my experience, that's not very helpful to anyone. Real help and comfort comes by articulating how in the world injuries can be good. Such an explanation works best when it is firmly in place before the accident or injury. Yet prayers are usually welcome in emergencies and clarity can be offered in prayer. Compare the following. On the one hand, someone might pray for God to heal this loved one, if it is His will. But that seems to offer little comfort, since we don't know if that is His will or not. On the other hand, someone could pray, "Dear gracious Father in heaven, we are rightly afraid for our lives and the lives of our loved ones because we are so frail and the world around us is so dangerous. Yet you have given us eternal promises and an eternal living soul that cannot be touched or threatened. Grant us grace at this time to rest our confidence completely in you and in Your Son's resurrection to life, so that we are not afraid of what lies ahead. Give us and others wisdom to care for the physical life of this loved one, knowing that their soul and eternal life are always safe in your grace." There are, especially in such circumstances, unique opportunities to grow in faith and bear witness to that faith, if we are articulate. Similarly in marriage, a husband or wife can do about as well as their minds can clearly articulate what they should do and why they should do it.

Faith tells me I can love/submit to my spouse without fear, because God is able to restore what may be sacrificed and forgive what I may fail to do.

Both Paul and Peter ground faith in the resurrection of Jesus Christ from the dead (Romans 1:4–5; 1 Peter 1:3–5). Peter explains that Jesus gave His life freely for ours because He continually entrusted Himself to the Father, who judges righteously (1 Peter 2:23). Since we are joined with Christ by connection with His Word, we have already endured Judgment Day with Him in His crucifixion and death. We, in turn, are free to continually entrust ourselves to Christ, who will raise us up. The resurrection from the dead is so powerful and liberating because it means that everything, except faith, can be sacrificed for the good of others because anything can be restored (Hebrews 2:14–16). But only the Spirit of Christ can inspire us to use that freedom to its fullest.

> Faith tells me how to love/submit by holding before me God's explicit Word, which reveals His order in creation.

Faith is well-informed. The true faith that God inspires is not the deception of the world, nor the deceit of cults who practice their arts in secret. Christian faith in the role of man and woman bears the testimony of God's Word and nature. These two witnesses are insurmountable, positive, and constant. Men and women are not simply duplicates of the same species. Men and women are complimentary in a way that provides for the life of both as they invest their lives in children. Sexual immorality produces consequences that chastity and monogamy never know. Sexual intercourse outside marriage is never good for a person. Marriage for selfish purposes is never good either. Homosexuality is never good because sexual self-indulgence is at the root of a combination that can never be one. (Note: The real issue with homosexuality is the sexual aberration, not companionship. Human beings have always had the closest of loving relationships with the same sex without the sexual self-gratification; we call them friends.) Heterosexuality is no more beneficial if men refuse responsibility and women seek control. Only when we know our place with Christ and are united with Him can we know our place in the world and in the unique world of marriage.

> Faith moves me to gladly do what God desires by the very Word that describes His will.

Faith is not a sort of grudging self-denial required by the expectations of someone else. A husband is no more faithful if he cancels his bowling night because his wife expects him to than if he went anyway. Faith includes the insight (part of articulation) that recognizes the real benefits of God's design. Faith considers the options of bowling with the guys or being a husband to one's wife, and sees that there is no comparison. To be a man is to be mature and responsible. To be a man is to leave the boys and their games in order to take up a purpose that deals with life and death, in this world and in eternity. If I feel uninspired or grudging about my life, the cause is either that I am still failing to see the good of what I should do or that there is no good there at all, because it contradicts God's

The Creed: The Nature of God Related to Marriage

will. Faith is not getting myself to like doing what I should. Faith is the overwhelming conviction of what should be done and the inspiration to eagerly pursue it.

At this point, we have covered one-third of the Small Catechism as it concerns marriage but have used two-thirds of the pages of this book. From this point on, the material moves much more quickly. The reason is twofold. First, the Commandments and the Creed contain the watershed of divine revelation. The Commandments tell us what is expected of us and the Creed tells us what is provided for us. Upon that foundation we consider the related gifts of God: Prayer, Baptism, the Lord's Supper, and the Keys.

6

The Lord's Prayer
Petitions for an Eternal Union

VI. The Lord's Prayer (Workbook p. 32)

> "... *Ask and it will be given to you* ... *If you then, who are evil, know how to give good things to your children, how much more will your Father in heaven give good things to those who ask Him!*"
>
> Matthew 7:7–12

The Lord's prayer flows out of the Commandments and the Creed, particularly the First Commandment and the first article. We have no God but the One True God, and that God has provided abundantly for us, including making Himself accessible through prayer. The first article of the Creed tells us the nature of the one to whom we pray and relieves us of a concern to pray for physical needs, hence the text from Matthew 7. The second article tells us that we may freely approach the Father in prayer because the Son has reconciled us to Him. The third article tells us how and what to pray, as the Holy Spirit raises our consciousness to seek God according to His will. For a better look at the integration of Father, Son, and Holy Spirit in prayer, take some time to study the Lord Himself praying in John 17. In that prayer, the Son appeals to the Father for the union of His disciples and their lives, which depend on remaining in His Word. Marriage is a parallel or reflective union that equally depends on the providence of God, Word of Christ, and presence of the Spirit. From this perspective we consider how this shorter version of the Lord's Prayer speaks to marriage.

According to Jesus' words in Matthew 6–7, the purpose of prayer is not to inform God of our physical needs. The purpose of prayer is to help reorient us toward the kinds of issues that put physical needs in their small and relative place. Spouses do show love and care for each other in physical ways, but such care is no substitute for a comprehensive and spiritual care from which it flows. The challenges of our physical life together are the place and medium by which we exercise love.

The Lord's Prayer is indicative of the optimism that Christianity brings to life. The rising of the sun each day is a constant witness to the resurrection of Christ and God's will that we too should live. God's invitation for us to pray is also a product of His will that we should live and thrive. Husbands and wives (and parents) do well to remember that before we ask, God hears (Isaiah 65:24; Matthew 6:8) and that He does abundantly beyond all that we could think or ask (Ephesians 3:20). The kind of imagination and creativity that is encouraged within God's image for husband and wife is supported by God's desire that we call upon Him, for whom nothing is impossible.

Example: There was a case of a woman who moved out of her home because she was having an affair with a co-worker. Her husband wanted her back for some of the wrong reasons (selfishness), but was also distressed for some of the right reasons. The wife was blinding herself from the fact that a man who would ruin her family in order to indulge himself with her sexually did not have her best interests at heart. In my conversations with the wife, it became apparent that more than anything she was confused by two men who were playing upon her emotions in their competition for her affection. What she needed was a time and place that was free from these pressures. As that became evident I thought of a classmate who was working on a small island in the South Pacific. Since the wife's career was in the medical arts I asked my classmate if there was a need for such a woman, and if he could take her in. He responded affirmatively. I consulted with her husband to make sure he understood how this would be the best course for her, and as a Christian husband, he agreed to provide this opportunity for her—especially to free her from the influence of the adulterer. What a marvelous experience this was for everyone to benefit from! The adulterer would have to deal with the fact that the woman he was using was gone and he had no way of finding her. The husband had time to reflect on what his real interest was in her—for his sake or for hers. The wife had time to find peace, while enjoying the satisfaction of providing medical care to islanders who needed it. She also benefited from the great model of marriage and family that my classmate provided while she lived with him. Now think about this: whisked away secretly to an island in the South Pacific? Why not? Why not use our imagination and connection with Christian friends around the world to make a positive impact on the lives of everyone concerned?

A. "Our Father who art in heaven . . ."

The word "our" reflects the unity that God intends to exist between Himself and the people of His creation. The term "Father" describes two real relationships. First, He is the father of every human being, since He is the creator of us all. Second, He is the Father of every regenerate soul (Titus 3:4–6). Calling upon God as "our Father" often serves to remind husband and wife of a few things in particular. First, our God is not an invention of our own minds nor is His created universe accidental or subject to human opinion. When we pray we reorient ourselves in our union with God and with spouse according to His one design. We are always working toward one another under the clear guidance of our creator. Think of all the different ideas people have about relationships and role, the multitude of voices in the media that flood our homes and minds with competing ideas for what will work best for us, and the conflicts we have over them at all different levels: political, career, home. A Christian family must constantly deflect or dig out from under this continual assault of opinion and agenda. Second, as our Father, we remember that God can be trusted with our well-being. We are free to learn, to fail, to be forgiven and to try again. We have access to all help, beyond what anyone could imagine. Third, as our Father in heaven, we consider how to help each other set our eyes on things above (Colossians 3:1–17; note that Paul discusses this right before he speaks to husbands and wives!). If we can remember that heaven is our home and that we are strangers and sojourners on the Earth, then we can well discern what to make priorities and what issues are worth the devotion of our energy (Hebrews 11:13–16).

Example: No matter how devoted we intend to be or how well we know that the world's ideas of roles are mistaken, our human nature is inclined to anything that satisfies itself. Consider an activity as basic as mealtime. Who will cook, set the table and clean up afterwards (today this may not even be an issue, since family life has so disintegrated that families hardly eat together, and if they do it's rarely at home)? Too often settling this question means war and sometimes the taking of hostages (sometimes all liberties are denied until the dishes are done!). But why should people who claim to love each other quarrel over an opportunity to show that love in a real way? Trying to fight our way out of doing essential and noble tasks dishonors the task and perpetuates selfishness. What if a husband taught his family respect by always assuming that the responsibility for meals, from start to finish, was his? Rather than argue over the tasks or demand that others do them, he could make the tasks inviting by the time that is shared. Good conversations take place over kitchen chores because the setting of love and concern is obvious. Setting the table can be creative. Cooking can be great fun and an artistic expression, besides giving us the chance to make our favorite meals. Cleaning up afterwards can be therapy for stresses, since the work is easy and conducive to thoughtfulness. If we are children of our heavenly Father, the basic elements of our life in the home should express that best.

Hebrews 12:1–4: ". . . Looking to Jesus, the author and finisher of our faith . . ."

The order of creation sets the race before us: men, to be responsible for and take care of women and children, women to be faithful helpers of their husbands. This race can only be won by laying aside the burdens the world would impose on us (busyness, commitments, distractions) and the sin that so easily ensnares.

This is the prayer that the Lord taught us, so when we pray this we are looking to Him, the Son, as well as our Father. Jesus is the perfect husband. In all ways He exemplified the fulfillment of this prayer. Since we pray this prayer often and since it is so well known, we can teach ourselves to call to mind the image of Christ as we pray.

We will find fulfillment for every petition of this prayer if we hold fast to both the author of our faith and the same joy that was set before Him. Jesus, in His person and work, and now through His Word and Spirit, does hallow God's name, brings His kingdom to us, affects His will among us, provides for every need, forgives, holds back from temptation, and delivers us from the Evil One. Knowing and remembering this means we adopt the same mindset toward spouse and family. What a magnificent life is possible for the ones we love when we act as agents to fulfill these petitions in their lives. My spouse doesn't need to respect my opinion as much as she needs the inspiration of God's revelation. My children don't need to meet every expectation of their teachers as much as they need the kingdom of God to support and inspire them. Asking God to deliver them from the Evil One reminds me that my purpose in their life is the same.

The most difficult thing to do after reorienting our life according to this prayer is to keep that orientation. When we wake up in the morning our minds typically go to work on all the sorts of physical details that are coming at us: breakfast, dressing, commuting, work, car repairs, home repairs, and the like. But from the orientation of this prayer, eating, dressing, and earning a salary are only the settings within which we practice love. Let's say the husband is going to love his wife by making breakfast. What happens if he becomes resentful while doing so because he always makes it for her but she never makes it for him? Or, what if she doesn't come when he calls and now the eggs are cold? If he is resentful or angry over breakfast, then he has acquired the wrong target and will likely misidentify the enemy. He will think his wife is inconsiderate, but what happened to his consideration? If he is making breakfast because he loves her, then that love should endure. Love doesn't ask, "Hey, when is it my turn for you to do something nice for me?" Love says, "I am so mightily loved by God that no one needs to do anything else for me." Every moment of every day we live in a fallen human nature we will have to battle our way back from disorientation. What really matters for eternity and for now in our relationship? What hasn't God done for me already that would give me cause for complaint about anything else at all? These are the kind of questions that the Lord's Prayer helps us answer and keep in mind.

Looking steadily at Jesus gives us both the path to follow and the will/means to follow that path. Image must always be sacrificed for the sake of affecting a good (joyous) reality. Happiness in marriage does not come from being treated the way I thought I should be, but by serving as God intended me to.

With very few exceptions, the idea of success in our culture has to do with getting what I want and getting it now. Consider the fact that even when television or movies portray someone working hard for something, what they want is still selfish, often trivial, often vain, typically at the cost of everyone else around them, and accomplished in a time frame between a half-hour and two hours. Looking at Jesus offers the polar opposite. Jesus wanted only what the Father willed, which was all about our lives. Nothing Jesus did was ever trivial or vain; he healed the sick, fed the hungry, and raised the dead, mostly in private. Jesus did nothing at the cost of anyone else, but rather bore all our debts and obligations Himself. Jesus did not endure such service or suffering for a couple of hours. Even Mel Gibson's film, *The Passion of the Christ*, only gives two hours indication of what Jesus spent thirty-three years accomplishing. On the other hand, love for others gives us a motivation that selfish pursuits could never know. Most people change their minds regularly about what they want, discarding one thing and devoting themselves to another. They also tend to quit if there is too much difficulty, since they are only serving themselves and difficulty is not considered a service. Love for others cannot be abandoned so easily nor can it be traded. God's enduring love for us inspires us to focus on the care of others with endurance.

If I compare what I think I am suffering wrongfully in my marriage with Jesus, who endured such hostility from sinners, I find that I have really neither served nor suffered, but have only felt sorry for myself.

Our human nature prefers to make comparisons that are in our own interest—I am better than that person, I deserve better than those people. But Christ is the measure of what human nature was intended to be, so He is the standard. "Considering" Jesus includes remembering that the hardships I pity myself about are embarrassingly slight compared to what the Lord endured for me. Somehow when we are slighted we feel like a monumental injustice has been done. Keeping an accurate perspective on what we experience compared to what real suffering is helps us manage the challenges of daily life more matter-of-factly. If more is expected of you (husband, wife, or child) than anyone else, why not interpret this to mean that you have more to give (Matthew 13:12)? Challenges are the means by which we learn and develop our potential; they define our character. How could you know how strong, patient, clever, or well organized you are unless love for your family needed you to be one or all of these? At the same time, how else can we remain humble and honest before our family and God without occasions that bring us to honest admissions: "I need help," "I can't keep up with all that is expected of me," or "I'm sorry for lacking the ability to . . ."? Looking to Jesus not only puts our situation back into perspective, but it also keeps us connected to His Word that puts us back into our situation renewed and inspired.

The Lord's Prayer: Petitions for an Eternal Union

Hebrews 12:5–11: ". . . shall we not much more readily be in subjection to the Father of Spirits and live? . . ."

The "OUR" in our Father reminds us that we have a common almighty, ever-present Father who works righteously to correct everyone. I may appeal to this Father to help correct my spouse. I accept this Father's correction of me.

The text in Hebrews turns its attention from Christ to us by asking us to consider God's role in our lives. Do we understand as we say the "Our Father" every day that the source of our life really does come from outside of ourselves and from outside of our material world? Our life comes from invisible forces that God describes to us in His Word (Hebrews 1:3). As a loving Father, God corrects us so that we live in harmony with His created order. Now consider the difference in our appeals to Him as "our" Father. We tend to pray for others when we want God to correct them, and we tend to pray for ourselves when we want something. Thus, even our prayers for the "good" of others are generated by what we want: "I want them to be safe, healthy, and good to me!" Would it not be more consistent with our Christian confession to ask God to make me good and provide for others through me?

We may find as we pray for things that God answers by taking things away. I have noticed that human nature tends to become more selfish as we indulge its selfishness. For example, the more we let children spend time with the television (movies, cartoons, and video games) the less willing they are to do anything else and the more disrespectful they are when we suggest that they do something else.

Example: I spent some time with a good teenager from a good family, but he was angry because his parents refused their consent to some of his recent requests. I asked him to think about all the things he has ever asked his parents for, especially the things he really, really begged them for because he "had" to have them. Now I asked him about the role of those same things in his life today. Does he still cherish those things? Is he a happier, more content, and better-adjusted person because he had his way? No, in fact he is less of all those positive things. So, I asked him, "Why would your parents continue to give you things against their judgment when your own history argues that such a response is a big mistake?" The fact is, our own human nature is a poor guide to what we really want, since we don't know our own hearts and what we think we know is chasing a world that is passing away (1 John 2:15–17). By contrast, God does know our hearts and freely gives us the desires of them (Psalm 37:4). Being corrected or "righted" by God means saying no to many wants but aligns us with fulfillment of the needs that make life wonderful.

I heard once that we must do something forty-three times before it becomes a habit. Unfortunately, this only applies to good habits. Bad habits set in immediately because of the mis-orientation of our human nature. We have a lot to do and doing all of it forty-three times in a row is practically impossible. Still, we have a patient Father. Striving to live according to His design in the world and in our marriages means making little investments all through each day—and accepting small reversals. The progress may look small, but the cumulative effect is impressive. Just like depositing a little money each week in the bank builds into a remarkable investment, so God's investment in us and ours in each other will pay off impressively, but this takes time.

If I accept the chastening of the Lord, then I view my spouse and our difficulties as instruction—what there is to be learned from the difficulty (repenting of causes, practicing solutions) and what God is providing for me in my spouse (training in righteousness).

This aspect of the introduction to the Lord's Prayer parallels the first article of the Creed. We learn to be students instead of critics, inquisitors instead of prosecutors, and responsive rather than despondent. The difference is that most Christians say the Lord's Prayer much more often than the Creed. Connecting this difference in perspective with this prayer means we are that much more likely to keep it in our consciousness. Our muscles atrophy unless they exist with resistance. Love is exercised and realized in the tension of people in union with each other. Faith evaporates in the absence of the Word and challenges that drive us to it.

Hebrews 12:12–17: ". . . and make straight paths for your feet . . ."

It is a grave temptation to trade the long-term training of God for short-term remedies that are comfortable or easy. If we reject God's Word and discipline, then we reject Him as our Father and lose every blessing that we might have known.

"Making straight paths for your feet" is where the principles God gives are put into practice. There are principles that guide us, and then there are the mechanics of implementing those principles. For example, mechanics in a marriage means making sure we develop a pattern of living that provides time together—time in the Word, time to enjoy each other's company, time to relax together, and time to work out issues. Thoughtfulness is called for here, the kind that ponders what matters and how to navigate our lives in that direction. Major factors like career choices, housing, and schools need time for research and reflection. The mechanics of this include splitting up related tasks. For example, when we are moving, I take the time to research areas where we might live. Then, while my wife is at work, I do a quick drive-by to narrow down the number of houses that we will consider. This provides more productive time for the two of us to consider houses that are real possibilities. After a hard late afternoon of looking we take the time to have a quiet meal out and reflect on the day's results.

Mechanics also includes providing reminders and incentives for ourselves. We need to remind ourselves to focus on relationships with people rather than things. The broken dish can be mended or replaced but fury toward a husband over dropping it does damage to the union that is hard to repair. We can use incentives to help manage our contrary human natures. I found it very easy to encourage my wife to walk with a friend in the afternoons, especially after I found out how much fun and therapeutic it was for me to be home with our daughter baking or playing games.

Example: There was a man who was very devoted to being a good husband. His depth of devotion showed also in his work in social services. One of the problems this husband faced was competition for his time and attention. In the early years of his career he found it hard to get away from work and hard to leave work at work. At the same time his wife felt like the "other woman." He was giving the best of himself and his time to strangers, and she was getting the leftovers. The tension caused him to reflect on the cause of the trouble for the people he was trying to help—then he realized he was making the same mistake. Was he really helping society by jeopardizing his own home? He took to heart this biblical counsel: ". . . to strengthen what is feeble so that it may not be dislocated but healed, so that bitterness may not spring up" (Hebrews 12:12–15). This is the straight path he made for his feet. First, he took some significant time to make clear his intentions toward his wife and to apologize for not acting consistently with them. Thus, the past is resolved. Second, he explained to her how he had come to realize that he was giving the best of himself to his work and not to his family. Good, that clarified the present. Third, he pursued a discussion with her about how he could manage his work so that he was faithful to his convictions. Talking this over gave them both a chance to approach the challenges positively. The wife wasn't forced to "fight" for what was hers, but was invited to help him meet a challenge to their union. They decided that expecting him to work nine to five was simply not practical. A practical solution came in two parts. One, whatever extra time he spent on a given day was made up in his schedule that week. If he had to stick with a problem on Thursday afternoon, then he came in later or left early on Friday. Two, he invited her in no uncertain terms to call him at the office. Sometimes he needed a way to conclude a session or a reason to postpone. Schedules are like vacuums; if we don't fill them in with what is most important, they will fill in with what is not. If she called he could excuse himself, remind his wife that he loved her and that this was just the thing he needed to close his day. He would conclude matters at work and she knew he would be home soon and be glad to be there.

We are back to looking diligently toward God for counsel and strength. He shows us the straight path to follow. He strengthens us and teaches us to work toward healing. He gives us a mind that rejects bitterness, because bitterness contributes nothing to our well-being or our marriage.

Have you ever noticed that so many older people have faces that look bitter? Look at their faces and see how many mouths are drawn down at the ends—an inverted smile that clearly expresses the opposite of what a smile is all about. That face reveals bitterness, resentment, disappointment, anger, and frustration. But the people I see like this are Christian and have remained married to the same person their whole life. In my experience the cause of these long faces comes from a thinking that goes something like this: "I started out believing that God's design is the way to go, and that obeying Him is the right thing to do, and so I set out to do it. And then I found myself, over all these days and months and years, both trying harder than anybody else to get it right, and feeling worse than anybody else when I didn't get it right. And what I've found after all this time is that it really didn't matter; everybody else is just doing whatever they feel like doing. They're not feeling bad about how they're treating me, but they expect me to feel bad when I don't treat them the way they want me to. I have been doing all the giving in to what everybody else wanted, and never have been given anything." This sounds just like the older brother in the parable of the lost sons (Luke 15:25–32) and is precisely what the Hebrews text is warning about when it says, ". . . lest any fall short of the grace of God." Falling short of the grace of God does not mean that a person failed to do everything that God required in order for Him to be gracious in return. The grace of God is like the atmosphere we live in; He is gracious and His grace abounds. We fall short of the grace of God when we cannot admit the truth about our human nature and the truth about His gracious providence for us. To the extent that we protect any idea that we deserve or are entitled to certain things we are still justifying ourselves—on the basis of our own worth and not on God's grace. This accounts for half of the negative sentiments. Again, to the extent that we feel like we have suffered inequity we close ourselves off from appreciating or realizing new expressions of God's grace, which accounts for the other half of the negativity. Both sides of the mouth are drawn down, along with the whole heart.

    The way to turn our mouths upward in a smile is to realize that we are always getting better than we deserve. In fact, for years I have been saying "Better than I deserve" when people ask, "How are you?" If we admit the truth about ourselves, then we are the younger of the lost sons and as such we live fully in the gracious arms of our Father (Luke 15:11–24). He clothes us beautifully and receives us daily with joy and feasting. Only when we refuse to admit our waywardness do we make ourselves the older brother, refusing to enter the Father's house of feasting and joy.

Therefore, the introduction to this prayer asks us every day to consider the nature of our relationship to the Father. If we are not honest, we defeat ourselves twice: we rob ourselves of our potential within God's grace and we languish in our own self-righteousness. If we are honest with ourselves, then the possibilities for our lives are as abundant as God's grace. We need never justify ourselves. Only we have a perspective that recognizes everything as a gift of God, and we possess the conviction that the potential for our lives is limitless. This all flows from "Our Father" who is in heaven and continually looks for us to join Him there.

B. "Hallowed be Thy name . . ."

God's name is profaned if we submit to or make sacrifices to any other authority, not only because we have rejected Him as our head, but because this rejection will surely be seen in our marriage. So both our conduct before God and with our spouse will be a disgrace and denial of truth to all who witness it.

If marriage is based on the image of God, then any distortion of that image will ruin the marriage. As human beings made in God's image, our life is realized in relation to both Him and spouse according to His design. Whenever Israel traded the true God for the idols of the nations around them they inevitably traded fidelity in marriage relationships as well (Exodus 32:1, 6; 1 Corinthians 10:7–8). Idolatry and infidelity are both described as adultery and harlotry in the Bible. God forbids both, because trading the true God for something else leaves you with the devil and trading your spouse for someone else leaves you with a predator (note how both the devil and adulterers prowl about and bring their victims down to hell: 1 Peter 5:8; Proverbs 7:12–13, 24–27).

Consider how we profane God's creation be remaking it and then discarding it. Compare a national park to a landfill—God's handiwork compared to ours. This same comparison may be made between God's intent in marriage and what contradictory human conduct has made of it. If Christians do not faithfully convey God's intent in marriage, why would anyone else in the world value it? The divorce rate is dropping, not because fewer people are getting divorced but because fewer are getting married. It is very interesting that modern society idolizes nature and seeks to preserve it while it profanes God's design for human life and relationships. The challenge for a Christian witness is even greater because the media mainly serves the contradictions by flooding our world with the enticements of godlessness, from atheism to secular humanism, from sex on demand to homosexuality.

In order for God's name (Word) to be our life, all other names (gods/words/authorities) must be rejected.

Truth may be recognized by anyone, since all creation bears witness to God. The problem with relying on nature only is that you have only a partial witness. You may observe only a small portion of its witness and nature will not reveal to you God's redemption. A storm reveals God's power, but Christ reveals a salvation that no storm can threaten. The Bible is unique because it assures us that we have exactly what God wants us to know, no more and no less. The truth revealed in the Word is both consistent with and complimentary to the witness of nature. God's Word explains such things as the origin of the universe, the purpose of sun, moon, and stars, and why there is danger and death. God's Word also compliments the witness of nature by revealing His remedy for all the damage of human rebellion. There is no other God than One. Only authority that flows from Him is life giving, and competing words only displace the clarity and power of His inspired revelation.

C. "Thy Kingdom come . . ."

Matthew 13:44–46: ". . . the kingdom of heaven is like a merchant seeking beautiful pearls, who, when he had found one pearl of great price, went and sold all that he had and bought it . . ."

God's kingdom/paradise, comes to us whenever His Word and Spirit are present. God brings His kingdom/paradise into marriage when the husband sees his first responsibility as keeping his spouse (and children) in the Word and when the wife (and children) know that their chief responsibility is to hear the Word. God's Word is that pearl of great price for which we gladly give up all else. That

Word at work in the lives of our spouse and children allow them to be always more valuable and more valued in our sight.

Martin Luther explained that the kingdom of God comes of itself. In fact, the kingdom of God is always more willing to come than we are to permit it (Ephesians 3:20; Mark 9:22–24; 2 Samuel 12:8). I have never known a Bible to have blank pages when someone comes to read it. The witness of creation is loud and clear, but we have become deaf and blind (2 Corinthians 3:14; Psalm 135:13–18). The first key to opening your life and marriage to the kingdom of heaven is to be like the merchant in the parable. He recognized both the value of pearls and the value of having only the one of greatest price. As Christians we believe that there is value in life because God is the author of it (life is not a continual series of accidents). God's design for life means that there is an ideal life, the one in which all things work according to God's intent so that there is only life and no death. This may sound like intense idealism and it is! But life without ideals is like traveling with no destination (actually that's called wandering). My suggestion that husband and wife should never be their own advocate so that they are never adversarial is derived from this ideal.

This recognition that life is of inestimable value cannot be sustained by our own devices. Since the fall, we are oriented toward pessimism. Over history, ideals for life have steadily declined to the post-modern conviction that there is no value in anything (Consider the pointlessness conveyed by many movies, *Fight Club* for example). Only God's inspired witness to life and the clear ideals it presents to us can keep faith and hope alive. We hope for what we do not see because we believe in the invisible God who created all things living (Romans 8:24). Jesus demonstrated God's will that we should live by restoring life in the face of every opposition. We have life abundantly now and will realize the fullness of it when we cast off this contradictory human nature (John 10:10). Not surprisingly, the gates to heaven are described in Revelation as being made of one pearl each (thus, pearls make the most appropriate necklace for a bride!). So, as Christian men and women, we believe that paradise is found in our Lord and His Word. We also believe that His intent and His work in us are to reclaim that paradise even now.

The second key is realizing that while all pearls are pearls, there is just one of value so great that all the others are unnecessary. One merchant and one pearl provide a metaphor that is consistent with reality. There is only one God and one people of His creation. God's intent is for one man to be joined with one woman. While all creation bears witness to God in one way or another and while all philosophical and religious systems contain some truth (observations corresponding with reality), God's Word makes the quest for scattered bits and pieces of truth unnecessary. Nevertheless, the quest is essential. How would the merchant know when he found the one pearl unless he had examined all the rest? Real faith cannot and does not exist in a vacuum. Real faith exists as a product of the Word. The Bible has a character and history that is insurmountable and has endured every assault. Faith based on that Word thrives in the midst of opposition and contradiction (consider how faith dwells in a believer in spite of his/her own contrary human nature). The purpose of this petition in general and for marriages in particular is not to talk God into giving us something. The purpose is to remind ourselves that the Word of God is our access to the infinite and inexhaustible kingdom of God. The role of a husband is to open the windows of opportunity more and more in the life of the marriage and let that kingdom flow in, like a constant and refreshing breeze (remember that the Holy Spirit is the breath/wind of God—think Pentecost here!).

Example: In my experience, the problem for people who claim to be Christian is not that they don't possess the pearl of great price. The problem is that they don't know or believe it. One of the reasons God gave the laws of Sabbath and tithing in the Old Testament was to give Israel a means to be reassured that it was God, not creation nor accident nor idol, who was providing for their lives. The kingdom of God comes first for us in rest. His Word puts our minds, hearts and souls to rest with truth and grace. His kingdom is realized first by what He is doing, not in what we are doing. Therefore I recommend that Christians "exercise" their faith in ways large and small. Two examples follow.

First, take a whole day off. Any person can claim that their work is too important or too pressing to be absent from. I am arguing that the truth of such a claim reveals the danger of it. Are we serving others well when we fall into the trap of thinking that we are absolutely indispensable? I am not advocating irresponsibility. I would never consent to someone simply walking away from work that depends on them. However, the number one reason people give for not reading their Bibles is that they are too busy, and the center of that "busy-ness" is work. The strategy here is to keep working, to do so freely, but to keep this Sabbath strategy at hand. Reading the Bible daily provides for both; it inspires us to serve others diligently and it reminds us that Christians never do anything because we have to. When you feel like you are at your wits end, overwhelmed and drowning, that's the time to set aside a day for rest, ASAP. I recommend that my students do this once during the school year. When they feel they are at their lowest, they should sleep in, have a big breakfast, take in some sights in downtown Chicago, sit by the lake, and maybe take in a good movie. Most of all, they are to notice that the world kept turning while they rested and will turn better when they join it again.

Second, find rest in small moments. We can't take a whole day often, but each day is full of small moments when we can re-open those windows that have swung shut to the kingdom of God. One of the best times to do this is when we are waiting. Waiting in traffic, waiting in line, waiting for someone to meet us can be the most frustrating and enraging experiences for us. But they also hold the potential of being welcome and the greatest blessing if we use them to meditate on the Word, pray, and reorient ourselves. The luxury of a hot shower in the morning can bring to mind the blessings that God showers upon us and the invigorating nature of His Word, the Living Water. Sometime, while on your way walking or driving, take a few minutes (having pulled over if you are driving) to take in something beautiful that you see. Seeing the benefits God gives in all the small moments of our life replaces the need for a break with sense of appreciation.

> Matthew 13:47–52: ". . . therefore every scribe instructed in the kingdom of heaven is like a householder who brings out of his treasure things old and new . . ."

Remaining in the Word will keep us mindful of the treasures God has given us in creation: our image, worth, purpose, etc. Our first and elementary lessons in the Word remain the foundation of faith and life. Daily reading continually grants a fuller understanding, greater appreciation, and a more detailed application—something new to share with spouse and live by. Daily reading is essential for God's kingdom to be present in marriage.

One of the greatest characteristics of the pearl of great price is that the more you give it away, the more it is yours. Such a characteristic is entirely consistent with the nature of God and His Word. Notice that Jesus describes one who "brings things out." The beauty of the Word of God is that the more we give it away, the more we have it ourselves. When we read it to someone else, we hear it as well. The kingdom of God, like Jesus with bread and fish, increases as we give it to others. A husband's second responsibility (after hallowing God's name) is to be the agent whereby God's kingdom is poured into the life of his wife and children. The abundance of grace in the lives of the wife and children overflows, so the kingdom of God is returned again to the husband (as he appreciates the good his loved ones have realized) and is passed on to those outside the family.

The kingdom of God, having come, also provides us with the ability to bring things out of that treasury that are both old and new. The first and most simple expressions of God's kingdom form the foundation of our lives and remain with us. I still appreciate the Bible stories I learned as a child and still sing, "Jesus loves me this I know, for the Bible tells me so." Continuing to read and study the Word means that the Word will continue to show us new treasures—extensions of the profound, fundamental and simple graces we learned first.

What a great paradigm and reality this is for a marriage. Time with the Word brings the kingdom of God to us. The abundance of that kingdom brings rest and inspiration. That kingdom is expanded as we share it with others and that kingdom continues to confirm the truth we know and truths we have yet to see. In this context a husband, wife, and family grow together. The kingdom of God is a place wherein we appreciate what we always have about our spouse, but also discover new "gems" in their character.

D. "Thy will be done . . ."
Matthew 19:1–6: ". . . Therefore what God has joined together, let not man separate."

It is just as important to determine if God has joined a man and woman as it is to keep them from separating if God indeed has joined them.

The apostle Paul may have said all things are lawful, but Jesus said, "Oh no, they are not!" These words are not in contradiction to each other, but address the two natures in Christians, which live in tension. We are not asking God in this petition to do His will; He is already and always doing that. We are asking Him to accomplish His will through us, through a regenerate soul that wants to do His will and through a human nature that prefers to be contrary. Thus, we pray this petition in response to the opposition our human nature and everyone else's produces against God's will.

The first part of this passage, "what God has joined together," underscores the need for counseling before marriage. The second part, "let man not separate," underscores the need for great care after marriage. Confidence that God has indeed joined a man and woman in marriage is the foundation from which we may successfully endure all assaults that would rend us apart, just as knowing the true God and His grace in Christ protects our union with Him (John 10:29–30).

The second part of the passage addresses all those who would separate the couple united by God in marriage. The first enemy of this union is one's own human nature. The words of Jesus in this passage need to be loud and clear in the listener's wayward mind. When minds or hearts are tempted to see a happier life without the spouse or with someone or something else, marriage depends on the absolute conviction that God has joined the couple and united they will remain (provided the marriage is remains one of God's making; 1 Corinthians 7:15). The second enemy of this union is the world—the collective opposition of human natures that are contradicting God without restraint. Men in general still prefer irresponsibility and self-indulgence. Women, understandably, have responded to men in general by making an idol of their own nature (feminism) and competing with men for self-gratification. Evolutionary theory, secular humanism, and commercialism all mass-produce forces that pull spouses away from each other. Homosexuality and liberalism have gone so far as to deny that there is any such category of union that is uniquely of God's design. Conservative thinking is often too apathetic and accepting of the irresponsibility of men. Only when we recognize God's Word for what it is (hallowing His name) and provide time for that Word to be in our hearts and minds (His kingdom comes) can we be assured that His will for our marriage to be certain and blessed is being accomplished among us.

> The issue for the Pharisees was finding a reason or how small a reason to make divorce permissible. The issue for Jesus is finding FIRST all the reasons for avoiding one. Our approach to marriage should always be the same as Jesus'.

From a positive perspective, this petition provides enduring reinforcement of the fortress of union according to God's will. The preservation of our union with God and the union of husband and wife is the one box we should never think outside of! The problem displayed by the Pharisees is that, as men, they never committed to the marriage in the first place. But just as there is no end to the excuses a selfish human nature can make for wanting a divorce, so much more there is no limit to the grace of God to preserve a marriage of His making (Romans 5:17). Once the temptation toward divorce is dismissed, our minds can begin to work in positive directions. Behind the warning and prohibition of Jesus is a reality that says, "You're not going to do any better." After all, love for another does not depend on the other person, but on God who loves us. If we really believe that what every man needs is the same and what every woman needs is the same, then why would someone think that having a spouse in a different package would make their life any better? Faith and the love expressed because of it will make our lives genuinely better. The more we try to love our spouse well, the more we realize our need for God's help and the more loveable we will be to our spouse. Needing God's help drives me back into His Word and loving my spouse inspires her to love in return. Christian life and marriage is not so much about "self" improvement as it is about devoting and shaping our lives for the improvement of the lives of others. Conviction of God's will for our marriage supplies boundless positive energy to realize the blessings of God's will in that union.

Ezekiel 18:25–32: ". . . Repent and turn from all your transgressions, so that iniquity will not be your ruin . . ."

When my marriage is having a problem, I tend to compare my spouse's present fault with the whole history of my splendid performance. Even if I have done right in the past, I may have fallen from that righteousness and caused the problem myself. I can undo years of love with a few selfish actions. There is no benefit in comparing my actions (past and present) with my spouse's.

Ezekiel 18 is a fascinating text because it talks about turning away from those things that would be our ruin. It is essential to know that God's will and the law that reveals it are not arbitrary or trivial. It's not that God says, "Repent, and turn away from your transgressions because you're making me mad, or because I'm God and I get to say so." Instead, He says, "Repent and turn from all your transgressions so that iniquity (in other words, the things that you think you want so badly) will not be the ruin of you." Two specific problems present themselves here: the first is our propensity to displace God's will with our own; the second is our inclination to measure our spouse according to our will instead of God's. The dangers inherent to displacing God's will with my own are that I am usually unaware of it. If I am aware, I justify it. My will is going to be counterproductive for my marriage and there is no way to find joy or reconciliation in my system, since it is a product of selfish expectation rather than love. Measuring my spouse according to my measure has two advantages—funny they are both for me! One, I always look good according to my measure of things and two, if ever I do not, my measurement system blames my spouse; I look good, she looks bad. I am fine the way I am and she needs to make some changes and try harder.

Example: As a teenager, I spent a great deal of time trying to restore an old car. The horn wouldn't work so rather than consulting a wiring diagram, I simply tried reversing the wires. The horn still didn't work but I did see smoke coming from under the dashboard. I completely destroyed the wiring harness and almost burned up the whole car. We are "wired" by God to work a certain way as well. Ignoring the manual and experimenting with the wiring holds more promise of disaster than success.

God's will is that we compare our actions with His. Seeing His works and will in the Word shows us what needs to be repented of in our lives, so that we may turn and iniquity may not be our ruin. Iniquity is the ruin of every life and marriage. Repentance and grace from God are the only salvation and life of every person and marriage.

The will of God is not just described in His Word. It is also portrayed in the lives of saints, and most of all in His Son. But there is more. The Word of God not only reveals His will for us, it also accomplishes that will in us. God's will is not just concerned with the details of being husband or wife. His will begins with the whole proposition that we turn from our iniquity and live. Ezekiel will go on to tell us how God will take us as His own people (sanctify us), He will give us a new heart, He will put His Spirit in us, and He will cause us to walk in His statutes and obey His commands. The clear witness of God's will for husbands and wives confronts our contradictory ways and turns us (repentance), while His regenerative Spirit inspires and animates us to live in His image.

E. "Give us this day our daily bread . . ."

Here is the center or hub of the Lord's Prayer. As the sun is the center of our universe, so the Son/Word of God is the center of our lives. All the petitions flow to and from this one if we understand what Jesus means by bread. In Matthew 6 Jesus makes it clear that we need not ask God for those things which our physical life depends on. In John 6 Jesus makes it clear that He is the bread of life that we need because our whole life depends on it. The reason Jesus teaches us to ask for the one kind of bread and not the other is simple; it has to do with our two natures. There is no difficulty in God giving physical things to our human nature. The history of the Bible shows numerous accounts of God providing for the physical welfare of His people. What the people continually missed, refused, or despised was the truth and mercy that would save their life, body and soul (1 Corinthians 10:1–12; Hebrews 3:12—4:2). Jesus' own disciples missed the point of His miraculous feedings of the multitudes (Matthew 16:5–12). If we recognize God's Word for what it is, if we know that God gives us His kingdom in His Word, and that His will is accomplished by that Word, then the first three petitions are fulfilled in this one. If we are fed by His Word every day, then we have forgiveness and are forgiving, we have protection from temptation (Ephesians 6:10–20), and are being delivered thus from the Evil One.

We need not ask God for bread. We have more of it to eat every day than is good for us. What we do need every day is to remember where our life comes from, thus we turn to the text from John 6.

> *John 6:25–29: ". . . Stop laboring for the food that perishes; rather keep laboring for the food which endures to eternal life, which the Son of Man will give you . . ."*

Most people seek a spouse like these people sought Christ, not because they found someone to love (give life for) and serve, but because they found someone to make life easier for them.

The day before Jesus spoke the words of this text, He departed from the crowds because He knew they intended to come and make Him king by force. They actually intended to confine the life of Jesus to provide physical bread for their physical bodies, which were passing away. Sadly this has not changed. People still seek God as a means of making their physical lives easier, with no concern for and to the detriment of their whole lives. In the same way men and women seek a partner in order to get something they are missing—but the very thing they are missing is to give and not take! Jesus provided bread to show that He wills that we live and to show that He is able to provide for that life. His providence for our human nature, like the shining sun, is meant to turn our attention to how He provides for our whole life, body and soul. Therefore Jesus gave two imperatives, each with a rationale. Stop laboring for food that perishes, because it perishes. Keep laboring for food that endures to eternal life because it endures and because the Son of Man gives it freely in His Word. These two imperatives provide for a mindset that allow marriage to be a matter of giving and being given to—paradise.

The request to God for daily bread is first of all for God to give me strength (food) to give my life on behalf of others. It is not for God to give me whatever I want at this moment, like a spoiled child demands any whim from his parents.

Consider how short-lived the desires of our human nature are. When we are hungry, all we can think about is eating as if we were about to die. If we see something we don't have and want, it is as if our whole life would collapse into misery unless we have it. Yet we can eat until we feel worse rather than better and in a few hours we are "dying of hunger" again.

Attics, garages, basements, closets, and landfills are packed full of things everyone "just had to have" and then discarded. Knowing this, do we really want the desires of our human nature to determine the nature of our interest in and relationship to other people, particularly a spouse? Selfish prayer is a waste because God has no interest in providing for self-destructive behavior. Praying for daily bread will find fulfillment as surely as Jesus died and rose again for us and as surely as the blessings of that salvation flow to us through His Word. His abundance provides a life for us that overflows into the lives of others and still increases in doing so. He lives for me and I live for my wife and she lives for the sake of children, never to get something we don't have but always to give what we already possess in inexhaustible abundance.

Example: What if we trained ourselves to respond to physical hunger with living bread first? Jesus was forty days in the wilderness without food or water because his human nature was inseparably united with the Son of God, who is living bread and living water. When His disciples returned to him at the well in Samaria He told them His food was to do the will of His Father. How different our lives might be if we used our appetite for food that perishes to remind us to feast on the food that endures to eternal life and to drink in the living water that wells up in us and overflows to others?

> *John 6:47–51: ". . . I am the bread of life. . . . Your fathers ate manna in the wilderness and are dead. . . ."*

God has already stated that we are not to worry about physical needs since He provides them all without our asking (Matthew 6). What we are to seek is His wisdom/Word, which gives us life. Israel had miraculous bread in the wilderness, but it could not make them live because they rejected God's Word, promise, and Promised Land (Hebrews 4). If marriage is to live and be a "promised land," it can only do so when we are fed continually with the Word of God.

If you had your choice between a building full of free candy, soda, fast food and snack foods or a field full of gardens and orchards, which would you choose? The history of human nature consistently proves that we would choose things to eat that literally take away our lives (I didn't even include cigarettes, alcohol, or electronic forms of personal entertainment!). Fertile ground is being buried everyday under houses and stores full of all sorts of items of human invention, none of which can sustain life.

Luther said we run away from the things that chase us and chase the things that run away from us. This is true but need not be depressing, because there is gospel in the words, "There are things that chase us." The will, Word, and Spirit of God all seek us out in order to transform us from people who are dying even while we live to people who are always living, even through the process of dying. Like a diver who knows that his life under water depends on his air supply, so Christians must remember that our lives depend on the breath of God.

One way to respond to this petition is to practice it first thing in the morning. There is time after the alarm goes off to roll out of bed onto our knees and pray the Lord's Prayer. If husband and wife can do it at the same time, so much the better. Or stay in bed put prop up the pillows and read a Psalm or something from the New Testament. The main thing is that we take a moment, and it really does take only a moment, to open the windows of heaven as the first thing in our day. Along these lines, I advise Greek and Hebrew students to always leave their texts open and out on their desks. Then they can commit to reading at least one verse a day. Only one verse overrules the objections of our human nature that we don't have time for this. Even if we do only have time for one verse, it is one verse more than if we had not—and Jesus knows how to multiply bread. But in my experience, one verse is effective and enticing enough to keep us for a second or third. Spending this time can never be a mistake. If it means we must be more efficient with the rest of our time in the day, then the good Lord is well able to supply that efficiency (Ephesians 1:11).

Example: One of the things I have to do in order to have quality time with my wife in the morning is go to the office at 8:05 instead of 7:30. I'd rather go at 7:30 and prepare for the day of teaching. However, in order to spend more time in the morning with my wife, I have to be both smart and faithful. The smart part is to remember the day before to bring home what I need to get organized for work during the little moments of free time that present themselves in the evening at home. The faith part says, "Let's take faith out for a spin." It's not like I haven't been preparing over the whole course of my life to meet students with what God has to say about things. Let's say I'm going to choose to be a husband to my wife, and then see what God makes me able to do when I hit the classroom when I am not as prepared as I'd like to be. Many people agree that orienting our time according to the right priorities makes us more productive and efficient with all of our time. Regarding integrity, how can I teach students about proper priorities if I cannot or am unwilling to uphold them myself?

F. "And forgive us our trespasses as we forgive . . ."

My goodness, you'd think this petition would work for your spouse, wouldn't you? But not true. From a human perspective, we tend to think that because we have invested so much of our life in our spouse, we have a right to expect more from her or him. Expecting more means that if my spouse fails when I have worked so hard to make her succeed then she does not deserve to be forgiven. She's obviously not trying or not getting it, so our anger is justified and so is our slowness to forgive. But this petition binds us in our own self-righteousness. If we ask God to forgive us as we forgive others, then I would expect Him to be angry and slow to forgive me. But I depend upon God's readiness to be always gracious and quick to forgive. My spouse depends on that as well. This petition reorients this crucial aspect of our life together. We do want to be quick to confess our sins and be penitent. That can only be good for us. We want to be equally quick to forgive and put the best construction on things.

We also want to be careful not to review or belabor just exactly what went wrong and how mad we were about that. Such belaboring contradicts the very words of absolution that we need to say and our spouse needs to hear. What we can do after absolution is come back to "laying straight paths for our feet" (Hebrews 12:13). Knowing how detrimental something is in our relationship is powerful motivation to rearrange our thinking and way of interacting. A positive approach would reject an overstatement like, "You never give me phone messages on time or accurately" in favor of buying a memo pad so our spouse has a way of leaving accurate messages for us. On the other hand "making straight paths" means that I consider carefully whether accurate phone messages are as important to me as the messages my disposition send to my spouse. What if I put our wedding picture right next to the phone? Then every time I deal with phone messages I can think about US before I think about THEM. Forgiveness relieves the tensions that make us blind to solutions. Solutions and their implementation are so much more productive for a union between husband and wife than prosecution and defense.

> Matthew 7:1–5: ". . . first take the log out of your own eye, then you will be able to see clearly to take the speck out of your brother's."

Here Jesus instructs to judge not, meaning do not condemn a person to hell—because that is God's judgment alone to make. This does not mean we are not to judge one another—meaning we contend for what is right and renounce what is wrong, for the good of one another (James 5:19–20).

The term "judging" in the Bible has a range of meaning, from condemnation to observation. Judgment in terms of condemning a person is forbidden to us for at least two reasons. First, we cannot know what the eternal destiny of a person is. Second, our purpose is to do what we can to prevent a person's condemnation until circumstances prevent us from doing so.

On the other hand, Jesus' prohibition against condemnation does not mean that we need not or ought not to address conduct that is wrong. Jesus relieved the "sinful" woman of condemnation but He also told her, "Go and sin no more" (John 8:1–11). Paul makes it very clear that we bear responsibility for addressing wicked conduct in 1 Corinthians 5:1—6:4.

Love for others means that we are willing to do the difficult work of first learning truth and mercy from God's Word and then the even more difficult work of applying it to ourselves, and only then the still more difficult work of helping others in their acquisition of its blessings. For spouses this can be especially challenging, either because we feel like we shouldn't have to do this hard work or because we are convinced that it easier to avoid it altogether.

Jesus goes on to establish this meaning. He does not forbid us to remove specks from the eyes of others. Rather, He tells us to correct ourselves first.

Matthew 7 doesn't work unless you apply it to yourself first. The log in your own eye simply must come out before you concern yourself with anyone else. The beauty of Jesus' counsel here is that the lower your opinion is of yourself, the less critical you are of others. A second benefit is that even when you do see faults in others, you tend to be more understanding, sympathetic, and certainly less affected, because you have so many faults of your own. A third benefit is that from this perspective you also tend to notice the things that are right about your spouse and/or the people around you.

Approaching spouse or family according to this petition means that we can wait for a good time to deal with problems. We need not, perhaps even ought not, deal with things we see as problems in the moment. Better to give it some thought and if we still need to speak about it, we can do that in a productive setting. When we do approach an issue we are more conscious of addressing it from a context of grace. A healthy body can endure and recover from many kinds of accidents or illnesses that would kill a weak person. A healthy marriage supported by a sea of grace can easily manage the failings of husband and wife. Within that sea of grace that God provides, from a context of appreciation and love, we may offer a word of correction or even rebuke and find it accepted in the same spirit of love and appreciation. Finally, the honesty and perspective that Jesus' counsel provides makes it possible for us to see specks as specks and deal with them accordingly. "Taking it out of my brother's eye" may mean that I provide the means of correcting what keeps going wrong. If not, at least my spouse will realize from my disposition that what I am bringing up is very small in comparison to all that is right about her.

Example: I have found "cold war" very common among couples who are determined to remain married but are unhappy with each other. "Cold war" describes the practice of never talking about issues. Rather than being honest with each other and dealing with the shame of expecting what God has not or the shame of failing to do what God has expected, a couple avoids the shame by refusing to discuss the matter. In one case, I actually witnessed the wife "laying bare" the failures of the husband. His response was to say, "Why don't you take the log out of your own eye before taking the speck out of mine?" To this the wife replied, "Well, why don't you take the log out of your eye first!" Notice how both are completely misusing Jesus' word by imposing it on the other person. They both tried to hide their own shame instead of applying the lesson to themselves. They would rather hide their own errors than let God forgive them. They would rather dwell on the other person's errors than apply God's forgiveness to them.

It is truly remarkable how people who claim a Christian faith labor as if Christ had not taken away the sins of the world. When physicians find a cure for something, people can't wait to claim it by announcing their need for it. The great physician of body and soul has provided an ultimate and permanent cure for our shame, so why not cling to it in honesty?

G. "And may You not bear us along into temptation..."

James 1:12–22: "... But each one is tempted when he is drawn away and enticed by his own desires..."

This is the only petition of the Lord's Prayer that is not imperative—meaning a command. There is no need to ask God imperatively to NOT lead us into temptation since He never does that. What we are saying in this petition follows: "May the Lord not bear us along into temptation." It means we recognize God as the One who gives us life, breath, and all things. Life has become so easy for us that we forget God's activity and purpose for us (His desires). Therefore, we often eagerly pursue our OWN DESIRES, which ultimately are those of the world and devil. These desires all end in the destruction of our life and our relationship with others. We pray then in this petition that God would not keep life so easy that we run unhindered away from Him and into the world, e.g. God tripped me so I fell before I ran off the edge of the cliff. This petition then asks God to keep reminding me through the circumstances of my life to pay attention to His purpose instead of mine.

When you pray this petition and think about how it applies to your marriage, apply it to yourself first. It may be the case that dreams or ideas you had about your life or about your marriage (or a relationship you are pursuing) have been inventions of your own mind that are contrary to God's direction for your life. If we displace God's will with our own, then the sentimentality of disappointment can overwhelm us. Disappointment will look for satisfaction in temptations to blame our spouse, feel resentment, and seek fulfillment in another person. Praying this petition keeps us mindful of the traps we lay for ourselves in our own thinking. Praying this petition also reminds us to look for the good in the very situations that tempt us to make the opposite conclusion. Trials are the means by which we develop and assess our character. Rather than exploring the depths of disappointment and self-pity, the Lord would have us explore the potential of love to cover a multitude of sins and faith to move mountains.

We also need to recognize when God is working through trials in the life of our spouse. You may see things happen in the life of your spouse that is God's way of trimming him or her back. You can be of great assistance to your spouse if you know what to make of those things. The union of husband and wife means that one can still keep their eyes lifted up (Psalm 121) when the eyes of the other are wayward or downcast. Faith and wisdom give us the means and motivation to avoid the circumstances that tempt us and to use trials to help discover the path that God would have us walk.

Example: A young man in graduate school was pursuing an advanced degree, at least in part because his wife already had her doctorate and a very good career in her field. He was tempted by vanity and a misplaced sense of what people value. The temptation led him to feel like he had to compete with his wife on an academic level. During the course of his studies, he was forced to realize that he did not possess the ability to meet the requirements of the degree. Now the temptation of disappointment was overwhelming. At the same time, the necessity for him to re-evaluate his life opened his eyes to inquiries that had been made about his willingness to serve in his field of interest but in a position that did not require an advanced degree. With some encouragement he considered and accepted the position. In time he realized that he was much better suited to working with people than academics. He was well appreciated, successful, and at last content to compliment rather than compete with his wife.

> *1 Corinthians 10:1–13: ". . . but with every temptation He will provide THE means of escape . . ."*

The emphasis here must be on THE. God provides the one and only real means of escape from temptation—HIS WORD (see Matthew 4). While God is answering my prayer by pressing me down in my physical life, I may not know or remember how to understand that or endure. God's Word before me daily offers two means of help. First, His Word in my life daily decreases my need for big lessons (physical circumstances) because I am present before His Word to learn many smaller ones daily. Second,

> His Word teaches me to understand/remember that everything hard for my human nature is good, because it keeps it weak and dependent. Everything hard for my human nature is good for my divine nature because it encourages my love for God's promises and hope of heaven.

Most translations have only an indefinite article in verse 13: "God will provide a means of escape," which makes it sound like there is a means of escape, but you have to figure out what it is. The text declares that God will provide THE means of escape particular to each situation you find yourself in. Jesus demonstrated during His forty days in the wilderness that the Word of God is the means of escape. The Word of God is THE means of escape because it provides the wisdom to discern and strength to respond to the craft of the devil, world, and our own human nature. The combination of close contact with the Word while living in the world produces a perspective that sees challenges as opportunities rather than opposition. God's way of deliverance is rarely just a matter of taking us out of the world altogether, though that is the ultimate deliverance. Normally God delivers us from the devil even as we live in the world where he prowls about seeking someone to devour. Faith does not live in the absence of opposition, but in the presence of it. David said, "You prepare a table before me in the presence of my enemies" (Psalm 23:5). We're always going to meet opposition in the course of our lives. If you're a Christian, you're going to meet more opposition. If you are a Christian and married, you will meet still more challenges. If we lose our contact with THE means of escape, we will soon dread challenges rather than embrace them, we will become militant rather than evangelical.

Masters of martial arts discovered long ago that you can use the energy of an opponent to defeat their own purposes. From a Christian perspective, this means that we can use the energy of those who oppose us to make a witness that is all the more powerful, as Paul did in the Philippian jail (Acts 16:25–34) and as he wrote to the Philippians during a later imprisonment (Philippians 1:12–18). Within a marriage, we think first of the temptations produced by our own nature and the means God provides for escaping them. Next we think of our spouse, NOT as a temptation to escape from marriage but as a reason to face the challenges of marriage. Our spouse is our advocate in executing the means of escape that God's

Word defines. Together, husband and wife take up the means of grace to affect the means of escape from the rest of the evils that surround them.

H. "But deliver us from the evil one . . ."
1 Kings 18:20–22: ". . . and Elijah came to all the people and said, 'How long will you falter between two opinions? . . .' But the people answered him not a word. . . ."

If you compare your life and your spouse's with the Bible's teaching on marriage, and identify all the things that are wrong (evil) from which God would deliver you, you still have this question to answer—Do you want to be delivered? Our flesh has its own desires that war against what is right (our spirit—Galatians 5), and these desires are what make trouble for us/bring death into our lives and relationships. How can God deliver us if we prefer to keep faltering between obedience to Him and ourselves? There is no reason to pray this petition if we don't sincerely want what it asks. If we submit this petition to God without reservations, God will surely answer it and set His Word in our midst to lead us in that deliverance.

This petition begins by asking us if we really want to be delivered from anything at all. Many people actually seek God and pray to Him in order to obtain the very things God warns us about. Do you understand that when you pray this petition you are asking God to take your loved ones to heaven and this can (normally) only happen through the passing away of their human nature? So Christians pray this all the time, and then they are upset when someone dies. Death is a powerful means of revealing the true nature of relationships. A selfish person will be upset, angry, or even indignant about their loss. A person who loves, that is a person who sacrifices all for the good of the other, sacrifices their own sense of personal loss for the great gain of one whom God takes to Himself. We understand that labor and pain are involved in delivering a baby. There is just no other way to bear children. So also, arriving in paradise, there is no other way except by death (or a chariot of fire, in the case of Elijah). Talking about this now is imperative, because our minds can consider truths before a situation that they might not be able to tolerate within the situation. If you truly love your loved ones, if you want to get married in order to be an advocate for the other, then you will recognize God's greatest advocacy when He takes someone we love from this vale of tears, from the failings of their human nature, to paradise where the devil cannot accuse and the world cannot seduce. On the other hand, note well that God surely knows if we are asking Him to deliver our spouse through death so that we can be the ones delivered from them! We are always keeping in mind the distinction between the evil that dwells in our nature and the regenerate soul that dwells within that nature. We pray for, strain toward, and are grateful for all the deliverances that God provides in the course of our lives, most of all for the final deliverance in death. We have to remember that we are not yet in paradise, nor can we expect to create a lasting paradise here. We can be grateful for how well protected and provided for we are every day (which is amazing considering the devil's will). We can be even more grateful that challenging times work for our benefit even more than the easy times because of the eternal, spiritual nature of the life God has given us (2 Corinthians 4:1—5:21).

> *Romans 7:14–25: ". . . for I know that in me (that is, in my flesh) dwells no good thing. I find this to be a rule, when I want to do good, evil lies close at hand . . ."*

It is important to remember that this petition concentrates first on the evil in me, my flesh, not in feeling sorry for myself as if I were suffering innocently at the hands of others.

"Deliver us from the evil one" is a comforting and unifying petition because it sounds like we have a common foe, and we do. But a foe just as common but closer is our own human nature. So when I pray this petition, I start with myself; I think about the evil within. If I'm asking God to deliver me from my own human nature and the evil that resides in that, a number of solutions follow. First of all, it keeps me from struggling with saying, "I'm sorry" when I'm wrong. If I already know the evil within, why would I hesitate to take advantage of the remedy? Second of all, it keeps me from missing the blessings of my spouse that I otherwise wouldn't see because they challenge me. If I begin by seeing what is wrong in my character, your character looks pretty good to me. Third, when I look at the disposition of my own nature and the evil that lies within my own flesh, it peaks my consciousness again to be ready for troubles that the human nature is going to present. We have this human nature that is contrary to God, but we also have a spiritual nature that's oriented toward Him. The question is not whether evil is present nor whether good is. The question is which will be the dominant force in our life. What we don't want to do is think that feeling guilty about the situation is a Christian thing to do, or something that God expects us to do. Now, in a sense, guilt seems like the right thing, because it seems to be correct to feel bad about something I did wrong. The problem comes when we allow guilt to dominate, rather than grace. That's when the devil gets the upper hand and uses that guilt in two ways. One of the ways he uses that guilt is to discourage us about the future. In other words, look back at all the guilt that you drag along with you for all of the evil in your life, and what makes you think this is ever going to be different for you? Why not just give up? The answer is that there is no need to quit because God has not.

The other way the devil uses guilt is to make us negative toward other people so that comparing their evil with ours makes us feel better or at least the same. But holding another person under guilt to make ourselves look and feel better is completely contrary to the character of our Lord and to the kind of interaction that makes a marriage. Therefore, when I think of God delivering US from evil, I am thinking of how He is going to accomplish that starting with ME.

It is important to remember that my flesh is always with me and always instinctively does wrong. If this is to change for the good of my life and relationships, then God's Word must be equally present ("If you remain in My Word you will know the truth, and the truth will make you free" John 8:31).

Why pray to God to deliver us from evil and the evil one if we have in mind that we will do this ourselves? If we had the ability to resist or escape evil, wouldn't we exercise it consistently? God is the one who does the delivering, just as He showed Israel over and over again by conquering their enemies without them lifting a hand (2 Kings 19:35). The key to deliverance is the presence of the Lord. In as much as we have the Lord present in our lives, we have confidence and peace that He will deliver us. If we are worried or fearful about the Lord delivering us from evil, the

Word of God is available to relieve those fears while supplying the very wisdom and grace that delivers us. We do well when saying this petition to remember that the answer to this petition comes when we bring the Word of God into the lives of the people around us—especially when husbands do this for their wives and fathers for their families.

It is important to remember that once God has delivered me from proud, selfish, and evil thinking to know what is right to do, evil lies close at hand to keep me from doing well. After knowing what to do, I need to be ready for opposition to doing the right thing, and persevere through those temptations.

Paul supplies a priceless revelation when he tells us that evil lies close at hand when we want to do good things. Of course, why would the devil waste time on people who are already inclined to follow evil? The devil will surely concentrate his efforts on those who seek to oppose him and his kingdom by doing what is right. Therefore, wanting to good is only half the battle. The other half is being prepared for a surprise attack by the enemy. The hard part to realize is that the enemy lies within as well as without. It can be my spouse as well as a stranger. When Israel was rebuilding the walls of Jerusalem, it was necessary for them to carry a trowel and a sword. The trowel was used to do the good work necessary and the sword was to protect that work from the assaults of Israel's enemies (Nehemiah 4:17). If we are to succeed in loving our spouse, we will need to arm ourselves with protection against assaults that would undermine that love.

Example: Knowing that evil lies close at hand when we want to do good means that we are aware of the essential second step toward being delivered from it. First, God regenerates us and gives us the soul to do good works. Second, God gives us the insight to know that as we intend to do good, evil lies close at hand. I have observed countless times that a husband may think about how much he appreciates his wife on the drive home from work. He looks forward to embracing her when he arrives and telling her how much he loves her. He wants to show her as well, so he stops to buy flowers. In the meantime at home, the wife has considered similar appreciative thoughts about her husband, so she decides to make an extra effort to look her best and to fix a special meal. However, he took longer getting home than he thought, so when he arrives with flowers and words of love, she forgets about her appreciation for him because frustration is welling up inside. The dinner is cold and close to being ruined because he is late. In that brief moment his human nature reacts with indignation and responds with disgust that he should have spent his time and thoughts on her only to be criticized. She responds in self-defense, and he responds to that. At each turn they drag out past offenses in order to defend their anger and resentment. But why is there frustration, indignation, anger, resentment, or an argument at all? The situation began with the couple full of appreciation and good feelings for each other. The evil of self-satisfaction lies ever so close at hand. In an instant, that instinct of self-preservation can completely expel any thoughts of love. Yet in that same instant, an apology can be offered and accepted that protects and advances the appreciation felt and the attempts to show it. If appreciation is the climate of one's marriage, then that appreciation can be reinforced even more by graciously compensating for the failures. The flowers will either make the dinner already prepared taste that much better or they can provide beauty in the kitchen as husband and wife work together on a second attempt at a special meal. Loving someone means keeping focus on the love rather than misplacing our commitment to the means we have chosen for showing it.

7

Baptism
Confidence in the Potential of Your Spouse

VII. Baptism

A. What Is Baptism? (Workbook p. 41)

"All authority in heaven and earth has been given to Me. Therefore, as you go about, make disciples of all nations, baptizing them . . . teaching them . . ."

Matthew 28:18–20

Our Baptism confirms that we have been regenerated in the image of God's Son. We have been anointed in our Baptism as Christ (the "anointed One") was anointed in His. Therefore, the purpose of our life is NOT to prove that we can get a life or make a life for ourselves but to give the life that we have to others.

BAPTISM IS your proof that your spouse has a soul regenerated in the image of God. The Word of God in the life of that spouse provides the energy to make that life thrive in the face of contradiction from his or her human nature. So now we come to how we fuel the inner person. What fuels the inner person? On the one hand, truth fuels the inner person, as both David and Paul spoke of delighting in the Law of the Lord (Psalm 1:2; Romans 7:22). To the extent that we're honest with each other, the truth is going to be poking away at the human nature. We will be exposing failures or shortcomings, but this always comes off differently when one does so as a small part of a more comprehensive and positive endeavor.

Consider the difference between how we take the questions that a police officer asks and how we take the questions that a physician asks. I know that a police officer is about law enforcement. I know that a physician is all about health. So when the police officer asks me, "Did you know how fast you were going?" whether I did or didn't, I know where his question is going. I don't want to answer it because it's all about guilt, and guilt leads to a fine. I hate guilt and I hate fines! When a physician asks me, "What have you been eating for the last week?" it's not so he can write me a ticket or capitalize on my guilt. He is not asking so he can get me in trouble. I'm already in trouble. The physician is trying to find out how I got into trouble so he can prescribe a solution.

On the other hand, grace resolves the predicament of the human nature exposed by the truth and animates the divine solution. The Word of God generates a disciple and the Word of God sustains the life of a disciple. Jesus made that clear by saying that disciples are made by baptizing and teaching—that is to say, by keeping someone submerged in living water. Living water is a force that overpowers human nature and moves that nature according to the water's own course. Living water is uplifting and full of energy for our soul. Our spouse is the very first disciple we tend to every day (after ourselves). When husband and wife are disciples and are making disciples, their marriage is an unbreakable union (John 17:11; 1 John 1:7).

Example: Remembering that we have been anointed to make a disciple of our spouse is half the battle. One way to remember is by inverting our thinking about expectations and disappointment. Feeling disappointed in our spouse or having expectations unfulfilled takes no effort; these just come. But what happens if we invert the thoughts when they do come? Instead of dwelling on what my spouse didn't do, I could do something to help. Instead of dwelling on my expectations of my spouse, I could ponder some expectations for myself. Pondering leads us to seek food for thought, and the best food is the Word of God. I can say to my spouse, "How about taking a break from what you are doing (or not doing—but don't say that) for a snack and a little time with the Word?" As we read together, the Spirit has time to address my expectations, perhaps to reform them or at least to remind me of how abundantly God provides for me, in spite of what is lacking. That same Spirit may well work to convict my spouse of the very problem that was bothering me, perhaps reforming her behavior and conveying the abundance of God's grace to inspire loving activity. We take the truth about ourselves so much better from Moses, David, and Paul than we do from each other. Jesus, the prophets, and apostles express the gospel so much more powerfully and clearly than we do. Approaching each other in this way really addresses the problems we have for what they are and maintains clearly that we intend healing, not execution.

B. What Does Baptism Give or Profit?
Mark 16:16: "He that believeth and is baptized shall be saved, but he that believeth not shall be condemned."

Baptism provides confirmation of an invulnerable life that is eternal and oriented toward God's will. However, this life exists within a contrary human nature. Our consciousness of these two natures will determine whether we are problem solvers or problem magnifiers.

This section flows from the previous one. Rather than make disciples, our human nature prefers to concentrate on how other people are not disciples or how badly they are doing the job. We like to magnify problems for two reasons. One, magnifying what is wrong with others makes us look better and turns attention away from us. Two, magnifying the problem makes it seem like we are doing something about it, and if we don't do anything about it, who can blame us in the face of a problem so big? Notice how prevalent this is in politics. Politicians criticize and condemn each other's actions, but rarely propose real solutions. Marriage apart from the Word of God is bound to become political in nature because human relationships since the fall are all about competition for control. But if we are saved because Christ has taken away our guilt and declared us just, then we have reason to believe that problems can be solved—especially the problems with me! Since magnifying problems comes easily, we need to make sure our magnifying lens is focused on the Word, rather than on others. The Word of God describes its power to change, to save, and to reconcile. The Word of God says that Baptism proves the presence of a regenerate soul, which responds to living bread and living water.

Example: I have a good friend with seven children who once told me, "Every moment we spend with our children and every other moment they spend in a Christian environment puts building blocks into place—building blocks that the tides of change and storms of immaturity cannot cast away." Maintaining a Christian marriage and family in a culture like ours, which is so adversarial, is a task we cannot abandon for a moment. Nevertheless, marriage and family is something to seek, because it constitutes the whole fabric of our lives. The investments we make could not be more worthwhile. Human nature since the fall believeth not (1 Corinthians 2:14), and therefore cannot be saved except by death and resurrection. However, the regenerate soul believes, and the Baptism that confirms its existence reminds us to live and wait in hope within the ark of God's Word and Church.

C. How Can Water Do Such Great Things?

Titus 3:4–8: ". . . but when the kindness and the love of God our Savior toward men appeared, not by works of righteousness which we have done, but according to His mercy He saved us, through the washing of regeneration . . ."

Water exists and holds the properties it does because the Word of God created it so. Water is perhaps the most compelling witness of nature to the necessity of God's Word and to the properties of that Word to save. Thinking we can have a marriage without the consistent presence of God's Word is like thinking we can live without water.

The water of Baptism, like water in all of creation, is indicative of an essential, underlying reality. Our human physiology consists mostly of water. We need to drink water all day long. We depend on the water that is in the air (humidity). We depend on the water cycle, through clouds to rain to watering the earth. Water is the world's foremost cleansing agent. All these physical realities about water and the visible witness presented in nature are intended to indicate or point us to the necessity of our connection with God's Word, the absolute living water. "Baptism" is a Greek word that means wash. We would understand more clearly what the Bible teaches about Baptism if we understood the term as expressing the enduring circumstance of being "awash" in the living water of God's Word. The

Baptismal font at the church does a marriage about as much good as a lake in the distance. Today, it is common to see people carrying bottled water with them all the time—but that does little good in the long run unless they are carrying living water as well. Thus Baptism indicates the central necessity and purpose for Christians in general and spouses in particular. We need to keep each other "hydrated," that is "awash" in the Word of God. Jesus testified to the absolute necessity of remaining in His living Word with the conditional expression, "If you remain in My Word, you are My disciples . . ." (John 8:31). Psalm 119 bears witness to this in *every one* of its 176 verses and Paul does so by saying, "Let the Word of Christ dwell in you *RICHLY* . . ." (Colossians 3:16).

D. What Does Baptism Signify?

The significance of Baptism, like that of a wedding, is not meant to be frozen in time. Unless the significance of Baptism and our marriage moves forward with us, we will lose the image and benefits of both.

As discussed above, the significance of Baptism is made clear by the multitude of ways in which our life depends on water. The first and most essential characteristic of faith is dependence. If we know our dependence on something, then our life is ordered accordingly. Our dependence on water determines that we must consistently drink, wash, and water the ground, in order to remain healthy. Water is refreshing and beautiful. The sound of living water (i.e., moving water) in waves coming to shore or in a rushing river is unparalleled in beauty and therapeutic benefits (ancient Roman cities and many Greek cities today are filled with fountains so that people could always hear the sound of water). If physical water was created by God to be a constant witness to the real living water of His Word, then we do well to keep the sound of that Word in our hearing at all times.

1. Romans 6:1–11: "... likewise you also, reckon yourselves to be dead indeed to sin, but alive to God in Christ Jesus our Lord..."

If we fail to distinguish between our human nature and our regenerate soul and the desires of each, we are going to ruin our relationships by fighting the wrong battles.

Among the properties of water that bear witness to more significant underlying realities is its ability to cleanse or purge. God demonstrated that property of water in a profound way through the flood. The very same water that lifted Noah and his family to safety drowned everyone else. What was the difference? Noah knew his dependence on the Word of God and responded according to that Word. The world displaced God's Word with its own. The self-destructive consequence of doing so was already evident in the evil thoughts and violence that were so pervasive as to grieve God's heart (Genesis 6:5–6). Human beings who live contrary to God's Word simply cannot sustain a life in a creation ordered by that same Word. Therefore, the water that absolutely sustains life absolutely ended theirs. Peter confirms that the historical event of the flood was indicative of what happens in Baptism (1 Peter 3:18–21). The Word of God generates a new person within the old. The Word of God, like water, has the same effect as in Noah's day: God's law drowns the noisy rebellion of our human nature while it saves and buoys up our spiritual nature. Therefore, when Paul speaks of being "buried with Christ by Baptism into death" and reckoning "ourselves dead to sin" he is not speaking figuratively. Paul is saying that the law must remain in our hearts and minds to continually expose and renounce the self-destructive inclinations of our human nature. At the same time, the gospel must remain if our spiritual life is to have the energy it needs (remember the power of moving water).

Example: Paul is not being sentimental when he commands that we consider ourselves dead to sin. There is a thought process to this and it works. For instance, over the course of the years, I have learned how to maximize the wonder of the brown sugar, cinnamon, no frosting Pop-Tarts™. I know how to fix them and how to truly appreciate them. Though I love them, they are hard to find, so when I do find them I try to stock up, and I become a little possessive of them. One Saturday morning, I came downstairs only to find that my treasure had been looted. There it was on the kitchen counter, an already opened Pop-Tart box, empty foil wrappers, and crumbs. Where are the kids? There they were, watching cartoons and eating my Pop-Tarts. Did they fix them correctly? No. Were they savoring every wonderful bite? No. I came apart, grieving for Pop-Tarts unrecoverable and reading the riot act to the treasure looters.

Upon reflection that day, such conduct from a professor of New Testament studies seemed completely out of order. But what to do with my Pop-Tart disposition? Romans 6 provided the answer: "What interest does a dead person have in Pop-Tarts?" No interest whatsoever, and rightly so. My human nature is perishing in its own desires. Pop-Tarts offer no remedy and my desire for them only makes my condition worse, while spoiling any helpful witness I would make to my family. What would become of my family if I were teaching them that toaster pastry is what matters in life instead of the gospel? So, I swallowed the bitter medicine of reform instead of the sweet brown sugar cinnamon. I adopted the same disposition toward Pop-Tarts as a dead person would have, and exercised that disposition by having none myself while offering them to my children. At first the exercise was full of anxiety and desperation, but that quickly gave way to a new sense of freedom—freedom to see my life according to its effect on the lives of others. There is no shortcut to exercising the significance of our Baptism. The process of reckoning ourselves dead to sin has to take place for every desire that would work against our life, from Pop-Tarts to prioritizing our commitments.

Finally, once you have completed the process of reckoning yourself according to God's will, be prepared to take a hard hit broadside. One issue resolved tends to be replaced with two new ones. If there are no new issues for the moment, there is always the potential for relapse. One semester recently, after using this example with my class, a student who also appreciated Pop-Tarts brought me a box. The next thing I thought about was where to put them at home so the kids would not find them. As Paul said, "O wretched man that I am! Who will deliver me . . . ? I thank God . . . So then, with the mind I myself serve the law of God, but with the flesh the law of sin" (Romans 7:24–25).

2. Romans 6:12–23: ". . . what fruit did you have then of the things of which you are now ashamed? . . ."

Jesus said a bad tree cannot bear good fruit (Matthew 7:15–20). Many marriages are broken or breaking because one person expected or hoped that the other would change and become what he/she had hoped for. Change is possible, but good, genuine change can only come by God's grace at work through His Word. If a person is unwilling to give that Word first place in his/her life, what can be expected? There is no good fruit where God's Word is not actively at work. No good fruit comes from simply expecting a spouse to change himself/herself to meet our expectations.

Baptism allows us to look down from the deck of a sturdy ship into deep waters littered with sunken wrecks. What person has ever succeeded in taking a life from the people or world around them? Human nature is like a drowning person who, in fear, uses all his energy fruitlessly against his own life and against anyone that would swim out to save him. If there is no good fruit to be had according to the desires of our flesh, why be driven by it? If we know that our spouse's human nature is so oriented, why are we expecting good fruit from it? Looking for fruit in vain makes bad fruit in our life as well. From the moment we say, "I do," we begin to re-evaluate our situation from the very, very narrow perspective of self-satisfaction. As we look from there to the future, we may see nothing encouraging (like all the once beautiful but now sunken ships). Remembering Baptism keeps us mindful that God has provided for our past, present, and future. Both the past and the future of our human nature stand forgiven under God's grace. That same grace of God generates and fuels a new nature with a new future. The future of this new nature is not to expect fruit from others, but to bear the good fruit of tending to others so that they might be fruitful. Consider the example of Moses and the exodus. The Israelites never wanted to leave Egypt. They had adopted the Egyptian life and preferred the sinful indulgences it provided, even while they were suffering as slaves. Even after the miraculous Red Sea crossing, their minds could only think of returning to their old way of life. Thus, constant complaining and rebellion followed. But the children of the exodus followed Moses and eventually entered the promised land flowing with milk and honey. Our human nature is revealed in the adult Israelites. Our minds always suggest the bad fruit of being discontented. Single people long for a spouse. Married people long to be single. Our spiritual nature is like the children of the exodus. We have escaped the tragedy of bondage by passing through the waters of Baptism. Remaining in the living water of the Word means that errors or wrecks of our own invention remain buried under truth and mercy (love covers a multitude of sins). Now we feed every day on the real manna, the living bread that came down from heaven. This living bread of the Word constantly regenerates us into the image of the Son of God. This is the life that is oriented toward fruitful service to spouse and family first, then together as a family to the world.

Example: Many, if not most, couples discover that the adventure and excitement that ignited their relationship at the beginning is soon exhausted. This is because our physical nature is so limited. Our desires as human beings are fairly limited and become even more so over time. Many couples break up in search of a new discovery, but that one is just as limited as the previous. In contrast to such limitation, consider the potential of two people who are spiritually oriented. Instead of looking at each other only for gratification, together they look at the world for opportunity to serve—that makes a 360-degree view! The adventure for a Christian couple actually increases as time provides for experiences by which they learn more about each other, their potential, and God's will for them. For a Christian couple, the adventurousness in marriage doesn't find its essence in the physical interaction, but it finds its essence in the spiritual trajectory: where are we going with our lives? And the sky is the limit. Will we raise our own family or help other people raise theirs? Will we live near home, farther away, or halfway around the world? Will we travel or stay put? The life of a couple oriented to bear good fruit to God is forever expanding, not with possessions that have to be moved, but with experiences and enthusiasm that can never be taken away.

8

The Lord's Supper
Weekly Restoration of Confidence

VIII. Lord's Supper

A. What Is the Sacrament of the Altar?
(Workbook p. 44)

The Sacrament of the Altar is a matter of realizing unions that exist. On the day of the Son, at the rising of the sun, the body of Christ (believers) becomes visible to receive the body and blood of Christ in the visible form of bread and wine from the body of Christ in the visible form of the pastor. The Lord's Supper is a feast that celebrates the union between Christ and His bride, the church.

FIRST, THE Son of God joined Himself to His creation by assuming a human nature. Through that nature Jesus Christ demonstrated His character as the perfect husband by bearing absolute responsibility for the life of all people who were intended to be united with Him, like a wife. Now that reconciliation has been accomplished and Baptism has confirmed the regeneration of a faithful bride, the Lord adds yet another means of confirming His union with us. In the Sacrament of the Altar, the Lord joins Himself in a particular way with the elements of bread and wine. Wine and bread are the fundamental elements of a wedding feast. The public reception of those elements by people who confess their exclusive fidelity to Christ is a weekly proclamation of the union or marriage that exists between Christ and believers. All during the week, life in general and mealtime in particular sustain that same witness.

The Lord's Supper as a visible, physical, and collective event is a powerful means of restoring and reorienting marriage each week. When we kneel at the altar beside our spouse, we confess together the failing and troublesome character of our human nature. We are reminded that only the forgiveness of sins and the regenerate soul well fed hold a promising future for marriage and family. Seeing each other receive that forgiveness and spiritual food for the new person within confirms a resolution to offenses of the past week and assures us of God's presence to make the coming week better.

During the week, we do well to keep a consciousness of carrying forward that wedding feast. Why not consider every meal together a small manifestation of the Lord's Supper and of our wedding reception? What is more consistent, basic, and clear than love demonstrated by providing for the life of another with a meal? The conversation during preparations, during the meal itself, and afterwards may well be filled with further indications of love. Prayers before and after the meal can articulate that love even more clearly. Meals each day remind us (if we have forgotten) of our dependence on the living bread that came down from heaven—so we read the Word together especially around mealtime. If we are already reading the Word at mealtime, then the significance of eating together is enhanced. I am not surprised that the witness and benefit of mealtime have been practically lost in American family life. We have lost the simple but profound and steady witness to love that preparing meals for each other provides. We have also lost the union and benefits of that union that take place at mealtime. We have everything to gain by recapturing and protecting the steady union of our lives and witness of love that is meant to flow from the Lord's Supper through all the rest of our week, underscored and refreshed in our time gathered around the Word and the dinner table.

B. What Is the Benefit of Such Eating and Drinking?

Wine and bread are physical mediums by which God provides energy to our physical body. The body and blood of Jesus, like His Word, are physical means by which God provides energy for our whole life. God gave us bodies as a means of demonstrating love by providing for the lives of each other.

Martin Luther wrote that the food of Holy Communion is the opposite of normal food. Rather than being transformed and used by our bodies, this food transforms us and uses our bodies to serve God's purposes. There is a mystical aspect to the benefit of the Lord's Supper, to be sure. The Word, Spirit, and the body and blood of Christ are a means of grace that is beyond comprehension. Yet we can understand that He gave His body in service to us; He fed the hungry, healed the sick, and raised the dead. His blood was the life force within His human nature that supplied the energy needed to fulfill in His body all that the law required. His blood was also shed, because that is the penalty of failing to keep the law perfectly. That most capable and powerful blood comes to us with the wine. These elements of the Lord's Supper enter our system, along with the Word to refine and reshape us in the image of Christ, who gave His life in order to obey His Father's will. These elements then convey that determination towards obedience according to God's will for us, whether husband or wife, parents or children.

> *Exodus 13:7–10: ". . . unleavened bread shall be eaten seven days. . . . It shall be as a sign to you on your hand and as a memorial between your eyes, that the Lord's Law may be in your mouth; for with a strong hand the Lord has brought you out of Egypt."*

Egypt meant slavery for Israel. Sin is slavery for us. Our own sin is what keeps us in bondage to all of the ways of thinking, speaking, and behaving which ruin our life. As God delivered Israel from bondage through the Red Sea, so also God has delivered us from bondage to sin through our Baptism. Now He gives us a testament to keep us mindful of how essential and precious our freedom from bondage is. The Lord's Supper reminds us of our need to be rescued. By the grace of God that rescue is accomplished. The Lord's Supper brings that rescue into our lives and relationships by bringing to us the very body and blood of God, which saves us.

There is a common saying among language students that goes, "Use it or lose it." The same is true of the freedom and liberties we have as Christians. If we do not practice tithing, for example, we will lose our conviction that the Lord provides so abundantly for us that we can always give back at least the first tenth of what He gives us. Baptism is a great gift and I have already said that we need to keep the significance of our Baptism with us each day, but Baptism itself takes place only once in time (like our physical birth). God gave the Lord's Supper to provide a bridge to our daily life. Every Sunday God provides this sacrament again and again to confirm the life of His Son in our lives. Every week that sacrament reminds us that His Word is the living bread and our daily bread, while every meal is a chance to celebrate God's providence for us and practice our care for each other. In the next section we will see that confession and absolution are the third means God gave of conveying grace, which is available to us all week long.

In this respect the Lord's Supper provides a contrast between the faithfulness of Christ and the faithlessness of the men of Israel. Obviously 603,550 adult men who did nothing but body-building labor every day could have overpowered the Egyptians and left if they wanted to. The problem was and remains that human nature prefers bondage to freedom. We do not contradict God's will because we lack some anatomical structure or system. We remain bound to sin because we lack the will and spiritual presence to escape. This predicament means that men will perpetuate bondage in their families rather than liberating them from it. The Son of God (in this context appearing as the angel of death) provided the means of liberation in Egypt and gave Himself as the substitute for the death of the firstborn (the lambs without blemish that were slaughtered prefigured the real lamb of God, Jesus). The men of Israel at the time of Christ were living in bondage and holding others there as well (Matthew 23:13–15; John 8:33–37). In that time Christ demonstrated the work of a husband absolutely. Therefore the giving of His body and blood is an enduring reminder to men of their purpose, which is to serve. Forgiven, renewed, and strengthened by the Lord's Supper, Christian husbands take up the work of Christ to support and protect their families. Wives and children may then flourish within the freedom and orientation of that service.

C. How Can Bodily Eating and Drinking Do Such Great Things?

The significance of creation is as an extension of God that bears witness to Him. Life could have been some ethereal, immaterial existence and God could have created every human out of dust. But God created a physical world by which we might know Him more fully and made us instruments of His creative activity. Physical and spiritual properties do the things they do because God's Word established them so.

How does bodily eating and drinking do such great things? How does eating and drinking work anyway? Consider what wine and bread are. Wine is a medium by which the energy of sun, rain, and soil are brought to us, along with the added property of alcohol, which makes our heart glad (Psalm 104:15a). Bread is the flesh of grain, which is also a package for sun, rain, and earth to give us strength (Psalm 104:15b). Blood is the medium within our human physiology that brings both breath and nutrition to cells, which are constantly regenerating so we can live. Blood also takes away toxins that would kill us. Our body is the flesh by which we realize that our life is dependent and upon which others depend. The Word of God is just as much a means of communicating the power of the Son—living water and living bread—as was the flesh of Christ while He lived among us. Therefore the union of physical and spiritual elements in the Lord's Supper makes sense because the elements are parallel—blood and wine, body and bread.

Thus, the energy and image of Christ are communicated to us in the Supper, through the Word and through the witness of the elements. By this power Christian husbands apply their lives in the service of others, body and soul. Christian husbands and wives apply themselves to bearing witness to God's design by their relationship. Like the blood of Christ, we bring the breath of God (His Word) to others in our breath, and that breath of God makes hearts glad by communicating grace. Like the body of Christ, we harness our human nature to provide for the health and healing of the nations (Revelation 22:2). How marvelous to have the substance and the paradigm of this sacrament provided for us week by week!

D. Who Receives Such Sacrament Worthily?

I Corinthians 10:1—11:34: "... but I want you to know that the head of every man is Christ, the head of woman is man . . ."

In these two chapters of Corinthians Paul deals with worship, marriage, and the Lord's Supper. Paul's treatment of the three is interwoven because all three have the issue of union at the heart. Worship considers how we unite with God, marriage how we unite to each other, and the Lord's Supper how God unites with us. God and His Word, the Word and elements, the Word and believers—all these unions are made apparent and are celebrated in this feast.

In the middle of these two chapters Paul makes certain that the readers know that there is an order to relationships. Within that order there is union; outside of that order there is opposition. The devil opposes God by enticing people to idolatry. Men and women oppose each other by seeking to assert their own wills. The whole history of tragedy and destruction in the world has rejection of God's design for headship at its root. The remedy begins in the fact that the head of Christ is God. The headship of the Father means that the obedience of Christ will bring life for the world and that the Son need not fear for His life in accomplishing the same. The headship of the Son means that men obey Christ. Obedience to Christ means that men will carry forward the benefits of Christ to their wives and families. The headship of men means that women appreciate their husband's fidelity to Christ and cooperate in His will. Men and women come to this union with each other because they are first united with God by faith. People of faith recognize and connect with the substance and blessings of the Lord's Supper. Men and women thus united with Christ will be united with each other at all points, since the will of God for husband and wife is complimentary in every aspect.

9

Confession and Absolution
The Two Vital Signs of a Relationship

IX. Office of the Keys and Confession

A. What Is the Office of the Keys?
(Workbook p. 47)

> "*The Lord Jesus breathed on His disciples and said, 'Receive the Holy Spirit. Whoever sins you forgive, they have been forgiven . . .'*"
>
> John 20:22–23

As Christians, anointed in the image of our Savior, we are stewards of His grace. We are called by God to confirm His forgiveness, not to decide whether we feel like extending it our not. We forgive on behalf of God, not on behalf of ourselves, for we too live under and depend on the mercies of God.

You might think that having the cure for death would make a person eager to dispense it. Yet confirming forgiveness to another is often difficult. It seems to be most difficult for spouses, because they see themselves as deserving better from their partner than they have received or because they have endured what no one should have to. But we are not in a position to decide whether we will forgive or not, since God has already taken away the sins of the world through the death of His own Son. As people who depend on God's grace, we are called to dispense that grace to others. Note that the text says the sins of the person we forgive have been forgiven. Jesus means to underscore the fact that He has taken away all sins already. What we do for each other is not forgive, but confirm for someone that their sins have already been taken away. Our only task then is to listen to the confession and hear the request for forgiveness. Even if we feel like the confession is insincere, we forgive and leave God to catch the hypocrite (this does not mean we confuse forgiveness with physical consequences; an abused wife may forgive her husband but she still needs to move to safety).

There are several problems that confront couples when it comes to confirming grace. First, most couples do not have enough contact with God's grace. Apart from God's grace it is impossible to be gracious. Second, as mentioned above, apart from God's truth and grace, we tend to feel entitled to better than our spouse delivers or to feel overly affronted by their failings. Third, the more time we spend together the more we see of each other's failings, so they tend to loom larger than they should. Fourth, because we spend so much time together we tend to lose our tolerance for the failings and even suspect that our spouse doesn't care that their behavior is bothering us. Fifth, apart from the Word of God as a mirror, we tend to think too much of ourselves, so we slip into the mindset of a judge and executioner rather than a physician. The solution, of course, begins with the presence of God's truth, which reveals our own need for grace. Then we need to place ourselves firmly under the mercy of God, as in a deep, wide, cool running stream. From that vantage point we can well appreciate the discomfort and need of others and we can eagerly invite them into that living water, confirming their forgiveness with many words of the Bible that have been flowing over us.

B. What Is Confession?

I John 1:8–10: ". . . if we say we have no sin, we deceive ourselves and the truth is not in us . . ."

If the time we spend reading God's Word is the pulse of our life and marriage, then the time we spend confessing to and absolving each other is our blood pressure. If we are not confessing, it is not because there is nothing to confess (Romans 7). Rather, we are deceiving ourselves in order to protect our pride. If we deceive ourselves and avoid confession, then we are hiding from the truth and it is not long before everything wrong is someone else's fault—especially our spouse's (remember Genesis 3).

Confession and Absolution: The Two Vital Signs of a Relationship

If our time with the Word of God is the pulse of our life and marriage, then confession and absolution is the blood pressure. The Word of God and remedy it provides (the repentance it works and grace it applies) are the two vital signs of life. Ideally, a husband and wife would conclude every day with absolution (Psalm 4:4; Ephesians 4:26). The problem, if it is a problem, is that a Christian husband and wife get along well enough that trying to practice confession and absolution every night can seem forced and lose its sense of significance. Perhaps there is a parallel with Paul's admonition to pray without ceasing. Clearly Paul does not mean that we spend twenty-four hours every day in prayer. But there is a consciousness of a Christian that considers matters all day long in a manner of prayer. So also a husband and wife under the Word of God daily may keep a consciousness of repentance and a spirit of absolution all day long, even though they may not make a confession and declare absolution. Here is a place where praying out loud together can provide the best of both worlds. Prayer is an opportunity to highlight significant points from our Bible reading while also expressing a disposition of repentance and confirmation of God's grace in the specific terms of the texts just read.

Confession allows my spouse and me (and others) to live in the truth, not hiding anything, and not blaming others for what is my fault. Truth allows for mercy (Proverbs 3) and mercy presents no pressure. Mercy presents God's love and care to help, lifting up instead of bearing down upon.

Confession and absolution is not restricted to some sort of formal event. A humble Christian spirit notices its own failures all day long and says in each of those moments, "I am so sorry." In each of those moments the spouse confirms the state of grace we live under, by observing that there is nothing that needs to be forgiven ("that's alright, don't worry about it") or by confirming that we are indeed forgiven ("the Lord has put away our sin"). The more we are aware of the will of God (truth) and the grace of God (mercy), the easier it is to live in complete honesty. We are more conscious of our failures, not because we are assaulted by guilt but because we are determined to cast away everything that hinders us from realizing our potential as God's children and as godly husbands and wives. Of course, the only means of keeping this climate positive is by keeping the Word of God present so that neither guilt nor denial have an opportunity to undermine our intent.

C. What Sins Should We Confess?

Matthew 18:1–35: "... moreover if your brother sins against you, go and tell him his fault between you and him alone. If he hears you, you have gained your brother..."

Two wrongs don't make a right. God established the process for us to follow to keep one person's wrongdoing from moving others to do wrong. My spouse's faults do not give me the right to condemn, nor reject, nor be abusive. If I think something is wrong, I may inquire—ask for explanations and give time for understanding. If there is something wrong, I may bear witness to it with a view toward reconciliation (Leviticus 19:17). If I get nowhere, I may seek help from others and the church. The size of the problem makes no difference; God has given us counsel and a church to keep one person's trouble from becoming everyone's.

Matthew 18 can be hard to keep in marriages, because it's easier sometimes to talk to a good friend about what's the matter with our spouse than to talk to our spouse. Sometimes talking matters out with a close friend instead of our spouse is good, especially for Christians, because Christians understand that sometimes we just need to get things off our minds by saying them out loud and knowing that we have been heard by someone who understands. Understanding means knowing what we are talking about and knowing that we don't need to do anything else about it. While a close friend can be the best thing for a marriage, it can also be the worst in at least two instances. First, a friend is no friend at all if he or she listens and then adds fuel to the fire. Adding fuel to the fire means making things worse by sympathizing with our selfish human nature or by offering competition: "Your husband sounds like a monster for sure, but mine is the devil himself!" Commiserating only encourages our human nature in the course of thinking that made us miserable in the first place.

Second, great trouble can come when our friend is of the opposite gender. This is probably where the majority of adultery begins. Usually this

Confession and Absolution: The Two Vital Signs of a Relationship

happens in the case of a co-worker who likes us and we like him or her, because we always put on our best face at work. We like each other and seeing only the best of each other means that we never see the worst. So naturally we lend a sympathetic ear to even the smallest indication that something is wrong. If we indicate that something is wrong, the friend encourages us to confide: "I can tell something is bothering you. What is it? You can tell me." So we confide and that feels good, but the sympathy of this person of the opposite gender feels even better. He or she is relating to me the way I wish my spouse would; she is kind not angry, she is considerate not selfish, she is pleasant and beautiful not bride of Frankenstein. Then he or she puts a hand on ours to show concern, but the physical contact allows the electrons to flow. The sympathizing friend may enjoy this exchange as well because this kind of tenderness has been missing in their marriage as well. One thing leads to another—always gaining momentum because it feels so good and is hard to stop because we feel entitled to what our spouse has been denying us. Lots of chemistry is going on, but this is bad chemistry.

So, keeping the eighth commandment in mind, we consider whether our spouse has sinned or not. If we are convinced that there is a real problem, we seek to address that in the most opportune time: during devotions, in the readings, in prayer. If the problem remains, we place it plainly before our spouse—plainly and specifically with the clear intent of resolving the same. We are looking for healing, not dislocation. Anywhere along this line we may well confide in a friend, but only a friend of the same gender and one who is going to give us an unbiased, biblical consideration. If the problem is real and remains, then we may seek out help from those who bear spiritual authority in our lives. By this means we protect our commitment to always being our spouse's advocate and never his or her adversary and we protect our own life and well-being.

D. Which Are These (The Sins We Should Confess)?

Colossians 3:12–17: "... and forgiving one another, if anyone has a complaint against another; even as Christ forgave you. But above all these things put on love, which is the bond of perfection..."

Notice that the Bible does not command us to TRUST one another. It does tell us to LOVE—the love that sacrifices self for others. Why should we put our trust in other people or expect them to be trustworthy, when by nature we are not? Why should we expect of others what we cannot render to them or God? So we love one another and our spouse in particular because this alone—this love created and sustained by God's Word—gives us what is required for a permanent relationship.

The last part of Matthew 18 forms a bridge to this section by reminding us of what great mercy the Lord has shown us. Since we ourselves have received infinite undeserved mercy from God and since our life is protected by Him, we approach others as physicians, not judges (John 3:17). Physicians in the emergency room are not responsible for executing justice toward the patient nor do they take personally any resistance the patient gives. They are focused only on their purpose to serve the life of the individual. How much more should this attitude be between spouses (Philippians 2:5)? The key is to understand that we are called to love, NOT trust our spouse.

Most people are completely surprised, even shocked to hear that we ought not trust each other. The only time the New Testament speaks of trusting people is where John explains that Jesus did not entrust Himself to anyone because He knew what was in man—that is to say man is utterly untrustworthy (John 2:24–25). If we base our relationship on trust of another, then our relationship is going to fail because we are unreliable. Therefore the Bible commands us to trust God alone and to love our neighbor. Love for neighbor defines a relationship that is completely reliable, because our neighbor will always need to be loved and because our love for others depends on God's love for us, which is also absolutely reliable.

Confession and Absolution: The Two Vital Signs of a Relationship

(Note: Trust is not the same as honesty, though they are closely related. Relationships do depend absolutely on honesty; we know who we are in a relationship with, we get answers to our questions that are consistent with reality. Trying to make a union without honesty is like trying to glue two boards together that are covered with layers of wax. Honesty allows us to recognize and appreciate certain features of our spouse while compensating for or living graciously with the rest.)

10

Concluding Remarks
How to Keep This Mindset in the Mix

X. Conclusion (Workbook p. 50)

> *". . . for me to write the same things to you is not tedious, but for you it is safe."*
>
> Philippians 3:1

Man's purpose is to be responsible, loving, and the caretaker of God's creation. The root of all his sin is the avoidance of these duties.

OUR HUMAN natures, at their best, are like sieves. We read with our eyes and understand what the Bible is teaching us about our lives, but that knowledge drains away all the time. Paul understood this well, so he wrote the same things over and over again. This text is not unlike that. Much of the repetition in this book has to do with the comprehensive nature of God's image in our lives, and with the didactic approach of constantly reinforcing what we learn (Psalm 119 speaks of the necessity of the Word of God in every one of the 176 verses!).

The focus on men in this text is clearly lop-sided. This focus is as lop-sided as the dependence of people on Christ. We are completely lost without Him. Women always have Christ; He is ultimately and always a husband to them and protects their lives now and forever. But women were created to be submissive to the responsibility and care of a loving husband, which can only be realized as intended if the husband is faithful to the image of Christ. A wife may indeed convert her husband, and those who do are a special blessing from God (1 Peter 3:1–6). But a husband can—indeed must—be Christ to his spouse no matter how she conducts herself.

If he is faithful to his primary purpose of providing living water and bread from heaven, then there is good reason to hope for the best (Isaiah 55).

Woman's purpose is to remain before and help her husband. The root of a woman's contradiction to God's design lies in her determination to overrule this order.

Solomon wrote that a "wise woman builds her house but the foolish pulls it down with her own hands" (Proverbs 14:1). The word "foolish" in the Bible is a technical term that means unbeliever (consider the example of Job's wife found in Job 2:9–10). The unbelief of a woman's fallen nature insists that she knows best and is best able to order her life. The regenerate soul of a woman lives in the confidence that her life is safe with her Creator and Redeemer. The love of Christ and His inspired Word provide the means by which she conducts herself wisely and lives peaceably.

Satan deceives all people with the thought that both happiness and unhappiness come from the people and things around them. The source of unhappiness is, in fact, the disorientation of one's will. Real happiness comes from the power of God's Word to regenerate, reorient, and provide for one's life.

Abraham Lincoln once said, "People are about as happy as they make up their minds to be." I agree except for this: it is God who "makes up" a happy mind. The word "happy" in the New Testament is actually quite remarkable and different from "joy." Joy describes the kind of pleasure we experience because of good things that come to us; good weather, good news, good meals, good children all produce joy for us. Times that provide joy give us rest as well. "Happiness" is what we experience in spite of our circumstances because of what lies ahead. This is the term used by Jesus in the beatitudes (Matthew 5:1–12; Luke 6:20–26). The beauty of God's dominion is that He provides for us to be positive and enjoy life in every circumstance (Philippians 4:10–13). Times that challenge us drive us deeper into the Word and the care of our loving Savior, which makes us happy. I cannot control the world around me, but I can provide the Word of God to have dominion over the world within me. God's dominion insures a life that is ever improving towards fulfillment in paradise.

Movies Index

An Officer and a Gentleman, 110
Bridget Jones: The Edge of Reason, 114
Bruce Almighty, 116
Fight Club, 174
Meet Joe Black, 55, 116
Miracle on 34th Street, 114
The Passion of the Christ, 166
Rumor Has It, 114
The Stepford Wives, 64

Examples Index

Abraham and Job, 72
Advice from co-workers, 77
Alligators, 108

Car wiring, 180
Church wedding, 124
"Cold War" couples, 100, 187
Competing with one's wife, 189
Congregation's attempt to steal, 118–19
Control, 70
Controlling wife, 131–32
Counterfeit money, 32
Couple bearing good fruit, 205
Couple of one faith, 8–9

Deceitful groom, 13
Dominion and children, 34–35
Duty of pastors, 42–43

Excuses, 60–61
Exercising faith, 175–76

Faith and articulation, 156–57
Faith and assent, 154–55
Faith and knowledge, 154
Faith and memory, 156
Faith and obedience, 155–56
Father's home as Sabbath, 89
Forgetful minister, 153

Giving to those in need, 124
Guest or Servant, 127

Honest marriage, 49–50
Honoring God's command, 84–85

Investing time with family, 199–200

Joking about spouse, 76

Living bread and living water, 183
Lonely woman, 49
Loving husband, 147

Machinist, 42
Managing work and family, 169–70
Manipulation, 28
Marriage and the family business, 93–94
Marriage for the wrong reasons, 91–92
Materialism, 167–68
Mealtime, 163–64
Missionary marriage, 93–94
Mustang, 119

Nineteenth Century America, 59

Overpopulation, 36

Parental consent, 23
Pop-Tarts, 202–3
Proper priorities, 184–85

Reading Bible with spouse, 198–99
Rest in South Pacific, 162–63

Secular counseling, 79
Sexually active teen, 48–49
Showing appreciation, 194–95
Student's dependence on God, 152–53
Sunday morning wedding, 13

Examples Index

Teasing husband, 148–49
Teenage rape, 84

Uncertain fiancé, 12–13

Violent fiancé, 10

Woman as provider, 118
Woman's refusal to "obey," 9

Biblical Text Index

Gen 1:26–31	32	2 Sam 13:11–15	55
Gen 2	6, 9, 33, 103	2 Sam 13:15	120
Gen 2:15–18	37	1 Kgs 18:20–22	191
Gen 3	50, 51, 214		
Gen 3:1–8	51	2 Kgs 6:15–17	134
Gen 3:9–19	61	2 Kgs 19:35	193
Gen 3:20–24	73		
Gen 4:7	69	Neh 4:17	194
Gen 6:5–6	202	Job 2:9–10	222
Gen 19:11	31		
Gen 30:2	35	Ps 1:2	197
Gen 38	104	Ps 4:4	215
Gen 38:1–10	104	Ps 19	31
		Ps 23:5	190
Ex 32:1, 6	172	Ps 37:4	168
		Ps 103:6–14	105
Lev 19:17	216	Ps 103:10	73
Deut 4:6	75	Ps 104:15	211
Deut 6:4–12	76	Ps 106:34–39	91, 101
Deut 7:2–4	90	Ps 119	201, 221
Deut 7:3–4	91	Ps 121	189
Deut 12:8	52	Ps 135:13–18	154, 174
Deut 24:1–4	58, 107	Prov 3	215
Deut 25:9	105	Prov 3:5–7	27
Deut 30:1–20	75	Prov 7:12–13, 24–27	172
Judg 2	155	Prov 14:1	87, 222
		Prov 14:12	28
Ruth 2:1—4:12	94	Prov 15:16–17	124
Ruth 2:13	102	Prov 16:1	151
1 Sam 20:30–34	140	Prov 16:25	28
		Prov 18:1	40
2 Sam 11:1ff	138	Prov 21:30	71
2 Sam 11:1–25	108	Prov 22:6	90
2 Sam 12:8	174	Prov 26:20	148
2 Sam 13:1ff	108		

Biblical Text Index

Song 2:7	111	Matt 17:1–5	37
Song 3:5	110	Matt 18:1–35	222
Song 8:4	111	Matt 18:21–35	99
		Matt 18:23–35	50
Isaiah 40:2	102	Matt 19	52, 58
Isaiah 55	37, 65, 154, 222	Matt 19:1–6	177
		Matt 19:1–9	107
Isaiah 55:1–13	29	Matt 19:26	136
Isaiah 65:24	162	Matt 23	42
		Matt 23:13–15	210
Jer 8:8–12	78	Matt 28:18–20	197
Jer 23	53		
		Mark 7	97
Ezek 16	63	Mark 9:22–24	174
Ezek 18:19–32	101	Mark 16:16	199
Ezek 18:25–32	133	Mark 16:16–20	151
Ezek 36	122		
		Luke 6:20–26	222
Dan 2:35, 44–45	135	Luke 12:13–21	127
Dan 3:16–18	130	Luke 12:15	70, 155
		Luke 15:11–24	171
Hosea 2:16	102	Luke 15:25–32	171
		Luke 22:32	77
Mal 2:13–17	104–6		
		John 2:24–25	218
Matt 4	52, 195	John 3:2	155
Matt 4:1–11	71	John 3:16	154
Matt 5:1–12	222	John 3:17	218
Matt 5:38–48	136	John 4	61, 72
Matt 6	181, 183	John 6	26, 72, 181
Matt 6–7	161	John 6:5–11	109
Matt 6:8	162	John 6:22–71	65
Matt 6:19–24	115	John 6:25–29	182
Matt 6:25–34	81, 150	John 6:27	37
Matt 7:1–5	186	John 6:47–51	183
Matt 7:3–5	50, 83	John 8	50, 63
Matt 7:7–12	161	John 8:1–11	186
Matt 7:15–20	204	John 8:31–32	62, 156, 193, 201
Matt 10:39	144		
Matt 12:31–37	120	John 8:33–37	210
Matt 13:12	166	John 8:38	71
Matt 13:44–46	38, 173	John 8:42–47	50
Matt 13:45–46	135	John 10:10	174
Matt 13:47–52	176		
Matt 16:5–12	181		

Biblical Text Index

John 10:27–28	71, 156
John 10:29–30	178
John 13:4–5	123
John 14–16	151
John 14:13	81
John 14:26–27	150
John 15:13	83
John 16:14–15	150
John 17	81, 161
John 17:11	198
John 20:22–23	213
John 20:30–31	88
John 21:15–17	37
Acts 2:22–24	155
Acts 4:13–31	86
Acts 5	39
Acts 5:29	139
Acts 16:25–34	86, 196
Acts 17:11	71, 139
Acts 17:24–25	148
Acts 17:24–31	129
Acts 17:26	33
Acts 19:21	82
Acts 20:23	82
Acts 21:4, 11ff	82
Rom 1	31, 58
Rom 1:4–5	157
Rom 1:5	155
Rom 1:16–17	99
Rom 1:16—2:6	133
Rom 1:18–19	155
Rom 1:24, 26, 28	134
Rom 1:29–32	134
Rom 2:4	74
Rom 2:4ff	134
Rom 2:14–16	98
Rom 5:8	65
Rom 5:10	141
Rom 5:12–21	64
Rom 5:17	179
Rom 5:18	52
Rom 6	112, 203
Rom 6:1–11	202
Rom 6:12–23	204
Rom 7	214
Rom 7:14–25	192
Rom 7:21	121
Rom 7:22	197
Rom 7:24–25	203
Rom 8:24	174
Rom 8:28	55, 73, 143
Rom 8:32	109
Rom 8:38–39	130
Rom 9:33	48
Rom 10:1–17	153–54
Rom 12:2	82
Rom 13	110
Rom 13:1	140
Rom 13:8	82, 155
Rom 13:8–14	108
1 Cor 1	57
1 Cor 1:18–31	29
1 Cor 2:14	200
1 Cor 3:6	88
1 Cor 3:21–23	125
1 Cor 5:1—6:4	186
1 Cor 5:6	134
1 Cor 6:12	83
1 Cor 6:19	31
1 Cor 7	23, 90, 96
1 Cor 7:1	105
1 Cor 7:10–12	24
1 Cor 7:15	99, 178
1 Cor 10:1–12	181
1 Cor 10:1–13	155, 189
1 Cor 10:7–8	172
1 Cor 10:13	39
1 Cor 10:23	83
1 Cor 11:3	32, 137
2 Cor 3:6	87
2 Cor 3:14	174
2 Cor 4:1—5:21	192

Biblical Text Index

2 Cor 5:7	134
2 Cor 5:14	155
2 Cor 5:14–15	144
2 Cor 5:20	83
2 Cor 5:21	67
2 Cor 6:14	25
2 Cor 12:5–10	149
2 Cor 13:5	144
Gal 3:10–14	97
Gal 4:4	67
Gal 5	191
Gal 5:1	119
Gal 5:16–26	74
Eph 1	141
Eph 1:11	184
Eph 2:9–10	64
Eph 2:10	88
Eph 3:20	162, 174
Eph 4	77
Eph 4:4–16	77
Eph 4:26	215
Eph 5	2, 9, 12, 69, 83, 136
Eph 5:3	10
Eph 5:22–33	137
Eph 6:10–20	181
Phil 1:12–18	190
Phil 2:5	218
Phil 2:5–11	123
Phil 3:1	221
Phil 3:4–7	149
Phil 3:7–11	133
Phil 3:7–21	135
Phil 4:4–9	79
Phil 4:10–13	222
Col 3:1ff	116
Col 3:1–17	163
Col 3:12–17	218
Col 3:16	162, 201
1 Thess 4:1–8	110
1 Tim 1:9–10a	97
1 Tim 2:11–15	52
1 Tim 2:14	66
1 Tim 3	42
2 Tim 3:16	151
Titus 3	32
Titus 3:4–5	67
Titus 3:4–6	163
Titus 3:4–8	200
Heb 1:3	167
Heb 2:1	156
Heb 2:14–16	157
Heb 3:12—4:2	181
Heb 3:12—4:16	85
Heb 4	183
Heb 4:9	86
Heb 10	39
Heb 11:13–16	163
Heb 12:1–4	164
Heb 12:1–11	150
Heb 12:5–11	167
Heb 12:12–15	170
Heb 12:12–17	169
Heb 12:13	185
James 1:6	81
James 1:12–22	188
James 1:19	28
James 1:19–20	146
James 2:19–22	155
James 5:19–20	186
1 Pet 1:3–5	157
1 Pet 1:3–9	141
1 Pet 1:5	155
1 Pet 1:7	38
1 Pet 2:23	157
1 Pet 3	12
1 Pet 3:1–2	71
1 Pet 3:1–6	221

Biblical Text Index

1 Pet 3:18–21	202
1 Pet 4:11	152
1 Pet 5:8	172
2 Pet 1:20–21	79
1 John 1:4	88
1 John 1:6–7	62
1 John 1:6—2:6	148
1 John 1:7	198
1 John 1:8–10	214
1 John 2:15–17	168
1 John 4:1	139
Jude 6	66
Rev 12:9–11	67
Rev 22:2	211
Rev 22:18–19	53

Topics Index

Adultery, 12, 24, 25, 54, 101–11, 125, 131, 132, 172, 216
Advocacy, 5, 81–83, 95–96, 100, 112, 142–45, 174–75, 190, 192, 217
Arranged Marriage, 90–91
Artificial Contraception, 107–15

Baptism, 20, 77, 197–205, 207, 209, 210
Bitterness, 170–71, 203
Blame, 63–66, 180, 188, 199, 215

Chastity, 7, 10–11, 23, 25, 54, 71, 110–11, 114, 158
Confession and Absolution, 4, 15, 23, 27, 82–83, 210, 213–19
Consent, 2, 5–9, 13, 23, 25, 90, 94, 167
Consequences, 23, 51, 54, 56, 57, 63–64, 66–72, 106–10, 112, 132–34, 148, 158, 214
Control, 34, 53–56, 62, 70, 88, 91, 94, 113–14, 118–19, 132–34, 155, 158, 199
Creativity, 117, 162

Debt, 19, 108–9, 155
Dominion, 33–34, 36, 53, 54, 69, 80, 134, 222

Economy of God, 125
Eligibility, 3, 7, 8
Evolution, 9, 31, 33, 41, 43, 79, 133, 178
Expectations, 14, 50, 85, 87–88, 98, 138, 158, 198

Feminism, 9, 33, 58, 178
Free Will, 54, 56, 64
Fruitfulness, 36

Good Works, 194
Guilt, 15, 29, 50, 62, 67, 68, 73, 193, 198–99, 215–16

Honesty, 22, 45–50, 60, 76, 121, 132, 166, 172, 187–88, 215–16, 219

Image, 3, 9, 26, 31–40, 44, 63–67, 71, 73, 74, 81, 83–84, 92, 111, 117, 121, 148–50, 152, 162, 172, 197, 205, 209, 211, 221
In-laws, 95–96

Judgment, 58, 77–78, 123, 157, 186, 214, 218

License, 3, 5, 7, 11

Manipulation, 26, 28, 47, 94, 146

Natural Family Planning, 112–15

Prayer, 80–83, 143–44, 157, 161–62, 164–65, 167, 168, 172, 183, 184, 208, 215, 217
Proposal, 3, 8, 11–12

Remarriage, 24–25
Reorientation, 144, 161–62, 163, 165, 176, 185, 208, 222

Shame, 50, 56–57, 59–60, 62–63, 65, 66, 73, 76, 148, 177–78
STD Counseling, 3, 7

Topics Index

Submission, 12, 44–45, 66–67, 69, 73, 90, 101, 112, 134, 136–42, 145, 157, 158, 221

Violence, 106–9, 202
Virtue, 3, 9, 79–80, 83–84, 92

Water, 37–38, 72, 88, 102, 125, 176, 183–84, 198, 199, 200–202, 204–5, 211, 214, 222
Weddings, 4–6, 8–11, 13, 14
Worry, 81, 120–23

www.ingramcontent.com/pod-product-compliance
Lightning Source LLC
Chambersburg PA
CBHW070249230426
43664CB00014B/2460